REA

W9-CNG-185

SACRED FURY

SACRED FURY

Understanding Religious Violence

Charles Selengut

ALTAMIRA
P R E S S

A Division of
ROWMAN & LITTLEFIELD PUBLISHERS, INC.
Walnut Creek • Lanham • New York • Toronto • Oxford

AltaMira Press
A division of Rowman & Littlefield Publishers, Inc.
1630 North Main Street, #367
Walnut Creek, CA 94596
www.altamirapress.com

Rowman & Littlefield Publishers, Inc.
A wholly owned subsidary of The Rowman & Littlefield Publishing Group, Inc.
4501 Forbes Boulevard, Suite 200
Lanham, MD 20706

PO Box 317
Oxford
OX2 9RU, UK

British Library Cataloguing in Publication Information Available

Library of Congress Cataloging-in-Publication Data

Selengut, Charles.
 Sacred fury : understanding religious violence / by Charles Selengut.
   p.   cm.
 Includes bibliographical references and index.
 ISBN 0-7591-0361-5 (alk. paper)—ISBN 0-7591-0362-3 (pbk : alk. paper)
 1. Violence—Religious aspects.   I. Title.
BL65.V55S33   2003
291.1'78—dc21   2003012057

Printed in the United States of America

♾ ™ The paper used in this publication meets the minimum requirements of American National Standard for Information Sciences—Permanence of Paper for Printed Library Materials, ANSI/NISO Z39.48-1992.

Contents

Preface and Acknowledgements

My teacher at the graduate faculty of New School University, Professor Peter Berger, taught that social reality is constructed and maintained through ongoing human conversation, in the give and take of dialogue and social interaction. The most routine as well as the most momentous decisions are preceded by discussion and conversation. Talking with another, whether in agreement or disagreement, in a personal, face-to-face interaction, is, perhaps, among the most profound and uniquely human experiences. Books as social productions and images of reality, too, have their genesis in conversation and interaction. *Sacred Fury: Understanding Religious Violence* is the result of many conversations, dialogues, and even heated disagreements with friends, colleagues, and students, and I want to thank them and express my gratitude and appreciation.

I want especially to thank my colleagues Patrick Biesty, Paul R. Brezina, and Robert A. Weyer for their encouragement, scholarly contributions, and friendship. My colleagues Allan Nadler, William Stroker, and Christopher Taylor were most helpful in discussing the intricacies of Jewish, Christian, and Islamic theology, respectively, and I am thankful to them. Professor Muntaz Ahmad, the distinguished author and scholar of Hampton University, was extremely helpful in discussing Islamic history and culture, and I am most appreciative that I had his guidance. Charles Courtney of the Caspersen Graduate School of Drew University was especially helpful in discussing the work of Rene Girard. My friends Dr. Jonathan Helfand of Brooklyn College and Joseph Rappaport discussed with me many of the issues in the book, and I am grateful for their scholarship and friendship. They were, fortunately, never easily impressed and helped me clarify and appreciate the historical context of religious theology. Dr. Frank Kaufman of the World Peace Institute, a writer and expert in interreligious dialogue, was a wonderful conversation partner, helping me gain a global perspective on religious violence. Dr. Stephen Snyder helped me clarify the nature of the project and suggested creative approaches to the psychological study of violence. I want to thank him, deeply, for his scholarly insights and his personal encouragement.

I want to express my appreciation to Jeffrey Kaplan for first suggesting the project and to Erik Hanson of AltaMira for his advice and efforts in completing the project. I also want to thank the Drew University library staff, particularly reference librarians Bruce Lancaster and Jan Wanggaard for their help in researching material for this book.

Introduction: The Study of Religion and Violence

This is a book about the relationship between religion and violence. Most people consider religion to be the antithesis of violence and, in many places and times, religion has been a force for peace and social justice. The Ten Commandants, the ethical basis for many of the world's religions, forbids murder and violence. The Hebrew Bible, the New Testament, and the Koran—the scriptural foundations for Judaism, Christianity, and Islam—all have passages condemning violence and taking advantage of the weak and powerless. The scriptures talk about the life of faith as a way of love, kindness, and peace. We know, however, that despite being a force for goodness, charity, and reconciliation, religion also encourages and promotes war and violent confrontation.

The fact that religion is so frequently involved in communal violence raises intriguing questions about faith, religious organizations, and religious leaders. Why is it that religious communities whose holy scriptures call for peace are engaged in so many wars and violent conflicts all over the globe? What about the Golden Rule and the teachings in the world's religions calling for tolerance, acceptance, and loving-kindness for all people? At the center of all religions is the yearning for the *eschaton,* an end-time when all the peoples of the world live together in peace and harmony, without war or conflict. The Hebrew Bible talks about the time when the "lion will lie with the lamb" and "nation will not war with nation anymore." In Christianity, Jesus counsels

1

turning the other cheek and, suffering on the cross, he still seeks forgiveness for his oppressors. Islam venerates the prophet Muhammad as a messenger of peace, and the Koran describes the harmoniousness of Islamic society and tells us about the importance of hospitality and welcoming the stranger with warmth and dignity. And despite these central religious images which articulate nonviolence as normative religiosity, religiously generated violence continues unabated throughout the world. As Mark Juergensmeyer, the eminent sociologist of religion, puts it, "Only the most unreflective believer can fail to be jarred by the bloodiness of portraits of the Hindu goddess, Kali, and the dying Jesus. Nor are the bloody images limited only to religion's past: modern newspapers are crowded with pictures of Islamic and Sikh terrorists, guerilla Christian priests and revolutionary Buddhist monks."[1]

Elsie Boulding, the distinguished sociologist and peace activist, refers to this duality in religious life as the two contrasting cultures, which she terms the "holy war" and "peaceable garden" cultures, found in all religions.[2] Religions face an enduring tension between encouraging holy war, self-righteousness, and intolerance and championing tolerance, dialogue, and peaceful compromise with other faiths, as typified by the imagery of the peaceful garden. Every religion is caught in this sacred dilemma, establishing, by force and holy war if necessary, its particular view of the just and moral society based on its divinely revealed truths and an openness and tolerance for those individuals and groups that do not recognize these religious "truths." Religions preach love and respect for all people, but they also, at the same time, promulgate a divine view of the moral and social order that they take to be binding on all humanity. This is the dilemma of the faithful which the historian of religion R. Scott Appleby described as the "ambivalence of the sacred."[3] The faithful are sincere when they talk of peace and tolerance, for this is a message of the scriptures, but believers in the truths of their traditions and revelations are forced to fight, also, on behalf of their religion against those who refuse to accept these "self-evident" truths and who, in the eyes of the faithful, are violating God's directives to humanity. Religion can tell us that it is ultimately right to love our neighbors, but it can also instruct us that it is our sacred duty to kill them.

Religious violence is among the most pressing and dangerous issues facing the world community. The fervently faithful, acting in the name of religion, have, in the last decades, murdered hundreds of thousands of people throughout the globe, and groups of militants, in various religious communities, are organized into terrorist networks whose avowed goal is to destroy all those who oppose their religious goals. In the Middle East toward the close of the twentieth century, religious fundamentalists among both Jews and Muslims assassinated their political leaders, President Anwar Sadat of Egypt and Prime Minister Yitzhak Rabin of Israel, because these men were willing to make religious compromises and come to a peace agreement between Islamic and Judaic forces. Rabin's assassin, Yigal Amir, a law student and fervently orthodox Jew who was a student leader at the Bar Ilan University near Tel Aviv, claimed that Rabin was guilty of renouncing eternal Jewish rights to the Holy Land, which, in his view, was solely the land and territory of the Jews as promised by God in the Hebrew Bible. For Amir and his followers, Rabin had to be killed so that no sacred Jewish land would be ceded to the Arabs. Similarly, for the militants in the Muslim Brotherhood who were responsible for the murder of Sadat, compromise with the Israelis was against Islamic law and was an act of religious infidelity punishable by death. And the violence and killing continue to this day, with elements in both Islam and Judaism invoking religious justifications for armed conflict and terrorism. Each side claims that it has a sacred obligation to wage war against the other side in order to reach its religious goal of full control of the Holy Land.[4]

These religious wars have spread to the United States. On September 11, 2001, the twin towers of the World Trade Center in New York City, perhaps the world's most famous skyscrapers and a symbol of American prestige and world dominance, were attacked by Muslim terrorists of the al-Qaeda network, who hijacked four jetliners and successfully crashed two of them into the towers. The attacks destroyed the buildings and killed all the passengers in the two planes and several thousand people who were trapped in the burning buildings. Americans were under-standably shocked by the carnage and the destruction but also by the suicidal nature of the attack in which all the hijackers were killed. Many Americans were, similarly, mystified by the attack taking place on American soil. Why was the United States singled out for this suicide mission on the part of militant Islam? Why was America the enemy? There are, of course, no neat an-swers, but to the fundamentalist al-Qaeda network and its char-ismatic religious leader, Osama bin Laden, the United States of America was the "great Satan," whose modern culture, materi-alism, and secular morality were creating terrible consequences for traditional Islamic society and religion. The attack was a le-gitimate and religious act of war against a dangerous enemy.[5]

In Europe, religious violence between Christian Serbs and Muslims in the areas once controlled by the defunct government of Yugoslavia has taken many lives, and tens of thousands on both sides were forcibly removed from places where they had lived for centuries in campaigns of ethnic cleansing to ensure that a particular town or city would be populated solely by members of one religious group; killings and rapes were justi-fied as legitimate means to maintain ethnoreligious separation. In Ireland, a violent civil war between Irish Catholics and Irish Protestants has been going on for centuries, with periods of rela-tive quiet and times of great violence and destruction. The Irish speak the same language, look alike, and share much the same culture, but religious differences still matter and terrorism against militants and civilians in the name of religion is a regular feature of life in Northern Ireland. Though both sides are Chris-tian, each sees the other as perpetuating a false and illegitimate religiosity. Each, somehow, blames the other for the problems and shortcomings of Irish society.

In other parts of the world as well, religious violence contin-ues. In East Timor, a part of Indonesia which has been a place of peaceful coexistence between religions, serious and sustained violence occurred in the last decades of the twentieth century be-tween the Muslim majority and the predominately Catholic mi-nority, with massacres of the civilian population an almost regular occurrence. In the continent of Africa, religious battles between the Christian and the Muslim communities have taken place in many countries, with particularly violent encounters in Nigeria. New religious cults preaching apocalyptic suicide, with the deaths of hundreds of people, have mushroomed in Uganda and other parts of Africa. In predominantly Hindu India and Muslim Pakistan, two nations with nuclear capacity, continuing tensions over the disputed area of Kashmir have resulted in thousands of deaths as militants on both sides invade each other's territory. Extremists regularly call for total war so that each side can assert its moral, religious, and political rights once and for all. In the former Soviet Union, where religious tensions were kept under control by the authoritarian, atheistic central government in Moscow, religious conflicts have mushroomed throughout the former Soviet republics.. Perhaps the best known and bloodiest of these religious conflicts was in Chechnya, where a Russian Orthodox population united in war against the predominantly Islamic community. However, all over central Asia religious violence has broken out between various Christian groups and Islam and among the newly formed Christian sects and denominations.[6]

Even in the United States, a country founded as a place of religious tolerance and a society with a history of rigorous religious pluralism, there are unfortunate signs of growing religious conflict and violence, as evidenced by the rise of neo-Nazi and militant white supremacist militia groups. Timothy McVeigh, who was executed for his role in the bombing of the Alfred P. Murrah Federal Building in Okalahoma City, which resulted in the death of 168 innocent victims, had associated with such groups.[7] Members of extremist Christian antiabortion groups, motivated by their interpretation of biblical doctrine approving violence, have murdered physicians and nurses in abortion facilities in many parts of the country. These militant antiabortion groups have well-established websites and publicity campaigns, and, though they are officially rejected by mainline pro-life organizations, they continue to collect money and gain adherents.

The Unique Relationship Between Religion and Violence

Why is it that religion is so often involved in violent conflict and why is it that religion is used to justify war and violence? The answer lies in the unique nature of religious faith, organization, and leadership. Religious faith is different than other commitments and the rules and directives of religion are understood by the faithful to be entirely outside ordinary social rules and interactions. Religious faith and commitment, as the French sociologist Emile Durkheim explains, are based upon sacred and ultimate truths and are, by definition moral, desirable, and good.[8] For the faithful, religious mandates are self-legitimating; they are true and proper rules not because they can be proven to be so by philosophers or because they have social benefits but because they emanate from a divine source. Ordinary judgment, canons of logic, and evaluation of behavior simply do not apply to religious activity. This is something that highly secularized scholars, diplomats, and ordinary people, particularly those from Europeanized Western countries with a strong enlightenment tradition, find it difficult to acknowledge: different logics and moralities govern decision making in fervently religious communities. For example, while secularized Westerners may applaud the significant charitable work and social services performed by religious communities, they do not realize that secular motivation has virtually noting to do with religious charity. The faithful act charitably because their sacred tradition so demands, not because it is necessarily politically correct or socially utilitarian. To the shock and disappointment of many secularized people, that same community and tradition may call for holy war, where persecuting sinners and unbelievers and killing heretics is, similarly, a religious obligation. The critical motivation, then, for the fervently faithful is not utilitarian ethics, secular logic, or government legalities but the requirement to conform to the demands of religious law, whether or not it makes sense to those outside the faith community. The divine imperatives of the religious tradition, including violence, are not open to question by nonbelievers, and secular legalities can be breached if they conflict with religious truth. I recall a fervent Christian antiabortion guest speaker, otherwise a gentle and reserved person, telling my religion class that he contributed to and supported violence against abortion doctors and workers. My middle-class, suburban students were shocked and pressed him as to the morality of killing. He calmly replied, "I have talked to my pastor and this is what God wants us to do. We are protecting the unborn." Mark Juergensmeyer similarly writes of antiabortion radicals who support violence—some had been actually convicted of murder—telling him that they found their activities problematic and burdensome but that they had no choice, since it was their religious duty to respond with violence to abortion activity.[9]

Religious violence is also fostered by promises of rewards in an afterlife free of the disappointment and pain of everyday life. The violent actions carried out by the faithful may be considered criminal, entail long prison terms, and even result in one's own death, but the promise of eternal life, which only religion can provide, can break all legal and cultural restraints against crime and violence. Nasra Hassan, a social worker in the Palestinian territories, tells of a conversation with a Palestinian Muslim youth who volunteered and was chosen to be a suicide bomber. "S," as the prospective bomber was referred to in the report, explained that it was a honor to be chosen from among many volunteers and that this was his surest way to a perfect afterlife. "So by pressing the detonator, you can immediately open the door to paradise—it is the shortest path to Heaven," where one enjoys an eternity of spiritual and sexual bliss, he explained.[10] All religions have versions of an eternal life for their religious martyrs who die a sacrificial death on behalf of the tradition. In Judaism, such martyrs are called *kedoshim*, the "holy ones" who verify the truth of the faith by their willingness to die for it. Christianity, during its years as a minority and despised religious community in the Roman empire, actually encouraged religious suicide to prove the power and intensity of the Christian faith to the Roman authorities. In Islam, Hinduism, and Buddhism, as well, strong traditions of self-mortification and religious suicide continue. These otherworldly, supernatural rewards for violence and religious suicide on behalf of religious goals, as Rodney Stark and William Bainbridge explain, are not to be discounted, even in a scientific, secular age, for they can never be totally disproved; they are believed to occur in a world which is beyond scientific and rational understanding.[11]

All religion is ultimately about infusing the transitory and sometimes baffling experiences of human life with meaning and justification. Social scientists explain that a primary function of religious institutions is to provide social order and normative structure to human existence, protecting society from chaos and assuring the individual that life, with both its blessings and disappointments, has ultimate meaning and value. Religious systems, in the language of the sociology of religion, provide a theodicy, an explanation of human suffering which promises an ultimate reward, in an afterlife of eternal bliss and happiness, for the those who have followed religious teachings and have been faithful and obedient in the course of their lives.[12] These religious frameworks are so essential to believers that in the hands of charismatic religious leaders, this strong faith can be used to demand violent action by committed followers. The faithful, in these instances, are offered a terrifying choice: if you are a true believer and wish to remain a part of the community and be assured of heavenly reward, you must concur with the injunction to wage violence against the religion's enemies. It is difficult—frequently impossible—to refuse this religious "logic" in which violence is justified as an essential element of religious life. The cost of refusal is steep, for it means that one is no longer a part of a community and a hereafter to which one has dedicated oneself, psychologically and materially. Many militant religions put the matter starkly when it comes to calling for violent action: "You are with us or against us." In this sense, religion is eminently suited to exercise psychic, if not physical, coercion on members and followers.

The desire to remain connected to the religious community, to continue in the warm confines of its fellowship and theological understandings, results in acceptance of, if not outright participation in, the violent actions carried out on behalf of the group. The actual violence in any group is usually carried out by small cadres of zealots, as in the case with American militia groups or the antiabortion movement, but the larger group which supports such movements with financial help, safe houses, transportation, and respectability in the larger community is numbered in the tens of thousands and even in the hundreds of thousands and beyond. This is the case in the Middle East conflict, in the Catholic-Protestant conflict in Ireland and the Hindu-Muslim clashes over Kashmir, where powerful and respectable members of these communities, on both sides of the divide, aid, abet, and provide capital for the violent outbursts. We do not want to give the impression that religion, in all instances, is necessarily involved in violence. This is clearly not the case. Rather, religion, by its ability to provide sacralization of human activity and by its great power to infuse life with meaning, order, and security, can call upon the faithful to engage in what it sees as "holy terror" in defense of God and religious truth.[13]

Perspectives on Religious Violence

Defining violence, particularly religious violence, is a complex issue. The conventional definition tends to treat violence as observable physical injury. The problem with this definition is that it ignores the various forms of nonphysical, psychic violence in which religious beliefs, holy personages, and sacred places are desecrated or destroyed in religious battles. In this book, therefore, we will follow the approach of Mary Jackman as presented in John Hall's important monograph on *Religion and Violence: Social Processes in Comparative Perspective*, who defines violence as "actions that inflict, threaten or cause injury" and such action may be "corporal, written or verbal."[14] The "injuries," as Jackman defines them, need not be physical; they can be psychological, sociological, or symbolic, as in the case of religious desecration. Thus our approach to religious violence includes activity leading to (1) physical injury or death, (2) self-mortification and religious suicide, (3) psychological injury, and (4) symbolic violence causing the desecration or profanation of sacred sites and holy places. This is a relativistic approach to religious violence in which no judgment is made about the objective or realistic events that take place. Religious violence is a category and event so defined by a particular community and its religious culture. The experience of psychic violence will depend on the religious sensitivities, beliefs, and values of a religious community. Destroying imagines of Hindu deities in a South Indian temple would be, in this definition, an act of desecration, while some monotheistic, fundamentalist militants might claim the desecration of the images is no violation of religion.

This book presents a typology of theoretical perspectives and approaches used to interpret the relationship between religion and violence. Each chapter presents a theoretical perspective on religious violence, followed by an application of the theoretical model to contemporary case studies to explain the origin, nature, and dynamics of the conflict. Religious violence is a complex and varied phenomenon and no one interpretive scheme can legitimately explain the many forms of religious war, terrorism, and violent conflict. Such activity is frequently motivated by religious mandate and religious law, but what passes for religious violence may also be an attempt on the part of one community to utilize religious sentiment in order to gain political or economic advantage, to punish a historical rival, or to maintain power over a subordinate group. Violence against women and minorities and certain types of masochism may be justified by religious texts but frequently are best understood as serving the social and psychological needs of the individual and collectivity. The power of religion to motivate and mobilize can be used for religious as well as distinctly secular purposes. It is therefore essential in studying the phenomenon of religious violence to carefully analyze the underlying causes and motivations and not view it as monolithic. Focusing on the underlying etiology and genuine nature of these events will enable us to properly understand the specific cases and behaviors and hopefully to contribute to amelioration and resolution.

In this book, we consider the phenomenon of religious violence from five different approaches and perspectives:

- *Scriptural violence considers violence and conflict that is based upon the sacred books and holy teachings of a religious tradition.* Scriptural violence includes religious conflict that is seen as directly justified by divine mandate. We study here such phenomena as "holy war" in Christian tradition, *milchemet mitzvah* or obligatory war in Judaism, and jihad, or wars motivated by defense and support of the Islamic faith community. The scriptural perspective highlights the transcendental and sacred nature of religious violence. It focuses on the unique message and revelation of each religion and its task and goal to transform the world in accordance with that religion's understanding of divine command.
- *The psychological perspective sees religiously legitimated violence as serving critical social psychological needs and functions for the larger collectivity.* The motivations for such violence may be avowedly spiritual and scriptural, but psychological interpreters like Sigmund Freud, Rene Girard, and others see in much historical and contemporary religious violence collective, unconscious desires for revenge, honor, and power. The psychological theorists emphasize the discrepancy between the manifest justifications of religious violence and the latent realities which underlie religious conflict.
- *The civilizational perspective analyzes religious violence as a weapon of a religious, political, or cultural group that perceives itself to be physically or existentially threatened by more powerful cultural or political groups and that appeals to religious fervor to protect what it takes to be its legitimate historical and civilizational position.*
- *Apocalyptic violence studies death, suicide, and terrorism as religious acts which are thought to bring redemption and salvation for the individual and religious community.* Apocalyptic violence tends to be otherworldly, focused on the supernatural, with the goal that the violence will help believers transcend the limitations and boundaries of the material universe.
- *Religious violence, sexuality, and the body considers sexual vi-*

olence as an element in religious life and explores the range of self-inflicted pain and martyrdom that is part of many religious traditions. The perspective calls attention to the power exercised by religious institutions and personnel over members of religious communities. The perspective highlights the role of the body in religious theology and social organization.

Avoiding Stereotypes

Religious violence in our global age is very much in the news and the subject of endless analysis and interpretation. In efforts to make sense of these bewildering actions—what many people call "senseless" behavior—popular commentators often resort to simplistic and stereotypical explanations. One frequently given explanation, rejected by religious scholars and social scientists, is that religious zealots who engage in violent behavior or terroristic activity are mentally unstable. There is no scientific evidence for this and it is simply an attempt to stigmatize religious activists and deny their genuine religious motivation.[15] The militants who were involved in the September 11 bombing of the World Trade Center and the Pentagon, for example, were an educated, accomplished, and, by and large, successful and upwardly mobile group. Profiles of other violent religious activists in the Christian antiabortion movement and in Jewish militant organizations show their members similarly to be involved in communal life with no unusual psychiatric history and no criminal past other than their involvement in religious extremism.[16] This is not to say that mentally disturbed individuals do not join and participate in these movements. Some do, and they well may be attracted by the strong camaraderie and violence in intense religious communities, but one cannot legitimately label an entire movement in this way. Actually, studies of terrorist networks show that they weed out disturbed individuals and actually seek recruits who are socially adjusted and psychologically stable; for the most part, they are successful in attracting such types. The fact remains that it is religious motivation and religious goals, however misguided many outsiders consider them, that set the agenda for religious violence.

Some commentators have claimed that there are peaceful religions and "warrior" religions and that violence is not a problem of religion per se but only of particular religions which are historically and theologically drawn to violence. Islam is sometimes so described in Western writings, while Christianity and some other religions are presented as essentially nonviolent.[17] This is an inaccurate generalization, for, as we shall discover, all religions have themes both of forgiveness and peacemaking as well as demands for retribution and violence against their enemies. Violence in language and deed is an element in every religious worldview that, labeling alien faiths as evil or warlike and one's own as peaceful and godly, reinforces a community's sense of moral superiority. Christianity, as well as Hinduism and Buddhism, two Eastern religions ostensibly opposed to violence, have histories of involvement with violence, and there are continuing killings and rampages in contemporary Hinduism and Buddhism.[18]

Jack Hawley of Columbia University has called attention to another misconception in dealing with contemporary religious violence which we want to avoid. It is the refusal, particularly on the part of Western-educated and secular elites, to acknowledge the essentially religious nature of much global conflict. As a consequence of their view of worldwide secularization and their incorrect belief that religious faith is waning, diplomats and academics "want to separate religion from economics or politics and blame everything on poverty or politics but violence is part of religion and economic conditions and politics draws them out."[19] As Hawley and others have shown, it is religious history, religious sensibilities, and religious passions which drive religious conflict and turn other disagreements into violent confrontations. This type of reductionism misses the key issues in the conflict and can lead to major international misunderstandings and catastrophes, of which the September 11 terrorist attack on the World Trade Center in New York City is the most egregious example.

The approach of this book is to take religious claims, histories, and passions seriously but without making judgments about the legitimacy or ultimate morality of any particular religious position. Many works on religious conflict and violence are avowedly partisan and judgmental, sometimes in fervent defense and in others in militant opposition. We take a more neutral academic view, sometimes referred to as "value neutrality," in which we seek to understand the unique confluence of history, religion, politics, and group psychology that gives rise to religious violence; we will not render any particular judgments.[20] Consequently, our goal is to foster understanding and to present reasoned interpretations that will make sense of global religious conflict. The book offers no fixed answers, but we believe that a full presentation of the theory and dynamics of religious violence will provide much-needed information for informed and reflective decisionmaking.

Notes

1. Mark Juergensmeyer, preface to *The Spirit of Violence: An Interdisciplinary Bibliography of Violence*, ed. Christopher Candland (New York: Harry Frank Guggenheim Foundation, 1992).

2. Elsie Boulding, "Two Cultures of Religion," *Zygon* 21, no. 4 (1986): 501–516.

3. Scott Appleby, *The Ambivalence of the Sacred: Religion, Violence, and Reconciliation* (Lanham, Md.: Rowman & Littlefield, 2000).

4. Karen Armstrong, *The Battle for God* (New York: Alfred A. Knopf, 2000), particularly 317–364.

5. Roland Jacquard, *In The Name of Osama bin Laden* (Durham, N.C.: Duke University Press, 2000).

6. For a review of religious conflict in many parts of the world, see James A. Haught, *Holy Hatred* (Amherst, N.Y., Prometheus, 1995).

7. Mark Juergensmeyer, *Terror in The Mind of God: The Global Rise of Religious Violence* (Berkeley and Los Angeles: University of California Press, 2000), 19–43.

8. Emile Durkheim, *The Elementary Forms of the Religious Life* (New York: Free Press, 1965).

9. Durkheim, *Elementary Forms*, 20–30.

10. Nasra Hassan, "An Arsenal of Believers," *New Yorker*, November 19, 2001, 36–41.

11. Rodney Stark and William Sims Bainbridge, "Secularization, Revival, and Cult Formation," *Annual Review of the Social Sciences* 4 (1980): 85–119.

12. Peter L. Berger, *The Sacred Canopy: Elements of a Sociological Theory of Religion* (New York: Doubleday, 1969), 53–80.

13. Bruce Hoffman, "Holy Terror: The Implications of Terrorism Motivated by a Religious Imperative," *Studies in Conflict and Terrorism* 18 (1995): 271–284. See also Bruce Lawrence, *Defenders of God: The Fundamentalist Revolt against the Modern Age* (Columbia: University of South Carolina Press, 1995).

14. John R. Hall, "Religion and Violence: Social Processes in Comparative Perspective," in *Handbook for the Sociology of Religion*, ed. Michele Dillon (Cambridge: Cambridge University Press, forthcoming).

15. David G. Bromley and James Richardson, eds., *The Brainwashing/Deprogramming Controversy: Sociological, Psychological, Legal, and Historical Perspectives* (New York: Edwin Mellon Press, 1983).

16. See the extensive investigative report on the September 11 hijackers reported in *Frontline: Inside The Terrorist Network*, prod. and dir. Ben Loeterman, 60 min., PBS Video, 2002. See also Juergensmeyer, *Terror In The Mind Of God*, chap. 2.

17. See Robert Spencer, *Islam Unveiled: Disturbing Questions about the World's Fastest Growing Faith* (San Francisco: Encounter, 2002).

18. Haught, *Holy Hatred*, 47–60, 107–116.

19. Jack Hawley, "Pakistan's Longer Border," paper presented at the conference, "Understanding Religious Violence," St. Bartholomew's Church, New York, N.Y., February 2002.

20. Max Weber, "Science as Vocation," in *From Max Weber*, ed. Hans Gerth and C. Wright Mills (New York: Oxford University Press, 1958).

1

Fighting for God: Scriptural Obligations and Holy Wars

We begin our discussion of religion and violence by focusing on the earliest and most elemental expression of religious violence, holy wars. The holy war perspective deals with the scriptural call and religious duty to engage in war, violence, and mass murder on behalf of religion. This perspective highlights, as perhaps no other one does, the close affinity between religion and violence found in many of the world's great religions. It is not easy—and perhaps downright uncomfortable—for religious leaders, theologians, clergy, and just plain, ordinary, pious believers to admit that at the center of the most sublime religious scriptures known to humankind is the obligation to wage war, to kill and to maim others in the name of God and his teachings. The fact of the matter is that despite all apologies and excuses, the scriptures and sacred traditions of the world's religions prescribe violence. Martin Marty, the distinguished Lutheran religious thinker and historian, explains that violence is not something alien to religion but has been a feature of religion from its origins to the present day. "Positive thinkers and public relations officers with a face would repudiate this notion or evade the fact. They want religion to be nothing but Godspell, good news. Yet, if the pursuit of truth is still to be cherished, one must note the feature of religion that keeps it on the front page and prime time: it kills."[1]

The obligation to wage war, destroy the enemy, and dese-

17

crate their sacred places, is not a farfetched or an idiosyncratic outlook but something encouraged and justified by the earliest and most prominent prophets, saints, and religious messengers.[2] Holy wars and religious violence, in the view of the holy war perspective, are not aberrations or tangential to religious life but are at the very core of religious faith. This perspective insists that religious violence is not a cover-up for economic or cultural disputes or group competition and envy but a spiritual and theological essence of religious organizations. What this perspective teaches is that religious conflict and violent encounters are, above all, sacred struggles on behalf of religious truth and divine revelation. Holy wars are encounters between good and evil, between truth and falsehood, between the children of God and the offspring of Satan. In this encounter, pious believers are not free agents permitted to choose between violence and nonviolence but are drafted into God's infantry to fight the Lord's battles and proclaim his message to all the world. This is not a mantle easily assumed. The burden is heavy and the dangers great, but if believers are to be consistent and faithful to their God, they must answer the call to arms and use every means possible, including murder, assassination, bombings, arson, and collective punishment, to fulfill God's mandate for war.

Holy war is a serious business and the protagonists are aware of the stakes involved. The scriptures are explicit in their directions: killings, murders, and mayhem must be carried out. There is a kind of brutal honesty in holy war rhetoric and religious warriors do not deny the death, suffering, and destruction that their violence will bring. To the contrary, this is clearly acknowledged and glorified as essential to God's plan for the universe. The enemies of a particular religion, including other "false" religions, idolaters, and defectors from one's own camp, must be destroyed so that the sacred prophecies foretold in the scriptures will come to pass. Believers are expected, perhaps even driven, to fulfill the divine mandate for violent struggle so that they may be deserving of God's blessings and ultimate redemption. Violence and religious wars are, in this view, pleasing to the deity and will pave the way for the much-longed-for eschatological and messianic transformation, for the endtime, when the group's expectation of God's kingdom will be established. The faithful, however, are always in danger of the human temptation to substitute reasoning, compassion, and empathy for the victims in place of meticulous conformity to the religious direction to wage war. This is wrong and would only result in prolonged and perhaps greater suffering for all humanity, for these wars and violent outbursts, as bloody and terrible as they are, mysteriously will pave the way for ultimate peace and harmony.

The theologian Richard Rubinstein has shown that holy wars are not random and haphazard but are, to the believers, acts of faith which are eminently reasonable and "rest on a coherent principled theological rationale."[3] The motivation is religious and the waging of war is a religious duty comparable to other rituals of faith and religious obligation. Rubinstein argues that these wars and violent conflicts are not meant to inflict pain per se—which they surely do—as much as they are an effort to use violence in order to transform the world into a moral order in line with God's decrees. Holy wars, then, have religious goals which will bring about an improved human order, well worth the costs of the human suffering. Other religion scholars have argued, similarly, that religious wars have emerged from the desire of many religions to dominate all aspects of social and personal life and that victory in war will enable them to be the sole power to properly govern social, religious, and political life. Brian Victoria, a Soto Zen priest who has written about the strong involvement of Japanese Buddhism in Japan's wars, sees holy war as religion's refusal to purge itself of what he calls "tribal consciousness" and acknowledge a universal humanity. Victoria argues that so long as religion is attached to its own parochial view of truth and revelation, holy war will continue as a legitimate form of religious activity endangering the lives of countless people all over the world.[4]

The Phenomenology of Holy War

Holy war is a necessary and essential element in virtually all religious systems. What are its characteristics and functions in comparative perspective? How has the concept evolved over time? How is it justified and legitimated in the light of other religious teachings stressing peace and human brotherhood? The most helpful way to understand holy war is to appreciate how the faithful—those who plan, execute, and ultimately kill or are killed in these battles for God—conceive, interpret, and explain their behavior. Firstly, through *theological reinterpretation*, these religious battles, involving violence and killing, are redefined as supernatural undertakings which cannot be explained through human logic and secular reasoning. The violence in holy war is not conventional human violence, where individuals or groups contend with one another for secular goals such as money, power, or status; they are sacred events, being fought for God and his honor. Indeed, they are, in this theological view, not violence at all. It may look like violence, but these are battles to bring truth and redemption, to inspire truth and faith for which even the fallen enemies will eventually be grateful. The religious battles taking place on God's command are never defined by scripture as events of violence; they are battles for justice. The God of the Hebrew Bible, for example, though portrayed as a warrior God demanding warring action from his people, is above all a God of mercy and justice who uses battle to create a peaceful and just world.[5] In the case of Muslim holy wars, similarly, the religious conflict and the violence and killing that follows are carried on in the name of Allah and are meant to instruct and inform those who dwell in idolatry and ignorance.[6] The violence against infidels is actually a call to those living in sin and ignorance to acknowledge the superiority and truth of monotheism and the rule of divine law as seen in Muslim scriptures and teachings.

Religious traditions certainly acknowledge the religious justification for religious wars but redefine them as *situational* events limited to divine directive. This means that the violence is not meant to be an essential part of the tradition but is, merely, a response to a pressing emergency situation as directed by God. In this way, the scriptural injunctions calling for peace, tolerance, and respect for life can remain consonant with the call for battle. The situational and temporary nature of violence combined with the understanding that the war itself is not a fully human event but directed and sanctioned by God shows that the holy wars are not inconsistent with other religious teachings. For the religious community engaged in religious battles, holy war is a not challenge to the Golden Rule, "love thy neighbor as thyself" or of the commandment, "thou shalt not murder." Put directly, holy wars are not about murder, they are situational moments of divine–human cooperation in furtherance of God's plan for justice and human redemption. In religious thinking, holy wars are manifestations of what the sociologist of religion Peter Berger refers to as *cosmization*, activities that occur in the ordinary routine world of human existence but are simultaneously enacted in a supernatural realm of divine truth whose significance transcends all human understanding.[7] Holy wars, as terrifying and violent as they may be, are among the most profound experiences of religious awe and divinity, for they link the religious warrior with God and the transcendental powers of the universe.

The earliest textual expressions of holy war occur in the Hebrew Bible. In the very earliest passages, God is viewed as an actual person, in the guise of soldier and general, fighting alongside his faithful. Gradually, this view of God's presence amidst holy war battle changes to that of a spiritual presence. The earlier holy war narratives also describe God as personally ordaining the battles, whereas over time God's wishes are communicated to the faithful through religious officials and, particularly in the contemporary period, through individual charismatic leaders. The scriptural cases of holy war are generally seen as situational and highly selective, while modern holy wars have become almost routine in some religious groups. Christianity and Islam incorporated many of the holy war elements from the Hebrew Bible but have added many ideas and beliefs from their own traditions.[8] In the global world of the twenty-first century, holy war has become global and is a phenomenon found all over the world and in religious cultures far removed from Western monotheism and their tradition of holy war. Hinduism, Buddhism, and Zen Buddhism, as well, have now incorporated elements of holy war in their religious outlook. Each instance of holy war, as we shall see, has its own unique history, justification, and purpose. We can describe, however, three general, characteristic motivations for holy war:

- *Holy war is fought to defend religion against its enemies.* This idea of holy war is used to fight against those who are believed to threaten the spiritual or material well-being of the religious community. This includes governments and societies whose legal systems, political orders, and social organizations persecute and discriminate against one's religion or threaten the practice and free expression of religious life. These "enemies" of religion can also include, at times, secular governments that, though promoting the free expression of religion, encourage or tolerate cultural expressions like pornography, the sale of alcohol, or sexual practices which are seen as a danger to religious morality and the continuity of the religious community. "Enemies" is a relative term and a social organization or alien religion can be redefined, at any time, by religious authorities and be subject to holy war.

- *Holy war is fought to ensure religious conformity and punish deviance.* Here violence and war are pursued to protect "true" religion against heretics and those who challenge religious orthodoxy. This was frequently the justification for the post-Reformation wars between Protestants and Catholics and is today a major justification of jihad against modernizing Muslims in the Islamic world. It is also used to justify violence by ultraorthodox Jews against those Jewish groups they consider deviationist sects in their own communities. Christian extremists in the antiabortion movements have also justified violence against Christian prochoice groups on these grounds.

- *Holy wars fought under the direction of charismatic religious leaders.* This is a general and somewhat all-embracing category which legitimates violence as holy war when fought at the direction of charismatic leaders who are believed to represent the divine will. Charisma, the gift of grace, the gift of leadership, is a unique quality of leadership which enables special individuals to endow their directions with sacred meaning and motivate individuals to participate in religious wars.[9] Charismatic leaders often deviate from religious traditionalism and are frequently opposed by established religious authorities, but their religious and psychological hold on followers is so great that followers will obey the charismatic leaders' bidding, despite the objections of the traditional clergy. Rabbi Meir Kahane and Osama bin Laden are contemporary examples of such charismatic leaders. The traditional clergy by and large do not recognize their religious authority to declare holy war but their charismatic leadership enables them to declare holy war against those they define as enemies.

The Theological Basis for Holy War: Judaism, Christianity, and Islam

Judaism's approach to holy war is based on the biblical narratives which tell of God's covenant with Israel, where God promises the land of Israel to the Israelites as an eternal possession and commands them and their leaders and prophets, Moses and Joshua, to wage war against the indigenous inhabitants of the land, then called Canaan. God tells the Israelites to annihilate all the inhabitants and destroy all the Canaanite cities, leaving no trace of their civilization. To the Israelites, as the biblical scholar Harry Orlinsky once explained, violence and holy war was eminently reasonable, since they were to inherit the land by decree of the Almighty God, whom they called Hashem.[10] The Canaanite nations who were to be dislodged saw things differently, but Deuteronomy 20 records God's instructions as absolute. The Canaanites were evil and idolatrous and had to be destroyed. The Bible puts the matter as follows:

> But from the cities of these peoples that Hashem your God, gives you as an inheritance, you shall not allow any person to live. Rather you shall utterly destroy them; the Hittite, the Amorite, the Perizzite, the Hivvite, and the Jebusite, as Has-

hem your God has commanded you, so they will not teach you to act according to their abominations that they performed for their gods, so that you will sin to Hashem your God. (Deut. 16–18)

The book of Joshua describes in great detail the various battles for the conquest of the land of Canaan and the necessary killing and obligatory nature of extermination decreed by God as a way to root out the evil and idolatrous culture of the local peoples. Israel's periodic loss of will and lapses into mercy for the indigenous population are derided by God and Joshua and are seen as only leading to greater and more pernicious evil. Total destruction, as in the case of the Canaanite cities of Ai and Jericho, is applauded and shown to be a true sign of religious fidelity, while mercy for the Canaanites, occasionally shown, is derided as moral weakness and infidelity to the Lord, Hashem. The Bible records that residents of entire cities were to be killed, leaving no person alive. After the final destruction of the prominent city of Ai, special sacrifices were brought on behalf of the community to Hashem and the entire Torah, the extant scriptures and traditions, was read in reverent and joyous celebration. The destruction of the city of Ai is a milestone in the holy war quest of the Holy Land.

All who fell on that day, both men and women, were twelve thousand, all the people of Ai. Joshua did not withdraw his hand that he had stretched out with the spear until he had destroyed all the inhabitants of Ai. Only the animals and booty of that city Israel took as spoils for themselves, according to the word of Hashem, which he had commanded Joshua. Joshua burned Ai and made it a wasteland until this day. (Josh. 8:25–29)

In these narratives, we see the essential Jewish understanding of holy war. It is war ordained by God to conquer or restore Jewish sovereignty to the land of Israel, which is covenantally promised by God to the Jewish people. This original motivation for holy war has been enshrined in Jewish history and jurisprudence as *milchemet mitzvah,* an obligatory war, and has come to mean that whenever feasible, a religious war must be fought for the maintenance of Jewish sovereignty over the land of Israel. In the course of Jewish history other categories of holy war evolved, including holy wars of defense and religious wars fought in honor of religious teachings, referred to in Jewish theology as wars for the "sanctification of God's name," *kiddush Hashem* wars. However, all these later versions of holy war are based upon the original biblical formulation for the conquest of the Holy Land in ancient Israel.[11]

After the Babylonian exile from the land of Israel in 70 C.E. and the loss of Jewish political autonomy, the concept of holy war was felt to be irrelevant to a dispersed and stateless Jewish community. Many leading rabbis proclaimed the holy war obligation to be null and void in the historical situation of statelessness and claimed that only a miraculous and supernatural divine intervention could restore Jewish sovereignty in the land of Israel. However, other authorities, including the authoritative medieval commentator and jurist Moses Maimonides, go so far as to rule that despite the exile and the impossibility to wage war, holy war remained a religious obligation, if only through a ritualistic and liturgical reenactment.[12] The theological basis for holy war was deeply embedded in Jewish law and tradition and remained so during centuries of Jewish exile. The Zionist movement and the 1948 proclamation of an independent Jewish state of Israel in the Holy Land restored the practical relevance of holy war theology and showed once again how theological ideas and sacred history can influence international affairs.[13]

The Christian approach to holy war is based, in large measure, on earlier biblical traditions and, although Christian theology has preferred the term "just war," the just war doctrine has functioned effectively, as James Johnston illustrates, as holy war doctrine.[14] The Christian understanding, following the writings of classical thinkers, is that violence and a "call to arms" are justified to defend threats to Christian religion and to punish heretics. "The enemies of the church," wrote the authoritative Christian jurist Gratian, "are to be coerced even by war."[15] Although Christianity, in its beginnings, was pacifist and opposed to violence of any sort, many historians argue that only so long as Christianity was a sectarian and minority religion could it hold on to its pacifist sensibilities. When Christianity became identified with the Roman state, it was forced to defend its doctrines. Being in power and concerned with security and order gradually forced Christianity to articulate a holy war doctrine to justify violence in the name of religion.[16]

Theologically, as well, Christianity as a world religion had to protect its doctrines from theological contamination, and the just use of war and violence was understood as a way of preserving the genuine and authentic Christian faith. As a universalistic faith meant to offer the sole possibility of salvation for all humanity, Christianity viewed all other religions as false and therefore dangerous to the spiritual well-being of the faithful. Enemies of Christianity came to mean, over the course of Christian history, not only those who represented a material threat to Christianity but also sectarians and heretics who rejected conventional and official Christian orthodoxy. Non-Christians, including Muslims and Jews who rejected the Christian savior and continued their own religious beliefs and practices, were similarly enemies of the church, and force and violence against them were justified. The underlying idea in justifying Christian violence was that the church had the sacred obligation and divine mandate to oust evil and champion the true word of God and, in this way, continue as "God's obedient and faithful servant."[17] The various wars, persecutions, and inquisitions throughout Christian history need to be viewed in the context of the church's self-understood obligation to defend "correct faith" against the dangers of heresy and alien faith.[18] These wars, mass murders. and the planned destruction of towns and communities where enemies of the church lived were justified as a religious duty to protect the faithful and maintain Christian communal life and religiosity. The Crusades, while surely influenced by a variety of economic factors, were very much a holy war for Christianity to maintain theological and social control and to stop alien religions and heretical sects from having undue power and influence. On the way to conquer the Holy Land from the Muslims by force of arms, the crusaders destroyed dozens of Jewish communities and killed thousands because the Jews would not accept the Christian faith. Jews had to be killed in this religious campaign because their very existence challenged the sole truth espoused by the Christian church. The Jews, in the words of the liturgy, were "perfidious" and were seen by the masses as responsible for the Christian savior's death. Their very existence amidst Christendom was seen as a challenge and threat to Christian faith and intermittent violence pursued them throughout the medieval and early modern periods of Christian history. The Muslims were seen as a threat to the Christian faithful and murder and mayhem were religiously justified as the crusaders made their to the Holy Land. The Christian-Muslim wars were frequently fought over territory, but an underlying motivation, as historians have shown, was the religious goal to remove their alien spiritual presence from Christian lands.[19]

In its role of defender of faith, the church declared war during the medieval period on any deviationist sect, orthodox or liberal, within the precincts of Christianity. Two such Christian groups persecuted and killed over the course of several centuries were the Albigensians and Waldensians, who espoused a more rigorous piety than the medieval church thought justified. This involved, in the case of the Albigensians, complete celibacy for all Christians and, for both of these groups, the establishment of alternative clerical hierarchies. Members of these groups, who were defined as threats to the church and to genuine faith, were labeled heretics, persecuted, and burned at the stake.[20] During the Reformation, wars between Catholics and Protestants were fought all over Europe. This was a particularly stressful time of religious competition between Christian groups, and each side appealed to holy war arguments to justify violence against the other side. The influential sixteenth-century Swiss Protestant theologian Heinrich Bullinger, defending Protestant theology, argued that wars against Catholics were justified, for Catholics were blasphemers and violence against them could be regarded as the "defense of true religion against idolaters." In almost the same characterization, the distinguished contemporary of Bullinger, William Cardinal Allen, justified violence against Protestants for their "wilde condemned heresies."[21]

The Christian ethicist Jean Bethke Elstain is perhaps the leading contemporary Christian proponent of the "just war" doctrine. Elstain maintains that Christian values justify military strikes against terrorists and criminal regimes that engage in indiscriminate violence against innocent victims. Elstain makes the case that by not responding to the genocide in Rwanda in the 1990s, for example, the United States was avoiding its moral responsibility to use its power to stop mass murder. The al-Qaeda attack on the United States, as well, permits military retaliation. Christians, argues Elstain, are not free to avoid confrontation but have a Christian religious obligation to engage in just, reasonable, and focused wars to prevent greater bloodshed.

However, Jacques Ellul, a highly influential French Christian thinker, has argued that a widespread sense of remorse over the violent events of European Christian history, together with the rise of secularization and the modern nation-state, has appropriately resulted in Christianity's virtual retreat from engagement in holy wars.[22] This view, now popular and influential in Christian mainstream theology, sees holy war violence as a relic of the past, part of Christian religious infancy. But recent and continuing events in Bosnia, Croatia, Ireland, Nigeria, and the United States put this conclusion in question. Be that as it may, Christian violence and just wars continue, although some Christian circles seek to distance themselves from these conflicts. Indeed, religious violence as scriptural obligation is now enjoying something of a renaissance in radical Christian liberationist movements, particularly in Latin America. These movements continue to invoke holy war justifications in their struggle for increased equality and material well-being for the world's poor and needy.

Islam's approach to holy war can be traced to the pre-Islamic polytheistic religious culture of Arabia. In the view of Islam, Arabian society at that time was living in an age of *jahiliyya*— an age of ignorance and a culture bereft of ethics and morality.[23] It was a time of indiscriminate violence and immorality, an age of barbarism where no person was really safe, and this state of jahiliyya was encouraged by the prevalent pre-Islamic pagan religious cults. The prophecy of Muhammad and the message of the Koran constituted a call by Allah to reject pagan practices and immorality and establish an ethical and moral order in accordance with the will of God as delineated in the messages contained in the Koran. This meant that considerable effort and struggle—jihad, in the Muslim understanding—would have to be expended to transform a pagan, immoral society living in jahiliyya into a Islamic state governed by laws and authority which emanated from the one supreme God Allah. Practically, this meant that the struggle or jihad fought on behalf of Allah might have to involve coercive and violent battles in order to destroy the culture of jahiliyya and achieve the goals and society ordained in the Koran. Jihad could involve political or ideological battles, but jihad also could be a holy war resulting in death and destruction in order to obliterate an immoral social and political order and replace it with a Muslim community governed by divine law, *sharia*, as interpreted by Muslim clerics. The Koran was aware of the difficulties of waging war and conducting violence on behalf of religion and did not suggest it lightly. Nonetheless, it had to be done to eliminate immorality and establish God's order.[24]

The scriptural call to establish a Muslim *ummah*, an embracing Muslim community, has led Islam since the time of the prophet Muhammad to divide the world between the lands and states under Muslim control, referred to in Muslim jurisprudence as *Dar al-Islam*, the domain of Islam, and those lands and territories not under Muslim jurisdiction, called *Dar al-Harb*, the domain or abode of war. The faithful Muslim's duty is to engage in religious struggle, jihad, to transform non-Muslim lands, the Dar al-Harb, into Dar al-Islam lands, governed by Muslim law. The goal of jihad is not to force individual conversions but to bring about the transformation, by force and violence if necessary, of non-Muslim areas into Muslim-controlled states, whereby they become part of the Islamic world, the Dar al-Islam. Islam from its earliest periods permitted monotheistic religions like Christianity and Judaism to maintain their religious institutional life within Muslim societies, but these communities, known as *dhimmi* communities, while permitted religious and economic rights, were consigned to an inferior status and subject to special taxes and obligations. Unlike dhimmis, citizens of non-Muslim societies are seen as *harbi*, people living in a war zone and therefore subject to conquest. Bernard Lewis, the distinguished Islamic historian, has explained that holy war, in appropriate settings, is an essential element in the Muslim religious mission. "There is a canonically obligatory perpetual war," Lewis writes, "between Islamic civilization and non-Islamic societies which must be fought by faithful Muslims" until the whole world either accepts the message of Islam or submits to those who bring it.[25] The world, in the Muslim view, is divided between "Islam" and "war," and the devout believer must answer the call of jihad to advance Allah's message for all mankind. From a classical Islamic perspective, believers should throw themselves into an unending jihad until their religious duty of world transformation is complete. Despite these theological considerations, political reality, military strategy, and evolving religious understandings have modified Islam's approach to holy war. Throughout the course of Islamic history, the precise contexts and meanings of jihad and Dar al-Islam and the concomitant justifications for holy war have changed. In the earliest periods of Islamic history, when Islam was steadily advancing in the ancient and medieval world, it was assumed that all non-Muslim lands would be conquered and take their place in the greater Dar al-Islam. After the Spanish *Reconquista* and the expulsion of Islam from the European continent, the classical view of total and constant jihad was modified to fit the gradual loss of Muslim hegemony. Despite these changes and many other theological adjustments and controversies throughout the centuries to this day, the call to jihad and holy war remains central to Islamic doctrine and religious culture.[26]

Contemporary Holy Wars: Case Studies

Judaism, Islam, and the Middle East Conflict

We now turn to a series of case studies describing and analyzing holy wars being fought around the world. We begin with the Middle East conflict, which is, perhaps, among the most serious and dangerous religious confrontations. It threatens not only the immediate region with war and destruction but could envelop Europe and America in a global war, with the possibility of the use of nuclear weapons. This is not a new conflict and it has its origins in the rise of modern Zionism in the nineteenth century and the return of Jews in increasing numbers to the biblical Holy Land in the late nineteenth and early twentieth centuries. Palestine, as the territory was known, was then a sparsely populated land with both a Muslim and Jewish populace but under the governance of the Muslim Ottoman empire. After World War I and the dissolution of the Ottoman empire, the governance of Palestine was given over to Great Britain as a League of Nations mandate to run affairs until the territory could be equitably divided between Jews and Muslims. Earlier, in November 1917, the British government had issued the so-called Balfour Declaration promising a national homeland for the Jewish people in their ancestral homeland in Palestine, and Jews from many lands, particularly from Eastern Europe, emigrated to Palestine in the 1920s and 1930s. World War II and the European Holocaust, in which six million Jews were killed in European death camps, accelerated migration to Palestine and convinced Western governments that a national home for the Jewish people was necessary. After much diplomatic negotiation between representatives of the Jewish and Arab communities and because of the impossibility of establishing a pluralistic binational state, a partition plan organized and approved by the United Nations was put into effect and the historic land of Israel was divided between Jews and Arabs. One state, Israel, became a Jewish state, while the other was to be an Arab state.[27]

The Jewish community in Palestine accepted the partition plan but the Muslim world, believing the partition arrangements to be unfair, refused to participate, and the first of several Arab-Israeli wars broke out in 1947 after the announcement of the partition plan. An armistice, but not a permanent peace treaty, was agreed upon in 1949, but violent clashes continued, with major wars breaking out in 1956 and again in 1967. The 1967 war, sometimes referred to as the Six-Day War but also considered by Muslims to be a "war of humiliation," was to have major repercussions, as it changed the geopolitical arrangements between the two sides. Israeli forces occupied the entire Muslim territory in 1967, and several years later, under pressure from religious nationalists like the Gush Emmunim, the Bloc of the Faithful, began settling lands in the Palestinian West Bank, which the Jewish settlers called Judea and Samaria, the sites of ancient Jewish cities in biblical times.[28] By the beginning of the twenty-first century, some 250,000 Jews lived in dozens of communities on the West Bank or, in the Jewish nationalists' view, in the ancient Jewish homeland of Judea and Samaria. The new Jewish settlements on the West Bank exacerbated an already tense conflict between the two sides and considerable violence erupted as Arab groups organized a series of *intifadas*, violent protests, to force the Israelis from what they saw as their ancestral Muslim land. The Israeli army was called in to stop the rioting and protests, and this in turn resulted in a seemingly unending chain of violence and counterviolence. Some elements on both sides turned to terrorism and killings, justifying these actions in the name of holy war. Suicide bombings, in which religious martyrs are wrapped in explosives and blow themselves up in public places to cause death and destruction to the religious enemy, became not-uncommon events. As the twenty-first century dawned, the violent confrontations became more serious as both sides began using increasingly sophisticated weaponry, including rockets and massive suicide bombs able to kill hundreds of people in civilian settings.

Both sides have many justifiable political arguments and legitimate historical grievances, but the conflict, at its root, is a religious conflict over rights to a land both sides consider holy and exclusively their own by religious fiat. The Jews, given their theology and holy scriptures, consider themselves to be God's "chosen people," to whom God has given the entire land of Israel as an eternal inheritance as part of the covenant which God made with their biblical patriarch, Abraham. The Hebrew Bible in Genesis records the promises which traditional Jews consider binding to this day:

> I will ratify my covenant between me and you and between your offspring after you, throughout their generations, as an

everlasting covenant, to be a God to you and your offspring after you; and I will give to you and your offspring after you the land of your sojourns—the whole of the land of Canaan—as an everlasting possession; and I will be a God to them. (Gn. 17:7–9)

Even earlier in the biblical text, as part of God's initial encounter with Abraham, who is to bring the message of ethical monotheism to the entire world, God tells Abraham: "For all the land you see, to you will I give it, and to your descendents forever." For Zionist Jews throughout the world these divine reassurances are indeed eternal and no political arguments can alter the divine arrangements. Foreign armies and nations have come to the Holy Land and with superior weaponry and power have taken possession of the land but all this is transitory, in the Jewish theological understanding, as the divine bond between the land of Israel and the Jewish people can never be broken. Rabbi Zvi Yehudah Kook, one of the twentieth century's most authoritative Zionist thinkers outrightly denied any other claim to the Holy Land. In his words, "This Land is ours; there are no Arab territories or Arab lands, but only Israeli territories—the eternal land of our forefathers which belongs in its Biblical territories to the government of Israel."[29]

The state of Israel, in this view, is not an ordinary political state and cannot engage in political compromise. The miraculous return to Jews to the land of Israel, in this view, is part of a divine plan for the redemption of all humanity, ushering in an age of peace and tranquility. The divine plan, however, is predicated on Jewish occupancy and sovereignty over the land of Israel. Consequently, the return of any part of the divinely promised land of Israel, any compromise over Jewish ownership, will retard messianic transformation and must be opposed.

> The State of Israel is divine. Not only must there be no retreat from a single kilometer of the land of Israel, God forbid, but on the contrary we shall conquer and liberate more and more. In our world encompassing undertaking there is no room for retreat.[30]

Islam, as well, is based on revelation and the special mandate of believers to create and maintain an ummah, an Islamic world community faithful to the sharia, the Muslim religious canon, and governed by the wisdom and learning of established religious authorities. In Islamic religious understanding, once an area has come to be part of the Muslim world, it is considered Muslim and should rightfully, forever, remain an integral part of the ummah. The areas of the Holy Land are, in Islamic understanding, Muslim lands, areas where Muslims have lived as an ummah for centuries and places where Islamic holy sites like al-Aqsa in Jerusalem and the Ibrahimi mosques in Hebron are located. The sacred site of the Haram al-Sharif in Jerusalem is located where the prophet Mohammed is believed to have ascended to heaven, and this sacred area continues to be under Israeli political sovereignty. These lands and holy sites are part of an extended Dar al-Islam,which may never be ceded to non-Muslims. Consequently, the Jewish state of Israel is an illegal and illegitimate entity in the midst of the Muslim world, an alien society foisted upon Islam by a military financed by a Christian West hostile to Islam.[31]

For the Islamic faithful, this situation cannot continue to exist. Palestine must be returned to Muslim authority and control and restored to its place as an essential and holy part of the Islamic world. In the Muslim view, the conflict can be resolved if the current Jewish government agrees to the full return of Muslim land. However, if Israel refuses, a holy war is to be fought to destroy the Jewish state and to remove the Jews, by violence if necessary, and take all their property. The distinguished Islamic scholar Ismail R. al-Faruqi, a committed Muslim and a professor of Islamic studies at Temple University, objects to indiscriminate violence and terrorism against Jews but insists that the state of Israel "had to be dismantled" and a war fought to destroy "the Zionist army, state and all its public institutions."[32] Al-Faruqi gives voice to deep elements in Islamic theology which would justify an all-out religious war, arguing that on moral, legal, and theological grounds, a Muslim holy war against Israel is justified.

Reality is recalcitrant of religious hopes and aspirations, and despite decades of conflict and negotiation, neither side, Muslim nor Jewish, has had its religious vision realized. The state of Israel is only on a portion of the homeland promised in the Bible and is, in many ways, a pluralistic, secular state with a substantial Arab population rather than the all-Jewish religious state awaiting the messiah envisioned by the faithful. For Islam, the holy sites and much of Muslim Palestine remain under Israeli domination, and the integrity of Dar al-Islam has not been restored. A Jewish government and powerful military supported by the United States hinders Muslims from reclaiming their lands and holy sites. Moderates and secularists on both sides are willing and able to compromise and work out some political solution akin to the 1947 calls for partition. For them it is a practical matter, a sort of win-win proposition. For the faithful on both sides, however, it is not a matter of politics at all but of divine imperative. The call, now, is for holy war on both sides, for the faithful to destroy and remove the other and realize, finally and totally, God's will.

The Christian War against Abortion

Christianity, in the view of many Christian and non-Christian scholars, appears to be eminently a religion of peace and reconciliation in the modern world. For most Christians, war is a thing of the past, and much of contemporary Christian theology has taken on a distinctly pacifist stance. Nonetheless, the just and holy war traditions of the Crusades and the wars against heretics in medieval and early modern Europe persist in sectors of radical Christianity. The desire to root out evil and establish God's order in this world with acts of what these believers consider sacred violence is still a not-unimportant part of Christianity in the contemporary world.

Radical Christian antiabortion groups approve and encourage violence and bombings against abortion clinics and justify the murder of what they call "abortion workers": physicians, nurses, drivers, security guides—in short, anyone who makes it possible, in any way, for a woman to obtain an abortion. In the view of these Christian activists, abortion is murder and the faithful Christian must act to stop this ongoing mass murder in America. Many Americans, surveys show, are similarly opposed to abortion, but while this opposition sometimes leads to civil disobedience and attempts to close abortion facilities, the mainstream groups all oppose violence as a means of opposition.[33] The radical Christian abortion opponents, however, consider the bombing of abortion clinics and the planned murder of abortion providers to be a religious obligation for faithful Christians. For them, mere protest and political action are an avoidance of the Christian's responsibility to create a Christian society faithful to the gospel. These Christians are members and followers of an informal confederation of ministers, churches, and antiabortion groups, many of which follow reconstruction Christian theology, which teaches that it is Christians' duty to transform secular materialistic society into a Christian theocracy which will eventually be able to properly welcome Jesus Christ when he returns in triumph to establish the kingdom of God. Followers of reconstruction theology have a postmillennial view of Christian history, believing that Jesus will return to earth only after Christians have reconstructed society to make it conform to the social and political morals and standards compatible with Christ's teachings. Not all reconstruction thinkers condone indiscriminate violence, but the movement urges its followers to do all they can to destroy secular American society and set up the Bible as the law of the land.[34]

The murder of abortion providers and the destruction of clinics are all part of a self-understood holy war which Christians are fighting to create a Christian society. Violence is indicated and appropriate under the conditions of contemporary America, which is portrayed in the literature as a neopagan society where the killing of unborn babies has become routine. Neal Horsley of the Creator's Rights Party, a spokesman for this extreme antiabortion movement, writing in defense of *The Army Of God* manual, a radical manifesto encouraging and justifying bombing and terrorism against government installations, contends that violence is necessary and justified in opposing abortion facilities. In his view, the government's support and legalization of abortion is, itself, a "declaration of war" because it gives people the right to "kill and slay" innocent babies. In a condition of war, Horsley argues, Christians have the right to fight back on behalf of the unborn and entirely innocent victims. *The Army Of God* position is correct, Horsley explains, in urging all sorts of terrorist acts because the "government of the United States has become a godless and apostate body" and violence is entirely appropriate to destroy such "idolatry."[35] A similar stance is taken by Rev. Michael Bray, a Lutheran-raised graduate of a Baptist Bible college in Colorado who is the author of *A Time to Kill*, the influential book laying out the theological justifications for violence against abortion facilities. Bray, who was convicted in 1985 of destroying seven abortion clinics, explained in an interview that "Americans live in a situation comparable to Nazi Germany" and that Christians need to call attention to the nation's depravity and immorality.[36] It is really only courageous Christians willing to serve time in prison or even be put to death by the state, in this view, who can save the nation from its downward spiral. Violence is, for these groups, a small price to pay for the ultimate transformation of secular, godless America into a nation living under Christian rule.

In reading the writings and speeches of these radical Christians, one is struck by how alienated, angry, and intimidated by contemporary culture they are. American culture and its separation of church and state, its values of tolerance and freedom of religion, its openness to non-Christian immigrants—all are seen as signs of moral decay and corruption and are, in this view, inherently anti-Christian. The United States, itself, has become a religious enemy. Paul Hill, a former Presbyterian minister who shot and killed a Pensacola, Florida, abortion doctor and his escort in 1992 and is now on death row in the Florida State Penitentiary, talks about "the inner joy and peace that has flooded my soul since I have cast off the state's tyranny." Hill, who willingly surrendered to police after his double murder, explains that the happiness and contentment he now experiences on death row is the result of the certainty of "having freely obeyed Christ after long being enslaved to fearful obedience to men."[37] Hill acknowledges his murders and accepts his imprisonment and perhaps his eventual execution but justifies his behavior as a "Phineas action" along the lines of the biblical priest Phineas, who killed an Israelite and his heathen consort for violating God's prohibition against consorting with foreign women. In the biblical narrative, Phineas's action is utterly pleasing to God and saved the Ancient Israelites from destruction. As recorded in Leviticus 25:10, God rewards zealotry, telling the assembled, "Phineas turned back my wrath from upon the Children of Israel when he zealously avenged Me so I did not consume the people the children of Israel in My vengeance." Murder and holy war against abortion facilities, are, in this view, acts of compassion and redemption for a sinning nation. The biblical story of Phineas has been made contemporary and the actions of those involved in the killing of abortion providers and the bombing of abortion sites are compared to the hero of the biblical narrative. In this view, engaging in violence is a religious act.[38]

While these Christian violent activists are outside the contemporary Christian mainstream, they nonetheless partake in a larger conservative and fundamentalist understanding of Christian faith which calls Christians to act against what they view as illicit and immoral political authority. This Christian imperative to stand up against evil, to wage war and engage in violence on behalf of the Christian mission, has been and remains an essential part of the Christian mosaic. Violence and murder in the antiabortion movement are understood by many as a direct continuation of the religious activism which once animated Christian history. When a Wichita judge in 1993 told the now well-known Shelly Shannon, a devout born-again Christian who fired at and wounded Dr. George Diller, a doctor at an abortion clinic, that what she did was morally and legally wrong, she replied, "That's what they said about Jesus." In speaking to sympathetic Christians, she proclaimed, "It was the most holy, the most righteous thing I have ever done."[39]

The American Christian antiabortion movement has been linked to about two dozen attempted murders and hundreds of cases of assault and bombings. From all reports there are not a very large number—probably only a few hundred—of active participants who are willing to participate in the planning and execution of violence. Nonetheless the movement, as *New York*

Times' writer David Samuels has shown, has a wide network of sympathizers and supporters.⁴⁰ Some provide safe houses and permit suspects to evade police by providing cover for the suspected assailants. Others help finance weapons purchases, transportation costs, and living needs. Still others provide public support by writing letters to newspapers and politicians in support of the religious violence or give large sums for the defense of those activists who are arrested. All see themselves—both those who contribute funds and those who pull the triggers—as Christian warriors motivated by religious faith and passion. They are convinced that it is God's work they do. The rather extensive infrastructure of faithful Christians who support the actual violence is critical to the success of the movement, which has in the last decade been able to severely limit access to legal abortions, and it is their continuing vision of an army of God marching to reclaim an idolatrous nation that empowers their struggle.

Al–Qaeda, Osama bin Laden, and the Holy War against America

Perhaps the most dangerous holy war is the war declared in 1998 by the radical Islamic sheik, Osama bin Laden, and his al-Qaeda organization against the United States of America. Bin Laden is a charismatic Muslim radical sheik, born into a rich and prominent Saudi family, with thousands of followers all over the world who are committed to his program of militant Islam. The al-Qaeda network itself is organized as a secret society operating in terrorist cells all over the globe, ready to strike against enemy targets. For al-Qaeda, the United States is a "satanic" empire, a land of *kufrs,* immoral infidels who in consort with the apostate Muslim elites in Egypt, Jordan, Saudi Arabia, and other Muslim states, cooperated with the United States in the 1991 Gulf War, and have, against Islamic religious law, permitted American troops to be stationed in the sacred precincts of Saudi Arabia. Moreover, the United States is a land of sexual immorality and idolatrous beliefs and guilty of exploiting Muslim countries for their oil and other natural resources.

The United States, moreover, is seen as the world power representing world Christianity and Judaism, "the Zionist-Crusader alliance," in Osama bin Laden's rhetoric, who are determined to destroy Islam. The United States uses all its power, influence, and foreign aid to subvert Muslim religiosity and Islamic institutions. Bin Laden's call for war and violence against all Americans is based on his fundamentalist but highly traditional and pious interpretation of Muslim texts, which he argues demand that all Muslims participate in a holy war which will bring violence and death to Americans as individuals and to the Unites States as a nation. In several of his formal *fatwas,* religious verdicts or proclamations, bin Laden makes a case for Muslim holy war against the United States because of alleged U.S. involvement in the arrest of Muslim scholars, the destruction of Muslim governments and economies, the violation of Muslim holy sites, and encouragement of the massive abnegation of sharia in Muslim society. Failure to participate in his call to jihad will, bin Laden argues, result in punishment by Allah and can lead to recalcitrant Muslims who cooperate with the enemies of Islam themselves being labeled sinners. There is great theological sophistication and deep insight into Islamic law and history in bin Laden's declarations, but also a complete rejection of the West as wholly evil and a civilization which conspires against Islam and all Muslim people and seeks to destroy them physically and spiritually. Western scholars and diplomats have underestimated the religious esteem in which faithful Muslims hold bin Laden. In his famous 1996 declaration to the Islamic world, particularly to the clergy and those knowledgeable of the sacred texts, bin Laden put it this way: "It should not be hidden from you that the people of Islam had suffered from aggression, iniquity and injustice imposed on them by the Zionist-Crusader alliance and their collaborators to the extent that the Muslims' blood became the cheapest and their wealth as loot in the hand of the enemies."[41]

Bin Laden's writings have argued that the proper Islamic answer to these Jewish and Christian enemies is not political negotiation or religious dialogue but violence and holy war organized by Islamic clerics and their faithful followers. In his call for holy war, bin Laden has been able to selectively interpret

Islamic history, demonstrating, from his point of view, that war is the required response to the threats now posed by the United States in its role of oppressor of Islam. The United States and its ally Israel imprison Muslim religious leaders like Sheik Abdul Rahman, who called for the 1993 attack against the World Trade Center and was involved in the assassination of charismatic fundamentalist Sheik Abdullah Azzam in Afghanistan. Bin Laden's essays and writings always touch upon the humiliation that the West, particularly America, has caused to pious Muslims and their leaders. This rhetoric has had great influence on faithful Muslims and helps explain somewhat his continuing popularity and religious standing. Bin Laden calls upon the ummah, the faithful Muslim community, to rise up "against its enemies as their ancestor scholars, may Allah be pleased with them, like Ibn Taymiyyah and Al'z Ibn Abdes Salaam did."[42] Invoking these great figures in Islamic history and scholarship has great resonance in the Muslim world, and sensitive and educated Islamic readers understand bin Laden to be part of a long line of Islamic warriors.[43] His Arabic poems are read and recited widely in the Muslim world and his language and style capture the flavor of the glory days of the caliphate and the era of Muslim world hegemony. For these reasons, bin Laden has gained respect, financial help, and protection from important Muslim constituencies who may disagree with his program of violent holy war and terrorism against the West. The al-Qaeda faithful are not viewed as outlaws or terrorists but as dedicated traditionalists who espouse a sectarian but historic view of Islam as presented in the Koran and in the teachings of the Prophet Muhammad. For many traditionally pious Muslims, Bin Laden's program of Muslim world dominance is a legitimate religious objective.

The al-Qaeda movement has translated their holy war declarations into highly organized and strategically successful terrorist attacks all over the world. The most spectacular, of course, was the September 11 suicide bombings of the World Trade Center in New York City and the Pentagon in Washington in which thousands were killed and the entire World Trade Center destroyed. Prior to the September 11 attacks, the al-Qaeda movement launched successful attacks on American naval vessels and U.S. military installations overseas and in 1998 carried out bombings of American embassies in Kenya and Tanzania, killing hundreds of people in the name of holy war. The al-Qaeda movement suffered a series of setbacks during the war in Afghanistan and many al-Qaeda members were killed or captured and imprisoned by American antiterrorist forces in that war. American troops, however, were unsuccessful in capturing or locating Osama bin Laden himself. It appears that bin Laden remains in hiding but continues to lead the movement, directing its holy war operations and regularly issuing religious proclamations and communiqués to his followers urging them on in their jihad campaigns. The al-Qaeda movement, from all reports, has been under severe attack but still operates as a viable movement with the ability and determination to continue its violent campaign of holy war against the United States.

The continuing al-Qaeda war against the United States was publicized dramatically during the January 2003 trial of the so-called shoe bomber Richard Reid, a British convert to Islam and a member of the al-Qaeda network, who concealed explosives in his shoes and was caught and captured during a transatlantic American Airlines flight as he attempted to detonate the bomb. Reid was unrepentant and claimed that he was not a criminal but a soldier fighting in a jihad battle. The United States was guilty of killing innocent Muslims all over the world, he told the court, and he claimed that " I don't see what I done as being equal to rape and torture or the deaths of two million children in Iraq." The judge in the case told Reid that he was a criminal and terrorist who would spend his life in prison, but Reid proclaimed his continued allegiance to bin Laden, yelling at the judge, "You will be judged by Allah. Your flag will come down and so will your country."[44]

Bin Laden's ultimate goal is the destruction of the United States, the dismantling of what he calls "infidel" regimes in the Muslim world, and the establishment of a worldwide Muslim society, a caliphate, under the rule of Muslim clerics and religious authorities. This goal and the hatred of America are rejected by many Muslims, but they have considerable appeal among radical and militant Islamic groups. It is among these groups, their mosques and religious schools, that bin Laden operatives and warriors are recruited. Though bin Laden represents a highly sectarian Islamic religiosity, his astute use of Muslim scripture and sharia and his appeals to Muslim pride and resentment of the West appeal to Muslims all over the Islamic world. His call for holy war resonates with many Muslims and his religious arguments cannot be easily dismissed. Bin Laden continues to attract recruits from all over the world, including the United States, Canada, and Great Britain. There are estimates that thousands of holy warriors have been trained in al-Qaeda facilities. From captured documents, it is clear that the training is technically sophisticated and severe, and commitment to the movement is expected to be total.[45] One document from an al-Qaeda house in Afghanistan captured in 2002 contains a written oath signed by an al-Qaeda soldier declaring, "I, Abdul Maawia Siddiqi, son of Abdul Rahman Siddiqui state in the presence of God that I will slaughter infidels all the days of my life." Indeed, some al-Qaeda warriors captured by United States intelligence in Afghanistan and elsewhere have refused to surrender and have sought to fight to their death in their war against the infidels.

Conclusion: The Significance of the Holy War Perspective on Religious Violence

The holy war perspective discussed in this chapter alerts and sensitizes students of religious violence to the continuing importance of religious scripture, tradition, and history in the modern world. While it may be true that secularization and the loss of religious faith and religious involvement in politics and society have taken place among educated elites in the United States and Western Europe, much of the rest of the world still takes religious faith seriously and desires that religion play a strong role in politics and society. Religious scriptures, which are viewed in highly secular societies as perhaps interesting and inspiring but still only literature or myth, are, in more traditional societies, taken to be the literal word of God. Faith and religious behavior are not based upon science, practical politics, or Western notions of logic and efficiency but on following the word of God regardless of the cost. Holy wars, as this perspective makes clear, may not be amenable to logical and rational solutions. Faithful holy warriors, whether in Afghanistan, Israel, Palestine, or Florida, live in a psychic and social reality entirely different from the world inhabited by secularized people. They think and feel differently about life and death, war and peace, war and killing, or dying a martyr's death. Perhaps Sheik Ahmed Yassim, the charismatic leader of the Palestinian Hamas movement explained it best. Pressed by a sympathetic *New Yorker* magazine journalist to explain the motivation behind suicide bombings, the sheik demurred, explaining that Westerners simply cannot understand religious martyrdom. They are so distant from a sense of connection with the divine, Sheik Yassim told the Arabic-speaking reporter, that religious sacrifice, instantaneous forgiveness for sins, and entrance to eternal life—the reward for suicide bombers—are entirely beyond American understanding. Tell your audience, the sheik instructed, that we do "all for Allah."[46]

For holy warriors, history is not a matter of the past, something to be studied for its inherent interest or even for the practical lessons that can be learned. History is the arena for the realization of God's blueprint, and things that have gone wrong must be made right. There is really no past and present for these believers, for they live in sacred time beyond the calculations of academic historians and journalists. The Beit Hamikdash, the Jewish temple in Jerusalem, destroyed two thousand years ago and the ancient center of the Jewish cult, remains a Jewish holy site and is worth defending in a holy war. For Muslims, the Haram al-Sharif, the place where Muslim narratives describe the prophet Muhammad ascending to heaven, is a Muslim holy site. Defeats or victories recorded in the Bible, the Koran, and the Bhagavad Gita, whether based on historical fact or religious myth, are indeed still to be taken as truth. Jack Hawley, the distinguished professor of Hinduism at Columbia University, explains that history always matters in religious disputes, but what is important is not what actually happened but what the faithful take to be the historical past. The holy war perspective, finally, forces us to confront the radically different realities in which warring religious groups exist. Religious conflicts and holy wars are ultimately battles over the nature of reality, truth, and values. Each protagonist sees its truth claims as absolute and within the parameters of the logic and calculus of its society; each group is convinced of its claims. Secularized people without a strong anchor in absolute reality and faith are often cultural and religious relativists, seeing no one commitment or faith as inherently superior. The continuing reality of religious wars fought on behalf of religious faith in the postmodern era demonstrates that in many quarters the old gods are very much alive, and despite the Western assumption of universal secularization, materialism, and rationality, many religions continue to maintain their own religious realities and are willing to die for them.

Notes

All biblical references in this book are from *The Stone Edition Tanach*, ed. Nosson Scherman (Brooklyn, N.Y.: Mesorah, 1996).

1. Interview by Rachel Kohn, *In the Spirit of Things*, Australian Radio National, August 13, 2000. See www.abc.net.au/rn/relig/spirit/stories/s163397.htm for transcript.

2. See Peter Partner, *God of Battles: Holy Wars of Christianity and Islam* (London: HarperCollins, 1997) for a historical survey of holy wars. Also see Gershon Gorenberg, *The End of Days: Fundamentalism and the Struggle for the Temple Mount* (New York: Free Press, 2000) for a discussion of holy war in the contemporary Middle East.

3. Richard Rubinstein, "The Temple Mount and My Grandmother's Paper Bag" in *Jewish-Muslim Encounters: History, Philosophy, and Culture*, ed. Charles Selengut (St. Paul: Paragon, 2001), 141.

4. See Brian Victoria, *Zen at War* (New York: Weatherhill, 1988).

5. See Harry M. Orlinsky, "The Situational Ethics of Violence in the Biblical Period" in *Violence and Defense in the Jewish Experience*, ed. Solo W. Baron and George S. Wise (Philadelphia: Jewish Publication Society, 1997).

6. See John Kelsay, *Islam and War: A Study of Comparative Ethics* (Louisville, Ky.: Westminster, 1979).

7. See Peter L. Berger, *The Sacred Canopy: Elements of a Sociological Theory of Religion* (New York: Doubleday, 1967), 23–25.

8. See John Kelsay and James Turner Johnson, eds., *Cross, Crescent, and Sword: The Justification and Limitation of War in Western and Islamic Tradition* (New York: Greenwood, 1991).

9. Hans Gerth and C. Wright Mills, eds. *From Max Weber* (New York: Oxford University Press, 1946), 245–248.

10. Orlinsky, "Situational Ethics," 45.

11. For an analysis of the development of the "holy war" doctrine in Jewish theology, see Ephraim Urbach, "Jewish Doctrines and Practices in Halachic and Aggaddic Literature," in Baron and Wise, *Violence and Defense in Jewish Experience*, 87–112.

12. Moses Maimonides, Law of Kings, 4, *Mishnah Torah*.

13. See Gershom Gorenberg, *The End of Days: Fundamentalism and the Struggle for the Temple Mount* (New York: Free Press, 2000).

14. James Turner Johnston, "Historical Roots and Sources of Just War Traditions in Western Culture," in *Just War and Jihad: Historical Perspectives on Peace and War in Western and Islamic Traditions*, ed. John Kelsay and James Turner Johnson (Westport, Conn.: Greenwood, 1992), 49.

15. Johnston, "Historical Roots."

16. See Partner, *God of Battles*, chap. 4.

17. Johnston, "Historical Roots," 54.

18. Edward Peters, *Inquisition* (New York: Free Press, 1988).

19. B. Z. Kedar, *Crusade and Mission: European Approaches toward the Muslims* (Princeton, N.J.: Princeton University Press, 1988).

20. Peters, *Inquisition*, 51–62. For a historical survey and sociological analysis of violence against sects and heretical groups see Rodney Stark, *For the Glory of God: How Monotheism Led to Reformations, Science, Witch Hunts, and the End of Slavery* (Princeton, N.J.: Princeton University Press, 2003), esp. chap. 1.

21. Johnston, "Historical Roots," 52–55.

22. See Jacques Ellul, *Violence: Reflections from a Christian Perspective* (London: SCM Press, 1970).

23. Karen Armstrong, *The Battle for God* (New York: Alfred A. Knopf, 2000), 218–258.

24. *The Meaning of the Holy Qur'an*, trans. Abdullah Yusuf Ali (Brentwood, Md.: Amana, 1989), 9:5.

25. Bernard Lewis, *The Jews of Islam* (Princeton, N.J.: Princeton University Press, 1984), 21.

26. Armstrong, *Battle for God*, 238–244.

27. Joan Peters, *From Time Immemorial: The Origins of the Arab-Jewish Conflict over Palestine* (New York: Harper & Row, 1988).

28. See "Jewish Zionist Fundamentalism: The Bloc of Faithful in Israel (Gush Emmunim)" in Martin E. Marty and R. Scott Appleby, *Fundamentalism Observed* (Chicago: University of Chicago Press, 1991).

29. Quoted in Ehud Sprinzak, *The Ascendance of Israel's Radical Right* (New York: Oxford University Press, 1991), 46.

30. Sprinzik, *Ascendance of Israel's Radical Right*, 116–117.

31. Ismail R. Al-Faruqui, "Islam and Zionism," in *Voices of Resurgent Islam*, ed. John L. Esposito (New York: Oxford University Press, 1983), 261–267.

32. Al-Faruqui, "Islam and Zionism," 263.

33. Faye Ginsburg, "Saving America's Souls: Operation Rescue's Crusade against Abortion" in Martin E. Marty and R. Scott Appleby, *Fundamentalism and the State* (Chicago: University of Chicago Press, 1993).

34. See Gary North, *Backward Christian Soldiers? An Action Manual for Christian Reconstruction* (Tyler, Tex.: Institute for Christian Economics, 1984). Also see Mark Juergensmeyer, *Terror in the Mind of God: The Global Rise of Religious Violence* (Berkeley and Los Angeles: University of California Press, 2000), 24–30.

35. Neal Horseley, *Understanding the Army of God*, www.christian gallery.com, accessed April 8, 2002.

36. Quoted in Juergensmeyer, *Terror in the Mind of God*, 23

37. Paul Hill, " Letter to White Rose Bouquet," www.christiangallery.com, accessed April 8, 2002.

38. See Jeffrey Kaplan, *Radical Religion in America: Millenarian Movements from the Far Right to the Children of Noah* (Syracuse, N.Y.: Syracuse University Press, 1997), 65–66.

39. Quoted in Anne Bower, "Soldier in the Army of God," www.monitor.net, accessed April 12, 2002.

40. David Samuels, "The Making of a Fugitive," *New York Times Magazine*, March 21, 1999, 47.

41. For an in-depth study of the history of al-Qaeda, see Yossef Bodansky, *Bin Laden: The Man Who Declared War on America* (New York: Random House, 2001). For a study of terrorism and an analysis of captured documents see Roland Jacquard, *In the Name of Osama Bin Laden: Global Terrorism and the bin Laden Brotherhood* (Durham, N.C.: Duke University Press, 2002).

42. Yonah Alexander, *Osama bin Laden's al-Qaida: Profile of a Terrorist Network* (Ardsley, N.Y: Transnational, 2001), app. 1.

43. See Bodansky, *Bin Laden*, 71–151, for an analysis of bin Laden's theological positions in the context of contemporary Islam.

44. Pam Belluck, "Unrepentant Shoe Bomber Given a Life Sentence," *New York Times*, January 31, 2003, sec. A, p. 13.

45. See Judith Miller, "Holy Warriors," *New York Times*, March 17, 2002, sec. A, p. 1, for documents and letters describing the organization and commitment of Al-Qaeda members. Also see documents in Alexander, *Al-Qaida*.

46. Nasra Hassan, "An Arsenal of Believers," *New Yorker*, November 19, 2001, 36–41.

2

Psychological Perspectives

In this chapter, we turn from studying scriptural and textual sources of religious violence to the psychology of religious conflict and violence. The psychological perspective does not focus on specific theological issues or matters of faith but analyzes violence as a way a social collectivity deals with envy, anger, and frustration. According to psychological theorists, the accumulated aggression, envy, and conflict within any society must find an outlet or the group itself will be destroyed by internal conflict and rivalry. Religious battles against competitors or those labeled enemies, in this view, are merely ways of allowing the human collectivity to express its pent-up anger. The violence expressed by the group takes religious form and is justified by religious vocabulary, but it is primarily a way to get rid of anger and aggression that, if left uncontrolled, would jeopardize social order and coherence. Put bluntly, religious battles are not about religion but about psychological issues and dilemmas that take religious form. There is the sense in this psychological approach that those involved in religious conflict and confrontation are themselves unaware of the underlying psychological forces and motivations which provoke and maintain the specific religious struggle.

The modern thinker who articulated many of these psychological ideas, particularly in *Totem and Taboo* and *The Future of an Illusion*, was Sigmund Freud, the father of psychoanalysis.[1] Freud saw civilized society as possible only in a situation where humans are forced to repress their instinctual desire to fully express their sexual and aggressive drives. In the Freudian view, human aggression and the propensity for violence do not have to be related to historical grievances or actual conflict. Human biology, social relations, and brain activity are intrinsically linked to aggression and violence, and despite all attempts at amelioration, aggression and violence remain an essential part of the human condition. The measure of social order we do enjoy, in the Freudian view, is made possible by the fierce demands of civilization, as seen in religious teachings, family socialization, schools, and the workplace. In his book, *Civilization and Its Discontents*, Freud summarizes his psychoanalytic view of human nature:

> Men are not gentle, friendly creatures wishing for love, who simply defend themselves if they are attacked, but that a powerful measure of desire for aggression has to reckoned as part of their instinctual endowment. The result is that their neighbor is to them not only a possible helper or sexual object, but also a temptation to them to gratify their aggressiveness on him, to exploit his capacity for work without recompense, to use him sexually without his consent, . . . to humiliate him, to cause him pain, to torture and kill him.[2]

Freud was an avowed atheist, and religion, in the Freudian system, is viewed as having no basis in empirical reality; it is an illusion fabricated to maintain social order by instilling fear of nonexistent, otherworldly punishments. Nonetheless, religion does have a positive function because it provides human collectivities with myths and rituals which help defuse the ever-present human aggression, which, if left without an outlet, would threaten social order and destroy society. Religious rituals like animal sacrifice and even human sacrifice were early religious attempts to enable the human collectivity to express its accumulated fury and aggression—instinctually always present—against a weak and unthreatening victim who could not retaliate. Later, rituals and myths developed to remember, commemorate, and vicariously relive these earlier real or imagined collective efflorescences of aggression and violence. In all these instances the sacrificial victim serves as a convenient outlet for the accumulated anger and sexual aggression engendered in the society that, if not expressed against the sacrificial object, would be taken out against members of the society. Sacrificial victims do not, in the Freudian view, represent an objective threat to the group; they are killed solely as a function of the group's need to gain release for the pent-up anger and aggression. In this way, Freud explains the ubiquitous nature of religious conflict and violence. Christianity, particularly, came under Freudian criticism as a religion preaching universal love but, like all religions, "showing the ultimate intolerance to all outside of it" and engaging, from time to time, in aggression against nonbelievers. In the Freudian view, the religious protagonists from time immemorial to the present are fighting, killing, and sacrificing in the name of religion, but the religious activity is an elaborate, if unconscious, cover-up.[3]

Girard, Mimetic Desire, and the Sacrificial Crisis

Rene Girard, the distinguished French literary critic, former professor at Stanford University, and author of such influential books as *Violence and the Sacred* and *Things Hidden Since the Foundation of the World,* is, perhaps, the most innovative thinker interpreting the relationship between religion and violence. His ideas are highly suggestive and controversial and all students of religious violence have had to contend with his significant ideas and analyses.[4]

For Girard, religious institutions are critical to the well-being of society because religion functions to defuse the anger and aggression that inevitably develop among people by providing rituals that serve as an outlet for actual and real anger and fury. Through ritual sacrifice and relived myths, religion encourages the expression of "safe" and controlled anger and aggression so that violence is not expressed against members of one's own group but against victims who cannot fight back, or the aggression is acted out in symbolic rituals in which aggressive emotions are acted out but no one is actually injured or killed. Girard takes the position that "sacrificial rites" are critical to avoiding war and violence. The classical example of a sacrificial rite is the killing of the scapegoat as part of the ancient Israelite Yom Kippur ritual. As described in the Hebrew Bible in the Book of Leviticus (16:2–30), one male goat was chosen by the high priest during the holiest service of the Jewish year in the Jerusalem temple to serve as an atonement for the sins of community. After a complex ritual in the temple, the designated sacrificial goat was dispatched to the Judean desert, where it was thrown from a cliff to its death. When news of the death reached the temple, the high priest announced that all sins for that past year were forgiven, and the masses congregated in the temple precincts rejoiced and celebrated their good fortune. In Girardian terms, the scapegoat ritual serves as an outlet for the collective anger and aggression that accumulates in social settings and if expressed within the group would destroy the social order. Through the collective expression of ritualized sacrifice, violence is removed from the group and directed against a safe "victim." Some form of ritual expression of aggression is part of every religion. Greek mythology and the Christian Gospels all partake of symbolic means of expelling violence through religion and myth. As Girard explains, it is never obvious how religion functions to provide outlets for violent impulses because "the function of ritual is to 'purify' violence; that is, to 'trick' violence into spending itself on victims whose death will provoke no reprisals"[5]

Girard takes issue with Freud as to the reason for human aggression and the need for violence. Where Freud emphasizes instinctual aggression, Girard sees violence as a result of envy and jealousy, what he calls "mimetic desire."[6] In Girard's understanding, mimetic desire is the wish to take on the positive attributes of another person, to be like that person in all the ways in which that person appears ideal, to act like that person, to have the high status, to be strong, wealthy, and socially desirable. This desire to emulate leads to envy, jealousy, and, according to Girard, ultimately to conflict and the desire to eliminate and destroy the model one so desires to imitate. Alternatively, we can become competitive with others in our society as to who is best achieving the ideal qualities of the societal model. Either way, mimetic desire leads inevitably to competition, comparison, and the desire to eliminate the competition. If the competition does lead to actual violence on the part of the desired other, violence will be responded to with violence and a never ending cycle of violence will ensue. It is important to recognize that, in Girard's perspective, aggression and violence emerge from the desire for sameness or even love and respect. The competitors begin by wanting to be like each other, but out of fear and envy they become enemies and want to eliminate each other. No society can tolerate this accumulated anger and violence. Religion, by providing sacred outlets for this violence in the form of sacrifices and holy war, is the means by which violence is kept out of the society. In other words, religion does not deny or repress violence in Girardian terms, but rather keeps it outside one's own social milieu by permitting violence against outsiders, those classified as enemies. As Girard tells us, "Ritual is nothing more than the regular exercise of 'good' violence."[7] However, should ritual and symbolic sacrifice not work, that is, if the collectivity no longer experiences the ritual and symbolic scapegoating as authentic and consequently it does not fulfill their need to express their violent and antisocial feelings, a "sacrificial crisis" ensues and society must now find real victims—actual rather than symbolic scapegoats—upon whom to vent their collective aggression. For Girard, it is essential that symbol, myths, and rituals be maintained in order to avoid the outbreak of actual violence. Both the historical cases of religious war and the many cases of contemporary religious conflict and violence are directly attributable, according to Girardian thinking, to the breakdown of symbolic rituals to defuse violence.

Girard's Theories Applied to Case Studies of Religious Violence

For Girard, the essence of religion and its essential function is to provide an outlet for the violence created by envy and competition. Religion, by sacralizing and legitimating violence against outside enemies or promoting ritual enactments of mythic violence, rids a society of its own intragroup violence. For Girard, as David Rapoport tells us, religion is a "stupendous collective deception" but an important deception, because it maintains societal stability by providing "unconscious" outlets for violence.[8] It is important to emphasize that in Girardian thinking what makes religious violence so functional is that those who engage in such violence see it as divinely ordained and feel no taint of shame or guilt. Religious violence is self-legitimating because it is based on sacred truth and does not need to be justified by secular or political logic or rationality. Religious warriors, for Girard, live in a Marxian "false consciousness" because they are unaware that by killing their enemies they are actually engaging in repairing and strengthening bonds of social relationships that make society possible.

Girard's work is controversial; a number of religious scholars have rejected his theoretical system as an insightful literary analysis of myth but one not supported by empirical studies of religious violence. Nonetheless as Mark Juergensmeyer has suggested, while the Girardian system may not apply in toto to a particular case, many elements of his theoretical model illuminate the nature of religious violence in contemporary societies.[9] Girard's work is particularly helpful because it incorporates myth, ritual, and the unconscious and refuses to explain violence as the result of logical goals or political strategy. His powerful insights on the role of mimetic desire involving violence which comes about through envy of those one admires and wants most to imitate, his insistence that violence has always been and remains an inevitable element in human relations, and his sensitivity to religion in its roles both to make peace and justify war highlight the conundrum of religious conflict and violence. In some way—and here one must remain sensitive to other elements promoting a particular conflict—Girard answers the eternal question, "Why are they killing each other?" Girard's answer would be, "While it might not make political or military sense, it may well make psychological sense and resolve a lot of internal and probably unconscious problems for the society."

A study of Israeli society and Israel's conflict with the Palestinians will help illustrate Girard's perspective, particularly his understanding of religious conflict as both an outlet for internecine conflict and a mechanism to create social solidarity and resolve intragroup tensions. Israeli society is ordinarily beset with considerable tensions between the strictly Orthodox Jews, *datiim*, who desire a Jewish state based upon *halacha*, Jewish religious law, and secular Jews, known as *hilonim*, who want a Jewish but secular democratic state. Datiim want Saturdays, the Jewish Sabbath day, to be officially observed in the orthodox fashion, with all commercial and recreational facilities closed and public transportation stopped. Hilonim see this as curtailing the enjoyment of the weekend, which for them includes mall shopping, visiting relatives and friends, and going to the beach, a popular Israeli pastime. Moreover, datiim demand rabbinical jurisdiction over marriage and divorce laws and insist that only their strict Orthodox Judaism be recognized as the state religion. Religion for the modern hilonim is a private and personal matter and not something to be legislated by rabbis or directed by government decree. The conflict and dissension between these two groups has resulted in their living in adjacent but separate societies. These divisions have caused segregation of neighborhoods, social circles, schools, and political parties, and in some cases even self-segregation in the Israeli army. Politically, the Orthodox tend to be hawkish and right-wing while the secular population is more open to peace negotiations with the Palestinians. The nationalist religious saw the Oslo Peace agreements of 1993, negotiated with Yasser Arafat and the Palestinians, as a sell-out and the architects of the Oslo agreement, including former prime ministers Yitzhak Rabin and Shimon Peres, as traitors for their willingness to cede Jewish land to the Arabs.[10]

Street fighting, verbal abuse, and actual physical violence between the two groups escalated throughout the 1990s, when the agreements ceding control to the Palestinian Authority was being implemented. The rhetoric in the nation's parliament and public forums reflected this tension, with each side calling the other disloyal. Some Orthodox rabbis enacted kabalistic ritual to put curses on leaders of secular Israel, and on at least one occasion, a famous rabbi gave approval for the assassination of Rabin. The secular camp, as well, went on the attack, calling the national religious camp warmongers and fanatics. One Hebrew University professor went so far as to call the national religious youth movement "Hitler Jugend," a reference to the notorious fascist youth movement in Nazi Germany. The professor claimed that the Israeli national youth movements brainwashed religious youth and encouraged them to engage in chauvinist, fascist, and warlike behavior.

The conflicts and confrontation within Israeli society virtually disappeared in the spring of 2002 when the Oslo peace process collapsed and the Israeli army invaded the newly autonomous Palestinian territories in Israel's fight against terrorism. This military action was justified, according to Israeli officials, as a defense of the homeland after suicide attacks against Israeli civilians in several Israeli cities. In their effort to eliminate the terrorist infrastructure, Israeli troops were deployed throughout the Palestinian areas, and the major Palestinian cities of Nablus and Ramallah were occupied by the Israeli army. As these troop movements and fighting were reported on Israeli TV and in the newspapers, the divisions in Israeli society began to recede into the background. Consensus grew and the unique contributions of each side were lauded in the national media. Former opponents of the datiim portrayed them as contributing essential functions to the nation by providing spiritual leadership and a moral compass during troubling times. Even those ultraorthodox who refused to serve in the military for religious reasons but worked in ambulance crews were praised for their contributions to the state and lauded for their love of their secular brethren. Secular Jews found themselves newly appreciated by their religious brothers and were portrayed as being the reliable backbone of the state, the sturdy builders and brawny types who made everyday life possible. Angry confrontations, conflict, and violence between the groups virtually disappeared. The national press agreed that the enemy must be defeated and even the nation's most liberal thinkers acknowledged that violence, however grim, must be undertaken to protect the state. The public mood was reflected in opinion polls. Instead of being a divided society on governmental and moral issues, 87 percent of Israeli Jews expressed strong support for government and its leadership and almost 90 percent said that peace cannot be made with the current Palestinian leadership. Yoram Hazony, writing in the *New York Times* about a month after the incursions into the Palestinian areas, described the new Israeli consensus in an essay appropriately entitled, "Israel's Right and Left Converge":

> Despite the suicide attacks on trendy hangouts . . . Israeli intellectuals still frequent Jerusalem's cafes. Conversations still linger into the night over espresso, served Italian-style with a small glass of soda. But the atmosphere has changed. Now many of the late-night heart-to-hearts are between lifelong members of Peace Now, the vanguard of the Israeli Peace movement, and veteran supporters of the West Bank settlers movement—people who were, until recently, bitterly divided enemies.[11]

Girard's work is most helpful in this connection. The greater harmony in Israeli society during this time of religious and national war is attributable to having an external enemy against whom to express the intragroup anger within Israeli society. The new harmony, in Girard's understanding, is purchased by engaging in violence against another so that violence is not taken out on one's own group. In Girard's analysis, the function of all religious wars is to keep the violence engendered in the community outside the community.[12] Wars that are fought for the most ideological and pure reasons are, in this view, merely elaborate attempts to defuse violence against neighbors so that social order will be maintained. This does not mean that wars are consciously fought to siphon off internal violence or to deny that there are political and economic triggers that generate violence. The power of Girard's work and his great contribution is his willingness, unlike many other scholars, to argue that religion is always involved with conflict and that the essence of religion is to enable societies to deal with their own internal violence. In Girard's view, religion does not have to be a force for violence. Genuine religion provides myths, stories, liturgy, and rituals that help a society express violent sensations symbolically so that actual violence need not occur. When myth and symbolical ritual do not work, religion will offer another solution to the crisis of excessive violence, and this solution will involve actual violence. Religious wars and conflicts are an example, in Girard's view, of religion's inability to do its work and resolve the problem of pent-up violence. The key function of religion for Girard is to purify violence, that is, to "trick" violence into spending itself on either symbolic victims or on outside enemies who will not challenge social harmony. Martin Kramer, in his study "Sacrifice and Fratricide in Shiite Lebanon," similarly found that conflict and rivalry between two feuding Muslim Shiite movements in the 1980s were halted when both groups came together to engage in the then-innovative tactic of suicide attacks against French, American, and Israeli targets in Lebanon.[13] The two militant groups, the Hezbolah, or Party of God, and the Lebanese Amal group had been feuding for years about who represented authentic Shiite Islam. In Girard's terms there existed considerable mimetic envy between the groups, and though to outsiders they shared much in theology and political outlook, each was envious of the presumed successful actions of the other on behalf of Shiite Islam. In 1982 both groups, for the first time and with the permission of leading Shiite clerics, began to engage in suicide bombings against Western targets, and immediately the conflict between the two groups subsided. As Kramer explained, the avowed goal of the suicide attacks was to drive Westerners from Lebanon, but "they also served to forestall the outbreak fratricidal violence from within."[14] The religiously sanctioned violence against enemies of Islam worked to contain the violence between Islamic brothers.

At first the suicide missions worked very well, in one case claiming 241 lives, and were well timed and coordinated. The military successes emboldened the Hezbolah and Amal leadership, encouraged increased clergy support, and gained widespread backing in the Shiite population. After a while, perhaps due to the Western military becoming better prepared to withstand the attacks, the suicide missions stopped achieving their military goals and increasingly younger Shiite were offering themselves as sacrifices. At a certain point leading clerics pulled away from this tactic, declaring it no longer useful and therefore illegitimate and against Islam. The suicide bombings continued for awhile, but without clerical support they ceased to be regarded as a viable tactic. The forced suspension of the bombings left the two groups without a sacrificial victim, in Girardian terms, as an outlet for their rivalry, and shortly after the suicide bombings ended, fratricidal violence between the two groups broke out. In January 1989, several hundred Hezbolah fighters entered an Amal stronghold and beheaded dozens of Amal followers and, in some cases, members of their families as well; others were tortured. Amal retaliated in similar fashion and the fratricide continued. Cease-fires would be pronounced periodically, but without another sacrificial victim the killing and violence between the two Muslim groups lasted for years. Without an outside victim, neighbors and Islamic brothers turned on each other, venting their fury and aggression. In Girardian terms, a sacrificial crisis must lead inevitably to violence.

Ehud Sprinzak, professor of political science at Hebrew University and a student of Israeli political extremism, applied Girard's notion of mimetic desire to the life and career of Rabbi Meir Kahane and his extremist Kach movement.[15] Sprinzak argues that the religious basis for the Kach movement was envy of gentile power and fury at Jewish persecution during the past centuries. Kahane and his followers, in Girardian terms, wanted to be as powerful and feared as they perceived the gentiles to be. While mimetic desire is based upon envy and the desire to be like one's competitor, there is always a fear, as Girard illustrates, that the attempt to imitate the object of one's admiration will not be successful. There is always the possibility that the fear of successful competition will lead to hatred and murder. The desire to imitate can be transmuted to a desire to destroy the completion, the very object of one's desire, as violence, envy, and love come together. The Kahane movement, as Sprinzak demonstrated, was driven by the mimetic desire to take on all the characteristics—power, honor, violence—they assumed were gentile, and in this attempt, the Kahanists justified violence as a religious obligation.

Kahane was an anomaly, an American-born Orthodox rabbi who held several advanced degrees from American universities and was an accomplished talmudic scholar. He emigrated to Israel in 1971 after establishing the Jewish Defense League in the United States. The JDL championed a combination of civil disobedience and vigilante violence to protect American Jews from anti-Semitic attacks. The JDL was listed as a domestic terror group by the Federal Bureau of Investigation; weapons and explosives were uncovered in JDL locations, and Kahane himself left the United States under suspicious circumstances, with some commentators claiming he made a deal with the government to be allowed to emigrate to Israel in order to avoid prison.[16]

Kahane arrived in Israel in September 1971. In his new country, he established the extremist Kach movement and began preaching his philosophy of Jewish might and the need for violence in defense of Jewish and Israeli interests. But now the enemy was not local hoodlums or neo-Nazi groups but Israeli Arabs, whom Kahane saw as a fifth column that represented a danger to the Jewish state. Kahane's solution was forced emigration for all Arabs from Israel, albeit with compensation and help. Kahane was never accepted by the Israel political elites or the intelligentsia, but his message of Jewish power and Jewish honor and his fierce justification of violence on behalf of Jewish interests resonated with considerable numbers of poorer urban Jews and with elements of the right-wing settlers' movement. Kahane's followers began a series of violent attacks against local Arabs in an attempt, in their view, to protect themselves and to show the Arab populace that Israel was an inhospitable place for them. Throughout the 1970s and 1980s Kach members living in the West Bank continued their campaign for "transfer," their term for the movement of Israeli Arabs to Arab countries, and demanded an immediate and violent response to any reports of Arab harassment of Jews. In the Kach view, negotiation, compromise, and a limited physical response to the conflict with their Arab neighbors would never work. They believed such tactics were the result of Jewish timidity and the mistaken Jewish emphasis on passivity. This Jewish refusal to stand up and fight, to be willing to kill and be killed, was a consequence of Jewish exile and statelessness for two millennia. For Kahane and his followers, this very fear and avoidance of violent confrontation led to persecution and Jewish victimhood.

Kahane articulated and popularized the now well-known phrase, "Never again," referring to Jewish resistance to attempts at mass murder and racial persecution. The need for legitimate defense and the danger of extreme passivity and cooperation with persecutors, as was the case in the European Holocaust, have been widely accepted. Kahane and his followers, however, were not content to protect Jewish interests with violence, if necessary, but argued that they were religiously obligated to be "tough Jews" and teach the goyim, the gentiles, that Jews could be as aggressive, violent, and bloodthirsty as any of their enemies. In Girardian terms, as Sprinzak explains, Kahane was the "epitome of mimetic desire" in that his greatest goal and the source of his religious passion was "to out-violate the violators of the Jews." He was driven by the desire for mimesis; he admired what he took to be the gentile sense of entitlement, authority, and honor. Jews, he believed, have been weak, displaying passivity, compromising their honor and living, without a sense of at-homeness and security. Only Jewish assertiveness and readiness to engage in violence could undo this historic denial of honor and respect. Kahane in a highly original way linked his call for Jewish violence with the classical Jewish theological emphasis on *Kiddush Hashem*, sanctification of God's name, and *Hilul Hashem*, profanization of God's name.

A Jewish fist in the face of an astonished gentile world that has not seen it for two millennia, this is Kiddush Hashem. Jewish dominion over the Christian holy places while the church that sucked our blood vomits its rage and frustration. This is Kiddush Hashem. An end to the shame and beatings and the monuments to our martyrized.

Do you want to know how the name of God is desecrated in the eyes of the mocking and sneering nations? It is when the Jew, His chosen, is desecrated! When the Jew is beaten, God is profaned! When the Jew is humiliated God is shamed! When the Jew is attacked it is an assault upon the Name of God.[17]

Kahane, in an unconventional but still traditional use of Jewish theology, was able to provide a justification for violence that was religious and identified violence with a defense of God. Kahane did gather a small but faithful following in Israel and was elected to the Knesset, the Israeli parliament, in the 1970s; his popularity was on the rise when the parliament and Supreme Court declared his party racist and therefore illegal according to Israeli law. Following his disqualification, Kahane became a somewhat marginal figure in Israel but continued to travel and meet with his followers. During one such meeting at a hotel in New York City, Kahane was assassinated in what later turned out to be a Muslim fundamentalist plot against American Jews. The plot was directed by Syed Nosair, an Egyptian follower of Sheik Abdul Rahman, who was the mastermind of the first World Trade Center bombing in 1993.

The tale of Kahane and his Koch party does not end with the death of Kahane. A small group of his most faithful followers formed a community in the West Bank settlement of Kiryat Arba, adjacent to the biblical city of Hebron and close to the shrine of the Tomb of the Patriarchs, revered by Jews and Muslims as a sacred site. Early on Friday morning, February 25, 1994, during Ramadan prayers, approximately five hundred Muslim worshippers were engrossed in prayer in the Isaac Hall of Tomb when a lone Jewish gunman from Kiryat Arba opened fire and killed twenty-nine worshippers and wounded another one hundred. The gunman was Dr. Boruch Goldstein, an American emergency physician and father of four children who had emigrated to Israel. Goldstein was a longtime follower of Rabbi Kahane and one of his most faithful disciples. Goldstein's murderous rampage shocked the Israeli public, which refused to believe that a family man, a distinguished physician, and by all accounts a mild-mannered and gentle person had committed such an atrocity. Yitzchak Rabin, then prime minister of Israel, pronounced Goldstein to be a "madman" and "insane." The media and political commentators went along with this ap-

proach, condemning the murders and expressing collective remorse but insisting that this was the act of a deranged killer.[18]
The facts of Goldstein's life and religious worldview did not
easily support this view. Goldstein was, until the attack, a much
sought-after physician and by all accounts a compassionate
caregiver who treated Palestinians as well as Jews and had no
reputation for violent behavior. He was no madman. Goldstein,
however, had imbibed the Kahane philosophy of Kiddush Hashem and Hilul Hashem. In the Kahane community, the Oslo
agreements were seen as a political sellout but even more impor-
tantly as a return to Jewish passivity. The Palestinians and all the
world had to learn that Israeli Jews were powerful and violent
and if the government could not stand up for Jewish honor and
assert Jewish power, then it was left to gunmen such as Goldstein to demonstrate that Jews did not cave in to gentile threats
and terrorism. If anything, the Jews in their own state would, as
Kahane taught, outdo the gentiles and in this way glorify the
name of God. In Goldstein's community and in many parts of
the traditionalist world he was seen as a hero, as having been
killed during his rampage for the sanctification of the name of
God and for having restored Jewish honor in a climate of Jewish
capitulation to Arab intimidation. A memorial site in Goldstein's
community of Kiryat Arba was erected adjacent to his gravesite
and quickly became a religious shrine attracting sympathetic
pilgrims from all over the world. "This was the man," reads a
sign at the memorial site, "who avenged Jewish blood."[19]
In practical political terms, Goldstein's rampage did not help
the Kahane movement nor did it advance the nationalist cause
in Israel. If anything, it unveiled the extremism in the Kahane
community, alienated some former sympathizers, and isolated
Kahanists from sectors of mainstream Judaism. Moreover, the
killings so frightened the Israeli government that sections of the
tomb were permanently closed to Jewish worshippers. But all
this really was not the concern of the Kahane followers. The
event was not, within their world, meant as an act of politics, nor
was it to be measured in worldly terms. The massacre was carried out to transform the uneven and immoral relationship between Jews and gentiles. In Girardian terms the desire to imitate

and outdo the historical treatment of the Jews provided religious legitimacy for this horrendous act. The Kahanists believed they were finally making things right and realigning history in accordance with God's will.

Religious Disappointment and Cognitive Dissonance Theory

All religions have, at their core, a sacred vision of the ideal community based upon their sacred scriptures, traditions, and laws. This is certainly the case with Christianity, with its vision of a Christian society organized according to the Gospels and faithful to Jesus Christ as Lord and Savior; with Judaism, with its view of the ideal Jewish society based upon talmudic traditions and halacha; and with Islam, whose history and theology call for establishing societies and states under the sole authority of Muslim leaders and governed by the Muslim sharia, religious law. Similar views are held by a number of non-Abrahamic religions as well, as is the case with Hinduism, with its emphasis on the sacredness of holy places and its rituals of sacred cleansing and rebirth.

What happens when these expectations do not come to pass? How do the faithful react when their most cherished dreams for creating a society based upon their religious traditions are unsuccessful? All human disappointments are difficult to bear but religious disappointments are particularly painful because so much commitment is invested in these beliefs and because these religious goals must be met in order for God's plan to be realized and for salvation to occur. For the truly faithful, the experience of living without establishing God's divinely ordained society is fraught with psychological distress. The famous social psychologist Leon Festinger terms the experience of this type of disappointment, "cognitive dissonance." As Festinger explains, "Two opinions or beliefs or items of knowledge are *dissonant* with each other if they do not fit together—that is, if they are inconsistent or if considering only the particular two items, one does not follow from the other."[20] Believers who take the prescriptions of their faith as ultimate truth, as obligatory rules to be followed by all and their leaders and prophets as messengers of God, face an enormous conflict between their most sacred beliefs and religious expectations and their experience as citizens of modern societies, which do not function according to religious law and theology.

In modern societies, the forces of pluralism and secularization and the values of individualism and self-expression have radically changed the status of religion. Religion in modern society has moved from the public realm of government and politics—"the public square," in Richard John Neuhaus's term—and is now limited to the personal realm, to leisure-time activity and rituals related to personal and life cycle events like marriage, birth, and burial.[21] Religion is important, but it is a matter of personal choice and there is no legal or even moral obligation to follow religious rules. Institutions like the family and education, once under the total control of religious authorities and organizations, now function independent of religious values and laws. The individual now chooses how she or he lives, marries or divorces, educates his or her children. Modernity means that no one religion can claim to be the purveyor of absolute truth. Christianity, for example, once at the epicenter of political and cultural life throughout Europe, now readily acknowledges even in countries like Italy, Spain, and France, where Christians constitute an overwhelming majority, that Christian doctrine and dogma cannot serve as the legal basis for the state or for rules governing civil society.

Consequently, to be a faithful religious believer who wants religion to govern the laws in a secular society is to be a "cognitive minority," a minority singled out for its unusual beliefs, and to be in a state of cognitive dissonance. What this means is that most people, particularly the intellectual and governmental elites, look down upon the cognitive minority religions, consider them "primitive," even irrational, and ignore or deny their beliefs, values, and morals. Peter Berger, the sociologist of religion, explains that to be in a religious cognitive minority is "not a very pleasant thing because people do not take you seriously. But it is also something much more fundamental. If you find yourself in a cognitive minority it becomes very difficult to take yourself seriously the longer the situation continues."[22] In other words, to have beliefs on particular matters of ultimate and religious concern which are widely dismissed as unimportant or as outright falsehoods is to be in a situation fraught with psychological stress.

Festinger, Berger, and others have demonstrated that human beings desire and depend on an established social network to sustain their sense of self and their conception of reality. What we consider "real" or "true" is indeed real or true when these factual statements are backed up by what everyone around us acknowledges as real and true. In the language of social psychology, truth and comfort about one's beliefs depend on a consistency between individual cognitions and cultural confirmation. Peter Berger explains that the efficacy of voodoo is true and real in rural Haiti and a voodoo follower there would have no experience of cognitive dissonance. The belief in the veracity of voodoo is socially accepted and confirmed by everybody, and there is no inconsistency between this belief and reality. However, an argument made to an annual meeting of the American Chemical Society that chemical reactions in a medical experiment are a function of voodoo intercession would be dismissed as nonsensical and unscientific. The scientific community would reject the reality of voodoo and contend that it has no basis in fact and is entirely inconsistent with scientific knowledge. Those researchers continuing to maintain the truth and reality of voodoo would be in a distinct cognitive minority, and if they chose to remain members of the scientific community they would certainly have to confront the cognitive dissonance between the beliefs and cognitions of the scientific community and adherence to the veracity of voodoo intercession as a scientific fact.

Dissonance, as Festinger and his associates have shown, produces profound psychic stress and discomfort. There is an inherent human drive for cognitive consistency and a concomitant desire to avoid the experience of dissonance. In experimental and sociological studies of dissonance, observers have shown that when placed in a situation of cognitive dissonance, individuals and cognitive minorities make a great effort to eliminate and reduce dissonance and thereby avoid the discomfort caused by dissonant cognitions and beliefs.[23] Essentially, there are three solutions to the experience of cognitive dissonance and chronic religious disappointment: (1) surrender, (2) reinterpretation, and (3) militant transformation.

Cognitive and theological surrender deals with these inconsistencies by rejecting beliefs which are felt to be causing the dissonant experience. The scientists mentioned earlier who had considered the efficacy of voodoo now reject it as a youthful mistake due to culture shock. They no longer need experience dissonance, having admitted their mistake and returning to normal "reality," and they are accepted back as legitimate members of the academic fraternity. Liberal Protestantism and its embrace of Enlightenment values and Darwinian evolution is a good example of the theological surrender of biblical literalism in the face of secular historiography and evolutionary biology. Biblical literalism and a supernatural view of biblical miracles as literally true are rejected and replaced with a scientific explanation. Biblically based norms, values, and behavior such as the Genesis creation narrative, the emphasis on authority in the family, or the prohibition on homosexuality are rejected—in our terms, surrendered—to be replaced by the now-contemporary values of enlightenment morality concerning human freedom and personal choice, equality, and scientific truth. Once scientific canons of truth are accepted and incorporated in liberal theology, Christian belief is made compatible with science and modernity and dissonance is eliminated. The creation narrative is now no longer an empirical reality but a myth that helps people make sense of life; it is certainly not to be taken as literally true. One can now be a faithful Christian and not have to confront positions or maintain beliefs which are incongruous with being a modern person.

Reinterpretation is a less dramatic response and does not call for rejecting the earlier beliefs entirely but rather reinterpreting the dissonant beliefs so as to make them compatible with other beliefs which define the common and acceptable social reality. The history of religion presents many examples of reinterpretation. In the case of Judaism and Christianity, the biblical account of a six-day creation ex nihilo is rejected and reinterpreted to mean that the creation stories in the Bible, while true in many ways, are not to be seen as conflicting with scientific facts. Creation took place but occurred within the framework of scientific truth. For example, the biblical narrative is reinterpreted to have taken place not in days but in six time periods lasting millions of years and the process described in the Bible parallels the evolutionary processes acceptable to evolutionary biology. In this fashion, dissonance between science and religion can be avoided by creatively demonstrating the compatibility of the two systems. Reinterpretation involves, in Peter Berger's phrase, a process of "cognitive bargaining" between the claims of religious truth and reality of secular society.[24] Some elements of faith must be abandoned but the overarching "truths" of religion can, in this way, be maintained.

Surrender and reinterpretation involve compromise and the recognition that critical elements of traditional religion are incompatible with modernity. Modernist believers are willing to do this, but what about fundamentalists and other religious traditionalists who refuse to compromise what they see as the word of God? These orthodox believers certainly face cognitive dissonance, but rather than compromise their beliefs they seek to remake reality to fit their religious cognitions and expectations. They engage in militant transformation to force all others to accept their religious beliefs and demand that society be based on their religious views. Militant reconstruction is the most active response to dissonance and the response which has the greatest propensity for violence. Militants seeking to transform society engage in politics and propaganda, but their strongest tactic is religious violence. The militants refuse to compromise, seeing themselves as solders for God, faithful warriors, and defenders of the faith. The militants champion violence to force society to conform to religion. Murder, bombings, and even mass killing are legitimate when it comes to asserting the dominion of God over society. From the psychological perspective of dissonance theory, the violence is an outgrowth of the believers' unwillingness—perhaps inability—to live with continuous religious disappointment. R. Scott Appleby has shown that treating faithful believers in a negative way, viewing their beliefs as nonsensical, and claiming that fervent religious expectations will never be fulfilled drives such believers to militant and violent confrontations which seek the transformation of society.[25]

Violence, Cognitive Dissonance, and Religious Disappointment: The Case of Militant Judaism and Islam

Militant Judaism and Islam illustrate how continued religious disappointment and the psychological traumas it engenders result in religious violence. Jewish theology and history, as we discussed earlier, take it for granted that the Jewish people have eternal rights to the land of Israel. At the core of Jewish faith is the notion that the Jews are God's chosen people and the land of Israel is the promised land, bequeathed to them, and only to them, by God. They will return there from exile to welcome their messiah, who will redeem the entire world as foretold in their scriptures. Jewish religious culture is entirely predicated on the idea of return to the land of Israel; the liturgy articulates this longing and all rituals, including marriage rites, have elements enacting this longing and return. All of Jewish history, it may be said, is a waiting period for the return to Zion and world transformation. In this sense the return of Jews to the land of Israel is miraculous, in their view, and, at the same time, empirical proof of the truth of their scripture and revelation. In this sense the Zionist movement and the return of Jews to the land of Israel has solved the centuries-old problem of cognitive dissonance. There is no dissonance between belief and reality.

In this context, the loss of any territory in the Holy Land or the sharing of sovereignty with gentiles is to deny God's promises, giving up the Jewish birthright and the inherent meaning and destiny of the Jewish people. All confessional Jews acknowledge this, but modernist Jews deal with the disappointment through cognitive and theological surrender and reinterpretation. Eliezer Schweid of Hebrew University in Jerusalem, a leading Zionist philosopher, has argued that the incongruity and dissonance between being an advocate for a democratic state and the belief in a purely Jewish state is so great that it is necessary to redefine Zionism as a state for all its citizens, regardless of religion. Schweid was aware that this meant the abandonment of the traditional Zionist vision, but he saw this as a way of reconciling the contradictions between a firm belief in democracy and the realities of a religious state which did permit full rights to all citizens.[26] Similarly, Yitzchak Rabin, and Shimon Peres spoke frequently about their sorrow and disappointment that the full land of Israel, with the ancient Jewish monuments and sites, would not be under Jewish jurisdiction, but they took the position that ending the occupation of the West Bank with its overwhelming population of Muslims and the signing of a peace treaty were more important than holding on to the biblical homeland. Some highly distinguished orthodox rabbis like Aaron Lichtenstein and Yehudah Amital, famed for their talmudic scholarship, also accept Palestinian autonomy and have called for compromise and the surrender of an absolute religious vision of full Jewish control over the entire land of Israel in line with the biblical promises.[27]

This attitude of compromise, of giving in to political reality, is anathema to Jewish militants. They refuse to compromise their beliefs and reduce their longing for the fulfillment of sacred prophecies. If reality challenges their beliefs, reality must be changed to fit the religious truth. This was precisely the case with twenty-five-year-old Yigal Amir, an Israeli army veteran and a brilliant law student at Bar Ilan University who assassinated Rabin on November 4, 1995, at the civic center in Tel Aviv after a massive rally in support of the Oslo peace accords signed with Yasser Arafat and the Palestinian Authority. Amir apparently was able to get into a secure area near the stage and as Rabin walked by, Amir shot him with two high-velocity bullets, killing him instantly. All of Israel was stunned. Rabin was the country's most highly decorated war hero, fought in all the countries many wars, and was an acclaimed diplomat. The initial response was that Amir was deranged, a lone and mentally ill gunman who was acting on his own.[28]

The reality turned out quite differently. Amir was a true believer and an articulate spokesman for militant religion throughout the country. He was a recognized scholar of the Talmud and had discussed the religious permissibility of assassinating Rabin with numerous friends, colleagues, and distinguished rabbis. He was no loner but something of a leader among Bar Ilan activists, with a very respectable military record in the Israeli army. Moreover, the act was not done in an hysterical or haphazard fashion. Considerable planning and careful organization took place as Amir contemplated the assassination and the entire event was planned to be in accord with Jewish religious law and was aimed at stopping the return of any Jewish land. Perhaps most surprising and frightening to the secular Israeli populace was that Amir's transformative religious politics were not idiosyncratic but were shared by a not-insignificant number of militant Jews all over the world.

Upon interrogation, it became clear that Amir believed he was acting in an entirely rational and controlled fashion because his goal was stopping the loss of his religious vision. In Amir's word's:

> [M]y general worldview is based on the path of the Torah, on the 613 mitzvoth, commandments. This leads to complete control of the body, the passions, the physical and emotional drives. The Torah is reason. He who acts emotionally acts like an animal. This is my morality. This is Judaism's general view and I implement it.[29]

"God gave the land of Israel to the Jewish People," he explained to his interrogators, and he, Yigal Amir, was making certain that God's promises, which he believed in with all his heart and to which he had committed his life, were not to be denied. He could not fathom, he declared, how a Jewish state would dare renege on the Jewish birthright, and he could not passively stand by as this terrifying religious tragedy took place. In Amir's thinking, his action was not a personal matter or an act of passion but a solution, albeit an extreme one, to a religious and psychological trauma brought about by the actions of the Rabin government. Amir was aware of the seriousness of his action but he explained that it was his fervent faith which encouraged and empowered him to commit this act of murder. He told his interrogators, "Without believing in God and an eternal world to come, I would never have had the power to do this." Rabin deserved to die because he was facilitating, according to Amir and other militants, the possible mass murder of Jews by agreeing to the Oslo accords. This placed Rabin, according to halacha, Jewish law, in the status of a *rodef*, a person about to kill an innocent person and therefore liable for execution by a bystander without a trial. Rabin was also a *moser*, a Jew who willingly betrays his brethren, and was guilty of treason by cooperating with Yasser Arafat and the Palestinian Authority in surrendering rights to the Holy Land. Rodef and moser are considered among the most pernicious activities in Jewish jurisprudence; persons guilty of such acts are to be killed at the first opportunity. Moderate rabbis disagreed with some of these conclusions, but some rabbis from the militant camp had, prior to Amir's act, made pretty much the same theological argument, though they did not conclusively call for the death sentence. As one group of rabbis put it prior to the assassination, "It is the obligation of the community leaders to warn the head of the government and his ministers that if they keep pursuing the Oslo agreement, they will be subject to the halachic ruling of *din moser* as ones who surrender the life and property of Jews to the Gentiles."[30] Amir, then, did not fabricate or innovate his argument for the assassination of Rabin. What was new and shocking to Israelis and to the international community was the image of Jews who had, historically, avoided violence to realize their religious visions and now, in the situation of religious disappointment, used violence and murder to pursue their religious goals.

Pious and traditionalist Muslims, as well, experience religious disappointment and inconsistency between their beliefs and the organization of most Islamic states. Militancy and violence are tactics some Muslim traditionalist groups and sects use to transform their governments and societies into orthodox exemplars of Islamic teachings. Islam, at its theological core, rejects the secular state and acknowledges no separation between a distinctly religious realm and a secular realm. The Christian approach of "render unto Caesar what is Caesar's and unto God what is God's" and the recognition that secular authority and ecclesiastical authority are both divinely ordered is rejected by Islam. For Islam, there is only the unitary realm of religion, which incorporates politics, economics, the military, and all other essential social institutions. The state apparatus is the public enactment of Islamic law, custom, and morality and should, according to classical Islam, permeate every aspect of society and human relations. For example, recreation and clothing which, in Western societies, are matters of personal choice are carefully prescribed in Islamic law and should rightfully be enforced by a Muslim government. Modern business and banking activities which operate according to their own secular economic rules and guidelines are to be carefully directed by sharia in Islamic society. Interest on loans and the conventional real estate mortgage are forbidden by sharia. The modern nation state as defined by majority rule of the populace is also rejected by sharia. The lay populace and the lay leadership can advise and consult shura, but all decisions, including those concerning war and peace, are ultimately to be made by the religious leaders themselves. The relative roles, responsibilities, and permissible activity of men and women are not open to personal or majority decision but, in an Islamic context, must follow Muslim tradition and law concerning modesty and appropriate gender behavior. In this connection marriage and divorce, too, must be under religious governmental supervision. Hassan al-Turabi, a founder of the Sudanese Muslim Brotherhood and former attorney general of Sudan expressed the traditionalist position in this way: "All public life in Islam is religious, being permeated with the experience of the divine."[31]

The Islamic state is the community of believers, the ummah, those faithful to Islam and living under the full gamut of Islamic law, the sharia, as interpreted by religious leaders and scholars steeped in learning and religious piety. From the Islamic political perspective, national boundaries and national states are irrelevant. Muslims may have state entities but the Muslim concept of ummah transcends national or ethnic categories and includes all who are faithful to Islam. Allegiance, then, is not to any national state but to the ummah and to those Islamic religious leaders who forge an Islamic entity which will be true, in every way, to the full gamut of Muslim law, custom, and politics. Practically this means the establishment and enforcement of sharia within all Muslim societies and in international relations. This Islamic civilization envisioned by faithful Muslims has not occurred in modern times, with the possible exemption of the former Taliban regime in Afghanistan, and, perhaps, in Iran as well. A stubborn reality involving the forces of cultural globalization, modern economics, international trade, and, not infrequently, the antagonism of fellow Muslims, has denied the faithful their deepest religious goals. Muslim states, as the militants see it, have abandoned fidelity to Islamic jurisprudence and have been co-opted by the United States and Europe to serve Western and not Muslim interests. The requirement to establish sharia as the law of the land and forge an international ummah in pursuit of exclusively Islamic goals has been stymied by secular governments and the westernized intelligentsia in Muslim countries. The leaders of Egypt, Pakistan, Algeria, and other predominantly Muslim countries, with populations of millions of faithful Muslims, remain disloyal to the tenets of Islam, in the militant view. Secular legislation abounds and the governments of some of the most traditionalist countries do not join in Islamic jihads against infidels and enemies of Islam but cooperate with Christian armies, as in the Gulf War in 1991 and in the war in Afghanistan, against pious Muslims. Particularly galling to Islamic traditionalists was the presence of thousands of American troops in Saudi Arabia in the Gulf War against Iraq. Saudi Arabia is the site of many Muslim holy places, most particularly the Ka'bah in Mecca, and as the birthplace of the prophet Muhammad is particularly revered by Muslims; the presence of non-Muslim combatants in these Muslim precincts was seen as a desecration.[32] The American-led 2003 war against Saddam Hussein's regime was a military victory which removed a vicious dictator but, to Islamic traditionalists, it violated the sanctity of Muslim space and was also seen as an Western intrusion.

The intrusions of secular Western thinking and lifestyle in government and politics is experienced as a danger to Muslim religiosity. For the traditionalists, the discrepancy and dissonance between Muslim traditional texts and lifestyles and the actual situation in Muslim societies cannot be tolerated. As in the Israeli case, Muslim modernists are willing to compromise; they are ready to surrender or redefine elements of Islamic belief so that Islam will not be in conflict with modern cultural norms and politics. Some modernists, for example, claim that the traditional obligations of the sharia for jihad are no longer applicable in the modern world. Some Muslim theologians have argued against the taking of more than one wife, permitted in sharia law, and other Muslim scholars have claimed that the institutionalization of sharia is not possible or required in the modern age and was limited in time to an older civilization. Muslim modernists frequently invoke the category of "silent sharia" to indicate that Muslims are given considerable leeway in decisionmaking because the Koran only prescribes broad principles, leaving details and specifics for the human community to decide. For example, in their rejection of a religious state, they argue that there is nothing in the sharia that compels one to bind religion to statesetting; the sharia does not demand a specific form of government. The modernists also invoke the silent sharia to show that Islam can be fully compatible with western democracy, pluralism, and equality. The modernists are often acclaimed scholars of the Koran and their work has shown a way of resolving the incongruities between Islam and modernity, but to the bulk of traditionalists they are viewed as blasphemers whose theology is a denial of orthodox Islam.[33]

Most traditionalist Muslims are, in our terminology, militant transformationists. They do not want to compromise their beliefs and texts and, facing challenges to their firm beliefs, they will seek to transform politics and culture, by violence if necessary, so that it conforms to their understanding of Islam. For them it is not religion that should change but the state and society that must be coerced to follow what is for them authentic, undiluted Islam. The pious transformationists simply cannot abide what is for them the incongruity and dissonance of a Muslim society not governed by the standards of Islamic law and procedure. Sayyid Qutb, perhaps the most important figure in twentieth-century revivalist Islam, argues that Islam and Western modernity cannot coexist. Modernity, in Qutb's view, is identical to the times of *jahiliyah* in seventh-century Arabia: the age and culture of ignorance, pagan immorality, and barbarism which Muhammad came to destroy and replace with the moral order of Islam. A Muslim cannot under any circumstance accommodate or compromise with jahiliyah. "In any time and place," writes Qutb, "human beings face that clear cut choice: either to observe the Law of Allah in its entirety or to apply laws laid down by man of one sort or another. In the latter case they are in a state of jahiliyah. Man is the crossroads and that is the choice: Islam or jahiliyah."[34]

In Qutb's view, violence and war are entirely justified in fighting the dangers to Islam. Qutb shows that traditional Islam has always stood against violations and threats to faith, and the Western threats are a legitimate reason for declaring war. Qutb was a literary critic and sophisticated thinker who did not underestimate the suffering, killings, and destruction that religious wars cause. Nonetheless, he argues, faithful Muslims cannot permit the continued violation and betrayal of Islam in the public arena. Qutb excoriates the modernists who seek to resolve the contradictions between Islam and modernity by adopting Western culture or seeking to define Islam in terms of Western religious categories. For him, Western culture is totally immoral. As early as the 1940s, Qutb referred to the United States, where he spent several years on a research mission, as a "vacuous and materialistic and depraved" culture and a country bent on taking advantage of the poor and underprivileged. He considers Christianity and "its notions of sin and redemption" as making no sense at all and the concept of the Trinity as idolatrous.[35]

For Qutb and the Islamic transformationists, the enemies of Islam include not only those who actively attack Islam from the outside but also all societies and cultures who remain in a state of jahiliyah. Societies and governments that tolerate violations of

Islamic law must be opposed by violent means if necessary. Islam has a liberating and divine message for all humanity and simply cannot stand by and permit the contravention of universal Islamic teachings. Not everyone must become Muslim but no society can be permitted to challenge, in any way, the standards of Islam. This is the hallmark of militant religion: the refusal to tolerate any opposing religious worldview. The militant sees violence as a legitimate means of establishing the truth and reality and in this way does not have to deal with any opposing or challenging views. As Qutb explains, "Truth and falsehood cannot exist on earth. . . . The liberating struggle of Jihad does not seize until all religions belong to God."[36]

Historically, the fear of *fitna*, civil war, among Muslims was so great in Sunni Islam that tolerance and cooperation among different sects was encouraged and applauded by some of the most influential theologians. The writings of Qutb and his followers and revolutionary activity against the Egyptian government in the 1950s changed this. Qutb presents a revolutionary view of violent jihad, claiming that revolt and overthrow of Muslim governments is just as much a duty of a faithful Muslim as fighting the infidels and pagans. Compromise and tolerance are signs of intellectual and spiritual defeat, while violence is a way of establishing God's order. Qutb and his comrades in the then-revolutionary Muslim Brotherhood organization were arrested in 1954 for conspiring to assassinate the Egyptian leader, General Gamal Abdel Nasser, and sentenced to fifteen years of hard labor. After his release, Qutb's emphasis on violence increased and he gradually came to the view that any Muslim state not entirely loyal to the full requirements of Islam had to be destroyed and its leaders killed. He was rearrested and executed by the Egyptian government in 1966 for his revolutionary writings and encouragement of violence. He was buried in an unmarked grave but today is a highly respected figure, seen as a religious authority and martyr by millions of Muslims all over the world.

Qutb's Islamic approach, which refuses any compromise and reinterpretation of what fervent traditionalists argue is authentic Islam, has been taken up by succeeding generations of militant transformationists, who see violence and coercion as *the* means of maintaining religious purity. President Anwar Sadat of Egypt was, by all accounts, a confessional Muslim who prayed regularly, followed a traditional Muslim lifestyle and calendar, and was not unlearned in religious matters. But he was willing to compromise some Muslim strictures and live with some dissonance in order to expand the Egyptian economy, increase tourism, and make peace with Israel. Among the complaints of the militants was Sadat's increasing military and economic cooperation with the United States, his support of the deposed Iranian shah, his liberal tourist policies permitting the sale of alcohol, the liberalization of dress codes, and, most pernicious of all, his trip to Jerusalem and his signing of a peace treaty with Israel which legitimized the presence of a non-Muslim state in the lands of Islam. Behind these and other disagreements lay a larger issue—modernity and westernization. The militants wanted only Islam; anything added was seen as a compromise of the Islamic vision. Sadat wanted a Muslim state but one which permitted, even encouraged, Western thinking and opened Egypt to the culture and economics of the West. On October 6, 1981, while reviewing his troops during an annual commemoration of Egypt's surprise attack across the Suez Canal in the 1973 war with Israel, Sadat was shot and killed by four men in what appeared to be a well-planned attack.[37]

The assailants, it turned out, were members of al Jihad, an Islamic militant group that was determined to establish an Islamic state and saw Sadat as a traitor to Islam for breaking ranks with other Muslims and making peace with Israel. In much of Europe and the United States, Sadat was seen as a hero, but in many traditionalist Muslim circles he was seen as selling out to the West and insulting Islam by what they took to be his pandering to his American supporters. In interview after interview, the assassins expressed the sense of loss and the trauma they experienced as a result of Sadat's action. As it turned out, his killers and those who masterminded the assassination were not from the margins of Egyptian society but included distinguished clerics, including Sheik Abdul Rahman, who was later to gain notoriety as the force behind the first World Trade Center bombing in 1993, and some of the actual gunmen were officers in the Egyptian military. The chief assailant was Lieutenant Khaled Islambouli, who, unbeknown to the military command, was a member of the al Jihad organization. Several dozen people were eventually arrested for the murder and brought to trial, where they defiantly justified their action as their religious duty to keep Islam untainted by Western influences, as represented by Sadat and his government. Asked for his plea at the opening of the trial, Islambouli proudly acknowledged his action: "I am guilty of killing Sadat and I admit that. I am proud of it because the cause of religion was at stake."[38]

The militant mood in Islam was not limited to the assassination of Sadat, nor were the militants just a small group of disenchanted rebels limited to al Jihad. There were literally dozens of militant groups, with members from the lower middle classes as well as upwardly mobile university graduates, that saw violence as the way of establishing religion's rights in society. Some of the groups specialized in attacking foreign tourists, who were seen as invaders in a Muslim culture. Attacks on tourists were also a way of wreaking havoc on the Egyptian economy and adding trouble to an already weak and increasingly unpopular government. A militant group inspired by the Sheik Rahman's preaching against the danger of any contact with infidel unbelievers killed fifty-eight European tourists in November 1996 as they were visiting the Pyramids and tombs at Luxor.[39] Al Jihad took it upon itself to rid Egypt of all non-Muslims, and a series of violent acts began against the Egyptian Copts, one of the oldest Christian communities in the world. Christian crosses were pulled from the necks of those who went out publicly wearing them, and many Copts were more seriously attacked and told to leave the country. The majority of the populace were against these actions, but the movement of militants had spread far enough and become strong enough that there was not much vocal popular opposition. Sadat was killed in 1982 and succeeded by his vice president, Hosni Mubarak, who throughout the 1990s was himself the victim of assassination attempts by these same militants.[40]

This militant, transformative Islam, given voice by Qutb in

the 1940s and 1950s, was given its most sophisticated contemporary expression by Abt al-Salem Faraj in his influential *Al-Faridah
al-Gha'ida, The Neglected Duty,* a booklet read by all the Sadat assassins and which provided the theological rationale for increased religious violence.[41] Faraj was executed by the Egyptian
government in 1982 for his role in the Sadat killing, but his work
remains the major inspiration for holy violence throughout the
Islamic world. Faraj's critical point is that jihad, violent and
physical confrontation with the enemies of Islam, is the neglected duty of Islam. Faraj puts it plainly: there is no Islam
without violent Jihad and it is a Muslim's duty never to permit
non-Muslim ways of thinking and acting to enter into Islamic
consciousness or society. A true Muslim, Faraj explains, cannot
tolerate the disparagement of religious ideals and the experience
of infidels ruling Muslim society. Violence is the Islamic way to
ensure, protect, and promote Islamic interests. The Koran is
clear, he tells us, in commanding, "Fight and slay the pagans
wherever you see them, beleaguer them and lie in ambush."
(9:5) For Faraj and his followers, there is no middle way. It is
Jihad and Islam or blasphemy and compromise.

The most profound innovation and expansion of the place of
jihad in Faraj's writings is his encouragement of individual acts
of terror and treachery (*fard ayn*), which, he claims, in contrast to
traditionalist Islam, need no explicit clerical approval. Moreover,
Faraj rejects earlier Islamic constraints against the murder of
children and other civilians, although he remains uncertain
about the killing of civilian women. Throughout his essay Faraj
is clear that jihad means "confrontation and blood" and that no
faithful Muslim may avoid the call of jihad. Here we see how
religious·violence is democratized in contemporary religious
conflicts and that it is now the ordinary folk who can engage in
violence without the need for permission from the official
clergy. While moderate Islamic scholars have rejected Faraj's
work as uninformed and untrue to Islam, militant transformationists have adopted this approach as an orthodox and legitimate way of protecting Islamic values and culture throughout
the world.

Christianity and the Inquisition

Unlike Islam, Christianity has gone through an intense and protracted experience with secularization. Christians, today, with some sectarian exceptions, recognize that religion in contemporary societies is primarily a private and voluntary matter over which the state and the clergy have no coercive authority. Individuals may or may not choose to affiliate with a church, may or may not follow Christian practices, and may even decide to convert to a competing faith. Faith is a private matter and no one religion can claim to represent the absolute truth and demand that the state or the ecclesiastical authorities enforce compliance with Christian dogma. Put differently, modern Christianity has come to terms with pluralism, which has radically relativized its truth claims. From a position in medieval Europe, in Peter Berger's term, as the "paramount reality," the absolute, true, and superior religion, Christianity has become merely one religion among many, with no one group able to claim ultimate legitimacy.[42] This transformation of Christian understanding did not come easily and it is not complete, as some groups still demand a return to the triumphant Christianity of the past, but for the bulk of Christianity the experience of secularization has resulted in new theologies of pluralism which encourage greater tolerance and decry violence in the name of religion.

However, the situation was very different in European medieval and early modern Christianity. In those periods, the Roman Catholic Church saw itself as the sole religious truth. The reality of Jesus Christ as Lord and Savior, a God incarnate who, acting with selfless, agape love for all people, grants salvation and eternal life for all who respond with faith, was a self-evident truth which could not be rejected. The theological formula that there is no salvation without Christ was not open to choice, discussion, or compromise. This was simply a fact of life. These Christian truths were not abstract matters of dogma and theology, they were the lifeblood of society. The earthly and eternal life of all, in the medieval period, depended upon the maintenance of proper faith and fidelity to Christian belief. In this sense all who did not subscribe to the exact formulas of Christian faith were enemies of religion and the state since they threatened the well-being of all.

The church hierarchy was the repository of truth and had a divine mission to maintain the purity of belief to ensure God's mercy and grace for the community. There could be no tolerance for disbelief, and any modification or alternation of Christian doctrine, however slight, had to be eliminated. The great enemy was heresy, from the Greek *haeresis*, or choice, for any changes in doctrine and practice from the official canon would bring religious and moral pollution to Christian society. If people began deciding what is truth, what is proper Christian belief and practice, if religion became a matter of choice and heretics were tolerated, the very fabric of Christian society and faith would unravel. The church hierarchy had to maintain, as the historian Richard Rubinstein put it, a "cognitive monopoly" within European Christendom. In this context, any deviation, even what appears to modern observers to be minor modifications in doctrine, liturgy, or ritual, was cause for great concern and stress. In our analysis, the cognitive dissonance engendered in the medieval church by any change in belief or behavior within the church was problematic to the point of psychological trauma, and Christian inquisitions lasting for centuries and involving religious investigations, censorship, and formal trials, as well as such punishments as banishment and death, became an essential part of medieval Christian society. The violent response was a way of dealing with fear and disappointment, rooting out what were considered to be absolute dangers to the continuity of God's true faith. From the psychological perspective, the inquisitors were making sure that their religious reality, their view of the supernatural, and their belief in the afterlife would not be psychically or cognitively threatened by the existence of alternative faith or interpretation.[43]

The Christian inquisitions, which in one form or another lasted from approximately the eleventh through the sixteenth centuries, were determined to maintain the purity of belief by investigating any possible deviations from proper doctrine and Christian practice. The goal was to set up an absolute and objective standard of Christian Catholic faith, doctrine, and practice which all would have to follow. Any suspected modification would be investigated to discover whether it remained within the acceptable parameters. Virgilio Pinto Crespo, in his study on inquisitional thought control in Spain, explained that "what was contemplated was an attempt to find the point of no return in matters of piety and fix precisely the limits in the search for religious truth beyond which the exercise of freedom of thought was at least ethically punishable."[44] The inquisitions were attempts at self-protection and were directed primarily against "internal enemies" of the church, whether those believed to be harboring liberal Erasmusian humanism, or the more strict, pious, and acetic religion of the Albigensians in the thirteenth century, or those who returned to pre-Christian forms of magic—ignorance and superstitions in the church's view—regarding healing and medical remedies.

The inquisitors generally saw themselves as educators helping people maintain correct beliefs by pointing out errors in knowledge and judgment. Once made aware of their errors and ignorance, those in error had to confess their mistaken beliefs. If they did, they were given various forms of penance, after which they were in good standing in the church. Punishment and death came only to those who refused to admit their errors, steadfastly maintaining their violations of doctrine and practice. Heresy, in the world of early Catholicism, had to be stopped by persuasion and, if necessary, by death. The experience of dissonance and the fear that such incorrect belief would spread and destroy society convinced the church authorities that torture and death were warranted for those challenging the faith. Violence was a legitimate form of social control because it was seen as self-preservation; it functioned to maintain the paramount reality of Catholic Christian belief.[45] In time, particularly during the Spanish inquisitions of the fifteenth century, the clear distinction between confession and innocence and remaining in error became muddled as large numbers of Spanish Jews converted to Catholicism but were under suspicion that they were secretly practicing Judaism. The investigators had to invent all sorts of techniques, including torture, to ascertain whether the beliefs of these new converts were genuine.

There were elements of political and economic motivation in the inquisitions but it is an error to think of the inquisitors as simply after material gain or the church merely as a foil for the newly emerging national states, as some historians have argued. It is similarly incorrect to consider the inquisitions as an example of the unique perniciousness of Christianity. The inquisitional period illustrates the nature of a universalistic religion at a particular point in religious evolution. The church prior to the Enlightenment and subsequent widespread secularization saw itself as *the* vehicle for salvation and took seriously its responsibility for maintaining an orthodoxy which would result in the second coming of Christ and world transformation. The existence of dissenters, those who were determined to reject this true and godly religious message, had to be dealt with not through compromise and tolerance but through the demand that all recognize the truths of the Christian faith. If dialogue could not convince dissenters, then violence was the legitimate way to get heretics to conform. The history of the inquisition is important because it shows how belief in one's own absolute religious truth leads to intolerance and dissonance which calls forth violent means to destroy religious dissent. The psychology of religious belief, throughout much of human history, demands unanimity and shows little tolerance for pluralism and individual choice.[46]

Victimization, Violence, and Symbolic Empowerment

Groups and movements that believe themselves to be victims, or even potential victims, of persecution, discrimination, and humiliation have a special penchant for violence and aggression. Such groups, particularly those with a history of marginality, have a collective sense that they do not matter to those in power, that they are, as the novelist Ralph Ellison put it, "nameless and invisible," not really seen, heard, or understood.[47] Their concerns, culture, and aspirations are never really dealt with by those who can help them. These groups feel ignored, abandoned, and humiliated. Their calls for help, their appeals for resolution, and their demands for justice never get a helpful response. These people are frustrated and humiliated and it is often these groups that develop an ideology and theology of religious violence to express their pent-up rage. The marginalized group becomes the specially beloved of God. They are God's chosen, endowed with unique rights to punish their oppressors, to kill and maim in order to gain a respectful place in society and undo their status as a persecuted and stigmatized community. Everyone else is demonized and identified with evil, all others are ontologically and spiritually inferior and therefore may be punished, imprisoned, or killed. Frequently these self-proclaimed victim groups have no realistic plan to transform society; their goal is to demonstrate their rage, to show how much havoc they can cause. In this way, their violence, dangerous as it is, does not change their situation but gives them a sense of imagined empowerment and self-worth.

John Mack, a psychiatrist studying the psychology of violence in victimized groups, explains that the pain of perceived inferiority and humiliation in these groups is so great that the group engages in a process of displacement and splitting whereby all rage and disappointment is directed against the group's enemies while the group itself is seen as totally pure and entirely good. This Manichean splitting of reality, according to Mack, while generally a gross exaggeration of actual conditions, serves as an elaborate defense mechanism, making it possible for members of the group to see all their troubles as coming from the evil intent and actions of their "enemy," thus enabling them to make psychological meaning of their unhappy situation. Mack referred to the violence these groups engage in as a form of "war as therapy."[48] They are caught in a passive and inferior state, feeling hopeless and depressed with their life conditions, and the violence and aggression against "enemies" revitalizes and energizes the group members, giving them a sense of power and visibility. Mack's point is important because he shows that in many religious and ideological disputes, it is the violence it-self, or perhaps just the language of violence, that is experienced as the liberating force. Frantz Fanon, a controversial black psy-chiatrist who was active in the Algerian wars of liberation against France, similarly urged what he considered the op-pressed colonial masses to engage in violence against the white colonialists even in cases where the French had an overwhelm-ing advantage in weapons and troops. Fanon's point was that the very acts of violence on the part of the oppressed, though unsuccessful, would cure the age-old feelings of inferiority brought on by colonialism and enable them to restore self-respect and honor. Once liberated by the heady experience of a violent outburst against the oppressors, the former colonial sub-jects would discover the way to their political liberation as well.[49]

Observers are frequently surprised that the violence perpe-trated by groups that believe themselves to be persecuted by to-tally evil outsiders bent on their destruction often has no realistic political goal. It is, as Mack puts it, "war as therapy" and not violence as an attempt to achieve a political goal or force a solution to an intractable conflict. Juergensmeyer describes this type of violence as an attempt at "symbolic empowerment" rather than a realistic and calculated attempt at transforming the social order or actually obtaining power for the group.[50] Mena-chem Begin, the former prime minister of Israel and the com-mander of the militant underground militia Irgun Zvai Leumi during the British mandate in pre-Israel Palestine, was a very shrewd, goal-oriented politician, but he acknowledged that the underground fighting, bombings, and occasional executions by Irgun Zvai Leumi were also attempts to convince the Jewish community that Jews did not have to be passive but could regain their self-respect by violent confrontation with their enemies. In his memoir, *The Revolt*, Begin explains, "When Descartes said: 'I think therefore I am', he uttered a very profound thought. But there are times in the history of peoples when thought alone does not prove their existence. A people may think and yet its sons, with their thoughts and in spite of them, may be turned into a herd of slaves—or into soap. There are times when everything in you cries out: your very self-respect as a human being lies in your resistance to evil. *We fight, therefore we are!*"[51]

The Christian militias in the United States are predominately made up of people from a white Protestant background, and many members have a long family history of birth and residence in the United States. Nonetheless, in many ways the militias fit the category of a victimized group.[52] Members of the militias feel American society is passing them by and the historically white, Anglo-Christian culture which defined America is disappearing. They feel they are rapidly becoming a minority in their own country. They view with fear and trepidation the changing demography of the United States, where some have predicted that Spanish will be the preferred language in most households by the middle of the twenty-first century. They see the large and successful immigration of Asians as challenging the standing of whites and fear the predictions that California and other West Coast states will have a minority of Caucasians by the middle of the century. The militias see affirmative action not as opening employment to groups who were historically excluded but as an attack on poor and middle-class Caucasians. The massive cultural changes of the last decades in family relations, the rise of feminism, and the removal of exclusively Christian symbols from public life also are experienced as attacks on white Christians who, by dint of family background, education, and social class, cannot find a secure place for themselves in contemporary America.

Someone is responsible for this sad state of affairs. All militia groups are convinced that the federal government has been taken over by enemies of "true" Christianity and that there is a conspiracy against white Christians to eliminate or completely marginalize them in American society so that they will be strangers in their own land under the authority of hostile races and religions. Some of these militias affiliate with Christian Identity, a rabidly racist, anti-Semitic, fundamentalist Christian movement blaming the takeover of the federal government on the Jews, nonwhite races, and the Zionist lobby in Washington.[53] Christian Identity considers white Christians to be part of the superior Aryan race, which also includes Germans and Northern

Europeans and which they believe are the chosen people with whom God made the biblical covenant. They see modern-day Jews as satanic impostors who are attempting to steal the divine birthright of the Aryan race and must therefore be killed along with other inferior races. The call for murder and violence in the militias and in Christian Identity is part of these groups' religious quest to reclaim their birthright as God's chosen, a birthright stolen by inferior races and religions. Christian Identity is the religious umbrella which articulates and legitimates their violence and racism, but other groups of militias are affiliated with the Ku Klux Klan and other white supremacist Aryan and religious organizations. What they all have in common is a sense of impending doom. Their members feel that if they do not act quickly and violently, as God has instructed them, to eliminate the dangers of racial pollution and retake their government and society, the foundations of Christian civilization will be destroyed. As one militia member put it: "This country will be a white Aryan homeland or it will not be at all."[54]

Typical of this genre is Timothy McVeigh, executed for bombing the Alfred P. Murrah Federal Building in Okalahoma City, where 168 people, including children and toddlers in a nursery school, were killed. McVeigh was a high school graduate who had a short but successful career in the United States military, serving with honor in Vietnam and receiving an honorable discharge. When he returned home from Southeast Asia, he had several entry-level jobs and drifted from job to job, never quite finding a place for himself. In conversations, he expressed his frustration with the unfairness of his situation. He was an American veteran who had been in battle, yet he could not find worthy employment, while foreigners and non-Caucasians were doing well. He came gradually under the influence of groups that gave him white supremacist readings, including the influential *Turner Diaries,* which convinced him that his situation was not unique but was the consequence of the federal government's falling into the hands of the enemies of white Christians. In this view, there is a planned conspiracy to impoverish white Christians and destroy their culture. There is a war planned to eliminate all Aryans, and in this situation, white Christians have to stand up and repel this danger, for it is a matter of kill or be killed. McVeigh was, in this view, a soldier in this war of Christian defense; after his execution, he remains a hero and model to the Christian white militia movement.[55]

Militia groups throughout the United States have planned a violent program of attacks against Asians, Jews, African Americans, and other nonwhite groups. Their version of racist Christianity has served to provide a justification for their planned violence, and the movement has attracted interest among Americans who see themselves as victims of globalization and the changing demography of contemporary America. These militia groups, despite their rhetoric and threats, are not very well organized and their organizations are heavily monitored and frequently infiltrated by law enforcement personnel. In interviews and studies of militia groups, members acknowledge their poor success rate; how, despite their fearsome rhetoric, many militia leaders have been imprisoned; and how American society appears not to have heeded their warnings and taken them seriously. They are convinced that a religious race war is coming, but in the meantime, they say, they are popularizing their program and ideology. John Porter, a former militia leader in Washington State who promised his followers an Armageddon-like war which would restore white Christian patriots to power in the year 2000 and who is now imprisoned in a federal penitentiary, told a reporter after his conviction, "If you get a piece of information out to two or three people—that's lifting the rock and letting in the sun"[56] Porter and other militia leaders have not been successful in getting the resources and recruits they desire, but the powerful sentiments and deep resentment against the government and minorities that they express can be exploited by extremist groups.

Nothing said here is intended to minimize the danger of racist religious groups. In an era of rapid social change, where many feel threatened by the shifts in the economy, social demography, and the moral order, the militias are an attractive option for providing meaning, a sense of purpose, and a social way of venting anger and frustration to a sympathetic audience. There are approximately three to four million militia members in the

United States; about a fifth of them are regular attendees at meetings and prayer services, have taken military training, and are willing to participate in violent confrontation. The bulk of members, to this point, are individuals who are moved by the rhetoric and fellowship of the militias and share the new religious ideologies but have not committed themselves to active violence. The language of violence and the exploits of McVeigh and other "heroes" of the "resistance" serve to give dignity and pride to these people who feel history is passing them by.

Conclusion

The psychological perspective on religious violence illustrates the significance of psychological themes in understanding the nature of religious violence and conflict. Mark Juergensmeyer in his essay on the logic of religious violence argues that political, economic, or sociological explanations of violence which emphasize the rational and practical gains to be gotten from violence are not always very helpful. He describes the violent confrontations between Sikhs, an Indian religion combining elements of Islam and Hinduism, and the largely Hindu government, which saw Sikh rioting and killings throughout the years of the Indian state, including the assassination of Prime Minister Indira Gandhi in 1984. Juergensmeyer concludes that religious issues and compromise were not at the heart of the conflict, and any deals made between the two parties could never be finalized. The militant Sikh community in various parts of India, Juergensmeyer reports, was searching for a Sikh identity, a feeling of empowerment, and a sense of honor that was no longer available in a transformed India. The Sikh religious violence, in this view, ultimately had no clear-cut, articulated goal but was a search for symbolic empowerment rather than a quest for religious ends. When in 1995 a militant Sikh, Dilawar Singh, killed the chief minister in Punjab along with fourteen others in a brutal attack, the assassin could offer no justification other than to say that his act had restored a sense of pride and honor that the government of India had taken from his people.[57]

Many conflicts in other parts of the world, similarly, have strong elements of redressing humiliation by religious means. Each conflict is complex, having a unique context and history, but religious justifications are frequently present in justifying violence. The Palestinian Muslim suicide bombers, who kill themselves in crowded public areas like malls, restaurants, and entertainment venues, killing many civilian Israelis, are thought to have restored honor and dignity to Palestinians who feel themselves humiliated by Israeli military power.[58] The suicide bombings are explained as acts of war against an implacable enemy, a way of effectively killing and maiming large numbers of the enemy with relatively very little cost. While this may be the case, many analysts, including some sympathetic to the Palestinian cause, have viewed these suicide missions as standing in the way of a political settlement. Indeed, the plethora of suicide killings in the beginning of the twenty-first century has hardened positions in many religious conflicts. The Irish civil wars, the wars and conflict in Bosnia, and the civil wars in Nigeria, among many, many others, have, as we shall discuss, many theological and cultural elements. But as Juergensmayer argues, the psychological elements must always be factored into the logic of religious violence.

Notes

1. For an introduction and analyses of the relationship between Freudian theory and religion, see Erich Fromm, *Psychoanalysis and Religion* (New Haven: Yale University Press, 1950). Also see Gregory Zilboorg, *Freud and Religion: A Restatement of an Old Controversy* (Westminster, Md.: Newman Press, 1958).

2. Sigmund Freud, *Civilization and Its Discontents,* trans. Joan Riviere (London: Hogarth, 1963), 58.

3. Sigmund Freud, *The Future of an Illusion* (New York: Norton, 1990).

4. Rene Girard, *Violence and the Sacred,* trans. Patrick Gregory (Baltimore: Johns Hopkins University, 1977). Also see his *Things Hidden Since the Foundation of the World* (Stanford, Calif.: Stanford University Press, 1987).

5. Girard, *Violence and the Sacred*, 36.

6. Girard, *Violence and the Sacred*, 143–168.

7. Girard, *Violence and the Sacred*, 37.

8. David Rapoport, "Some General Observations on Religion and Violence," in *Violence and the Sacred in the Modern World*, ed. Mark Juergensmeyer (London: Frank Cass, 1991), 118–140.

9. Mark Juergensmeyer, "Editor's Introduction: Is Symbolic Violence Related to Real Violence?" in Juergensmeyer, *Violence and the Sacred in the Modern World*, 1–8.

10. For the culture conflict between religious and secular elements in Israeli society, see Ehud Sprinzak, *Brother Against Brother: Violence and Extremism in Israeli Politics from Altalena to the Rabin Assassination* (New York: Free Press, 1999).

11. Yoram Hazony, "Israel's Right and Left Converge," *New York Times*, April 26, 2002, sec. A, p. 21.

12. Rene Girard and Mark R. Anspach, "A Response: Reflections from the Perspective of mimetic Theory" in Juergensmeyer, *Violence and The Sacred in the Modern World*.

13. Martin Kramer, "Sacrifice and Fratricide in Shiite Lebanon," in Jurgensmeyer, *Violence and the Sacred in the Modern World*, 30–47.

14. Kramer, "Sacrifice and Fratricide," 31.

15. Ehud Sprinzak, "Violence and Catastrophe in the Theology of Rabbi Meir Kahane: The Ideologization of Mimetic Desire," in Juergensmeyer, *Violence and the Sacred in the Modern World*.

16. Sprinzak, *Brother Against Brother*, chap. 6. Also see Robert Friedman, *The False Prophet: Rabbi Meir Kahane* (New York: Lawrence Hill, 1990).

17. Meir Kahane, *Listen World, Listen Jew* (Jerusalem: Institute of the Jewish Idea, 1978), 121–122.

18. See Sprinzak, *Brother Against Brother*, particularly 238–243.

19. The quote was taken from the title of a memorial volume published in honor of Baruch Goldstein. See Michael Ben-Horin, *Boruch Hagever* (Jerusalem: n.p., 1995).

20. Leon Festinger, Henry W. Riecken, and Stanley Schachter, *When Prophecy Fails* (Minneapolis: University of Minnesota Press, 1956), 25.

21. Richard John Neuhaus, *The Naked Public Square: Religion and Democracy in America* (Grand Rapids, Mich.: Eerdmans, 1984).

22. Peter L. Berger, "Some Sociological Comments on Theological Education," *Perspective*, Summer 1968.

23. Leon Festinger, *A Theory of Cognitive Dissonance* (Evanston, Ill.: Row, Peterson, 1957), 3.

24. See Berger, "Theological Education."

25. R. Scott Appleby, *The Ambivalence of the Sacred: Religion, Violence, and Reconciliation* (Lanham, Md.: Rowman & Littlefield, 2000), 281–307.

26. See Charles Selengut and Yigal Carmon, "Judaism, Islam, and the Middle East Conflict," in Charles Selengut, *Jewish-Muslim Encounters: History, Philosophy, and Culture* (St. Paul, Minn.: Paragon, 2001), 108–109.

27. Selengut and Carmon, "Judaism, Islam, and the Middle East Conflict."

28. Sprinzak, *Brother Against Brother*, 5–7 and 244–245.

29. Quoted in Sprinzak, *Brother Against Brother*, 282.

30. Sprinzak, *Brother Against Brother*, 278–285.

31. Hassan al-Turabi, "The Islamic State," in John L. Esposito, *Voices of Resurgent Islam* (New York: Oxford University Press, 1983), 241–251.

32. See Yossef Bodansky, *Bin Laden: The Man who Declared War on America* (New York: Random House, 2001).

33. See Charles Kutzman, ed, *Liberal Islam* (New York: Oxford University Press, 1998).

34. Quoted in Emmanuel Sivan, *Radical Islam: Medieval Theology and Modern Politics* (New Haven: Yale University Press, 1985), 24.

35. See Yvonne Haddad, "Sayyid Qutb: Ideologue of Islamic Revival" in Esposito, *Voices of Resurgent Islam*, 67–98.

36. Quoted in Sivan, *Radical Islam*, 68.

37. Karen Armstrong, *The Battle for God* (New York: Alfred A. Knopf, 2000).

38. Geneive Abdo, *No God But Allah: Egypt and the Triumph of Islam* (New York: Oxford University Press, 2000), 107–138. Abdo chronicles the growing importance of violence and the threat of violence in transforming Egypt from one of the most open Islamic countries to a society whose institutions are being transformed into models of Islamic orthodoxy. Abdo shows how the threat of violence has limited academic freedom and even foreclosed the possibility of religious debate in religious schools, which was historically one of the central elements of Islamic pedagogy and scholarship.

39. James A. Haught, *Holy Hatred* (Amherst, N.Y.: Prometheus, 1995), 81–94.

40. Abdo, *No God But Allah*, 107–138.

41. For a discussion and translation see Johannes J. G. Jansen, *The Neglected Duty: The Creed of Sadat's Assassins and Islamic Resurgence in the Middle East* (New York: Macmillan, 1986).

42. The term "paramount reality" is taken from Peter Berger and

Thomas Luckman, *The Social Construction of Reality* (New York: Double-day, 1967) to describe the official and establishment view of culture and religion. All other social views are considered deviant and receive political and social censure.

43. Peter L. Berger, *The Sacred Canopy: Elements of a Sociological Theory of Religion* (New York; Doubleday, 1969), chap. 5. See also Peter L. Berger, *The Heretical Imperative* (New York: Doubleday, 1979).

44. See Edward Peters, *Inquisition* (New York: Free Press, 1988), 40–44.

45. Virgilio Pinto Crespo, "Thought Control in Spain" in *Inquisition and Society in Early Modern Europe,* ed. Stephen Haliczer (Totowa, N.J.: Barnes & Noble, 1987), 17–188.

46. Peters, *Inquisition*, 77–97.

47. Ralph Ellison, *Invisible Man* (New York: Vintage, 1995).

48. John Mack, foreword to Volkan Vanik, *Cyprus—War and Adaptation: A Psychoanalytic Study of Groups in Conflict* (Charlottesville: University of Virginia Press, 1979)

49. Frantz Fanon, *The Wretched of the Earth* (Harmondsworth: Penguin, 1967).

50. Mark Juergensmeyer, *Terror in The Mind of God: The Global Rise of Religious Violence* (Berkeley and Los Angeles: University of California Press, 2000), 155–160.

51. Menachem Begin, *The Revolt* (New York: Dell Publishing, 1977), 85.

52. See Morris Dees, *Gathering Storm: America's Militia Threat* (New York: Harper Collins, 1996). See also Jeffrey Kaplan, *Radical Religion in America: Millenarian Movements From the Far Right to the Children of Noah* (Syracuse, N.Y.: Syracuse University Press, 1997).

53. Michael Barkun, *Religion and the Racist Right: The Origins of the Christian Identity Movement* (Chapel Hill: University of North Carolina Press, 1994).

54. Howard Bushart, John R. Craig, and Myra Barnes, *Soldiers of God: White Supremacists and their Holy War for America* (New York: Kensington, 1998), 290.

55. Juergensmeyer, *Terror in the Mind of God*, 30–38. Also see Bushart, *Soldiers of God*, 1–78.

56. Quoted in Jane Kramer, "The Patriot," *New Yorker*, May 6, 2002, 104–118. See also for an insightful interview with Porter and a report on the organization of a militia group.

57. Juergensmeyer, *Terror in the Mind of God*, 84–101.

58. Thomas L. Friedman, "The Core of Muslim Rage," *New York Times*, March 5, 2002, sec. A, p. 21.

3

Apocalyptic Violence

All religions have a vision of the ideal society which will come at the "end of time," the *eschaton*, when the universe will be in full harmony with God's plan and all the predictions for the ideal society described in the scriptures will come to pass. Judaism's vision of the eschaton is the messianic age, ushered in by the arrival of the Messiah from the kingly House of David, who will transform the whole world into a peaceable kingdom, where, as the Bible puts it, "they shall beat their swords into plowshares and their spears into pruning forks; nation shall not lift up sword against nation and they will no longer engage in war" (Isa. 2:4). Following an earthly messianic period of extended peace, harmony, and prosperity, the dead will be resurrected and all the righteous will join in an eternal life of heavenly bliss. Christianity adopted a good deal of Jewish messianism and proclaimed Jesus Christ as the messiah and savior who will return at the end of time to proclaim the kingdom of God, punishing sinners and rewarding faithful believers with eternal heavenly life. Islam, too, has its version of the end times when all will be judged for their faithfulness and redeemers will arise who will proclaim God's truth, punish the unfaithful sinners, and establish an eternal order where all will be entirely true to the prophet Muhammad's teachings and directives.[1]

The establishment of God's order will not come easily. The forces of good will have to confront the forces of evil and a terrifying, cataclysmic event causing great suffering and destruction—the apocalypse, literally "the lifting of the veil" from the

95

ancient Greek—will transform the universe and usher in the new age of peace and harmony. In Judaism, for example, the traditions describe an apocalyptic war between the two world empires, Gog and Magog, in which untold numbers of people will be burned and killed in the devastation, followed by the destruction of sinful empires and the return of the Jewish people to the land of Israel, where the ancient temple in Jerusalem will be rebuilt and all scriptural promises fulfilled. For Christianity, the books of Daniel and Revelation spell out the terrifying events of the endtime, the eschaton, in great and specific detail. There will be a series of divine judgments in which unbelievers and faithless sinners are severely punished and apocalyptic wars, the wars of Armageddon, take place to cleanse the world of evil and destroy immoral nations. At the conclusion of these violent, apocalyptic events, Jesus emerges triumphant and reigns in his glory and righteousness over all and the kingdom of God is finally established. The Koran does not speak directly about an apocalypse, but there are strong Muslim traditions about the coming immorality and unfaithfulness of the world during the "end times" and the fierce battles which will take place around Jerusalem between the forces of faith and those of false messiahs. At the conclusion of these battles and the elimination of Allah's enemies, Islam will triumph and the truth and harmony of Islam will prevail.

These apocalyptic narratives have always, and in all religions, greatly motivated and inspired believers. They tell of a time when faith will be vindicated and religious waiting for God's return will end. Human suffering will end and the patient waiting for divine rewards will take place. The apocalyptic events will end all troubles and do away with all sorrow, and the divine promises will be realized in the here and now. There can be no more desirable and welcome situation for the faithful than the realization of their eschatological expectations, with its promises of glory, honor, and eternal life. For this reason, the apocalyptic events, terrible as they are to be, are welcome as harbingers of the kingdom of God and the redemptive state to which all history is inexorably moving. Earthly life will end, but the apocalypse will begin a heavenly and eternal journey for the faithful.

Established religion has, historically, placed the coming of the eschaton outside human action. That the apocalyptic events will surely occur is the position of established religion, but this is God's work and it will have to come in God's time. Excessive concern with the end of the world ignores the task of religion in the here and now, ministering to the poor and needy, supporting the institutional needs of religious institutions and the clergy, and enabling people to deal with the sorrows and suffering of everyday life. In most traditional religions, human beings are forbidden to hasten or do anything which would invoke the terrible events of the apocalypse. Judaism, particularly, denies the legitimacy of human action to bring the messianic transformation it so ardently awaits. Christianity began in great expectation over the immanent transformation of the world, but it, too, had to come to terms with long-term, passive waiting for the return of Jesus and the establishment of the kingdom of God. Early Islam did put some of its apocalyptic fervor into practice as it fought a series of religious wars to extend Muslim rule in many parts of the world, but Islam, too, had to modify its apocalyptic visions as it fought a series of wars with Christians in the ninth and tenth centuries. Organized religion had good reason to limit the aggressive pursuit of the eschaton and the transformation of human society because in times of such great fervor, ordinary life, including working, building, education, family life, and even the rule of law, is denigrated and people refuse to live conventional lives, believing that all will soon be changed in the coming divine transformation. There is a sense, in times of apocalyptic upheaval, that ordinary life is not worth living and conventional norms and laws are meaningless given the liberated characteristics of the new reality. Religion has had to limit its own theological expectations and curtail apocalyptic aspirations so that conventional life continues and social order is maintained.[2]

Nonetheless, movements intent on hastening the coming apocalypse are part of every religion and have been active throughout history. The desire to break through the boundaries of everyday life and achieve a sacred reality and bond with the divine is a powerful stimulus to apocalyptic activity. Established religions may oppose these efforts, but the desire to force the end of history, to seek relief and release from the pains and travails of ordinary life and enter a new reality of ultimate truth and serenity, has motivated people throughout history. Thomas Robbins, a specialist in the study of millennial and apocalyptic groups, describes the mass suicide of thousands of members of the Old Believers, a group of Russian Orthodox traditionalists in the late seventeenth century, who killed themselves to protest changes in Orthodox practice. They believed their mass death would destroy the antichrist and pave the way for world redemption. Robbins describes how the Old Believers, who began by protesting relatively minor changes in church liturgy, eventually committed suicide or provoked government and church officials to murder them in an effort to hasten the coming Apocalypse.[3] Some apocalyptic groups do not participate in violence but are convinced that the end times are already here, withdrawing from ordinary life as they await world transformation. The Shakers, an American Christian sect founded by Ann Lee in the late eighteenth century, are convinced that the end of the world is at hand and Christ is returning to proclaim a new age; they give up marriage and procreation, living in communal settlements waiting for Christ's immanent return. They came to be known as Shakers because of their enthusiastic prayer meetings, where they shook strenuously in their excitement about Christ's return.[4] Some historians, interestingly, proclaim the Pilgrims to have been an apocalyptic movement, emigrating to America to create the new Zion in the New World, away from the evils and sinfulness of Anglican Britain.[5] Interest in the apocalypse is growing in modern societies, too; a best-selling series of novels, the *Left Behind* series, inspired by Christian fundamentalism, describes what happens after Jesus "Raptures" his true believers to heaven at the end of time and leaves others to torment and desolation on earth in the age of the antichrist.[6]

Apocalypticism and Violence

Not all apocalyptic groups actively engage in violence, but there is a strong propensity for the acceptance of violence, suicide, and armed conflict. Violence, in the apocalyptic imagination, is not necessarily evil. To the contrary, loyalty and obedience to a society and culture which are ungodly and continue to maintain beliefs and institutions which stand in the way of apocalyptic transformation is the real evil. For these faithful believers in the collapse of the current state of affairs, almost anything that will hasten its end is desirable and virtuous. It is, put another way, not violence and mayhem as ends in themselves of which they approve, but activities which will result in the passing of the old and the coming of the new order. For example, Kyle Watson, a Christian evangelist and writer, tried to allay the anxieties of contemporary Christian believers fearful about the coming apocalypse, with its global wars, by reminding them that the end of the world with all its terrors will bring about a time when believers will be united with "Christ in heaven."[7] The emphasis in all apocalypticism is not on the destruction of the old but on the glories and enchantments of the emerging order. Violence is therefore encouraged and theologically justified as a means by which the endtimes will occur. The basis for the acceptance of violence could be scriptural interpretation in Christian, Jewish, or Islamic apocalyptic groups or teachings based on the pronouncements of charismatic leaders, as is usually the case in new religious movements.

The issue of violence and apocalypticism is complex and, as many authors have pointed out, it is very difficult to predict which groups will actually engage in violence. Some groups with radical, violent rhetoric never appear to be involved in violence or terrorism while other groups with a passive theology end up involved in violent confrontations and, in some cases, in mass suicide. Three factors appear significant in understanding apocalyptic groups and violence. First, there is the response of law enforcement. Apocalyptic groups may take on radical lifestyles in the form of unconventional family arrangements, communal sharing of resources, and a refusal to follow established legal procedures. A certain amount of outside pressure can usually be handled by these movements and may even cement the camaraderie of the groups. However, should a group feel that its very existence is threatened by governmental officials and its sacred beliefs denigrated, the group may feel justified in violently confronting the police and political authorities. Robbins and Anthony see this type of violent response not as the result of group beliefs but as a consequence of what they refer to as "exogamous factors," violence caused by the external environment.[8] Second, apocalyptic groups are, in sociological terms, precarious social organizations because they are, generally, under the direction and leadership of charismatic leaders and prophets. Charismatic leaders are obeyed because their followers believe they have divine powers and have been chosen to be God's representatives. The usual restraints on conventional religious officials do not apply to charismatic leaders. Legal rules, religious traditions, and community pressure, all of which operate to restrain conventional religious authorities, do not inhibit the directives of charismatic leaders. Charismatic leaders are obeyed because they are believed to have direct access to divine truth and their followers are obligated to comply with all their directives. The charismatic leader is the final authority and his pronouncements are words of ultimate truth.[9] Therefore, the charismatic leader can, despite all religious convention, tradition, and law, direct his followers to undertake violent action. The charismatic leader needs no justification for his orders; they are legitimate because he says so. Finally, apocalypticism is a radical and alternative reality to the ordinary and taken-for-granted world in which most people live. The faithful followers of these leaders unequivocally reject the social world in which they reside and already live in an alternative world of their own making, with its own sense of time, space, and values. They are no longer of this world, and the logic and truths of ordinary reality do not restrain them. They have already left behind the meanings, interpretations, and restraints which govern people living in the ordinary everyday reality and their behavior, possibly including violence, makes sense to them in the context of their apocalyptic reality.

Apocalyptic groups are, by their nature, antinomian; they are opposed to the rules, norms, and legalities of the established order and they challenge the social and political status quo. Some apocalyptic movements are extremely aggressive, actively initiating catastrophic events which will, they believe, lead to the demise of the current order. For these groups, death and destruction must occur; they are necessary precursors to world transformation. Other apocalyptic groups retreat from society while they passively await the apocalypse which will take them, as a faithful elite, to eternal life. Sociologists consider all types of apocalypticism to be a unique category of religious organization having the following characteristics:

- The world is inherently evil;
- The rules, laws, and values of society are immoral and need not be obeyed;
- Adherents must follow only the rules and directives of their leaders and prophets, whom they believe are divinely inspired;
- The current social and political world must and will be destroyed; and
- Destruction and catastrophe are necessary and will be followed by the emergence of the new and redeemed order which will be superior in every way to current reality.

Catastrophic Apocalypticism: Aum Shinrikyo, Christian Identity, and the Temple Mount Faithful

Catastrophic apocalyptic groups believe it is their obligation to actively initiate the coming of the apocalypse through violence and religious confrontation. Such groups believe that they are the possessors of special religious wisdom or revelation that will enable them to bring about the endtime. Catastrophic apocalyptic groups acknowledge that their activities involve violence, but the violence and destruction caused by their program are seen, in their worldview, as ultimately guided by divine authority. There is a sense among these groups that their violence is a way of transforming and redeeming the human condition. In some cases, as in perhaps the Aum Shinrikyo movement, the catastrophic apocalypticism of the movement takes center stage and violence and catastrophe become ends in themselves. Apocalyptic movements all face this dilemma as they are pulled between violence and human transformation.[10]

The Japanese new religious movement Aum Shinrikyo was a dramatic example of this genre of apocalypticism.[11] Aum Shinrikyo was founded in 1987 by a blind Japanese acupuncturist and healer who took the name Shoko Ashara. Ashara had studied yoga and Buddhism and in the early years of his movement taught classes to small groups in meditation, self improvement, and methods of liberation from the travails of ordinary life. In the early years of the movement, Aum Shinrikyo was very much a typical Japanese new religious movement, providing fellowship and meaning in a rapidly changing Japan which was taking its place in a global world order. A major shift in the movement occurred in the 1990s, when Ashara claimed he had received a revelation from the Hindu god Shiva proclaiming him to be a messianic leader and redeemer who would transform Japan from a materialistic technocratic country into a utopian and perfectly harmonious society, which Ashara called the Kingdom of Shambhala. The way to do this, Ashara taught, was through the Lotus Village Plan, the development of independent communities all over Japan living according to Asahara's teachings. Thousands of spiritual seekers, including trained and talented scientists, were attracted to Asahara's communities and teachings and joined his group, living communally and following his leadership.

The somewhat optimistic teachings gave way a few years after its founding to a growing pessimism that peaceful means would ever transform the world and bring about the harmonious Kingdom of Shambhala. It is unclear as to why Aum, which began as a peaceful Asian meditative new religion, adopted an increasingly catastrophic view of the human condition. Most scholars attribute the change in the movement to its growing conflict with established Japanese society and its failure to attract really large numbers of followers who could have made Aum a significant force in Japanese society. Life in the Aum Shinrikyo communities was spartan, communal, and authoritarian, and the Aum communities were frequently in conflict with the townspeople and neighborhood associations where they lived. And although Ashara was a popular and much-sought-after lecturer and commentator—he spoke at several prestigious Japanese universities—his movement's membership remained static and he never reached a following of thirty thousand fully committed adherents, a number he said was necessary for Japan to be transformed into a peaceable and harmonious society. Ashara had laid down a strict regimen for members, and as is the case in many new religions encouraged his followers to sever close relationships with their families. When some members rejected this and wanted to leave the group, Ashara pronounced them evil and dangerous and, in several well documented cases, had them hidden, drugged, and occasionally murdered to avoid any public knowledge of defection.

The growing defections, community rejection, and police surveillance had a serious impact on the organization and ideology of the movement. The writings and speeches of Ashara increasingly rejected the possibility of peaceful transformation and he talked more and more about a coming nuclear war which would destroy the world. Only his followers, individuals who had been liberated by his methods, would survive the coming apocalypse, and he urged all to follow him if they wanted to be saved from the coming disaster. In 1992 and 1993, Ashara proclaimed that 90 percent of the Japanese population would be destroyed and that only those who had his special spiritual training and became "superhuman" would survive and repopulate and control the universe. "The genuine spiritualists," Ashara told his followers, "will grow full and shine like the sun, while the genuine materialists will be collected and burned."[12]

Ashara began predicting dates for an imminent world war in which much of Japan would be destroyed, but changed these dates to fit his growing apocalyptic rhetoric. At first the wars and destruction were predicted to occur in 2000, then 1998, then 1996 or even earlier. Eventually, Ashara grew even more disillusioned as his predictions and pronouncements were ignored and the movement came under more police surveillance and suspicion. Few new members came into the movement and defections became a critical problem. At some point, perhaps as early as

1993, Ashara and the movement turned from awaiting the apocalypse and seeking refuge for a selected elite to working to actively bringing about an apocalyptic catastrophe. Ashara adopted a good deal of extreme Christian right-wing thinking to justify his catastrophic goals, blaming world Jewry, the Freemasons and Western secularism for destroying traditional Japanese society and values and for seeking to take over the world for their perverted purposes. Ashara's conclusions were that the world had now become so evil and the Japanese leadership so perverted that the world had to be destroyed before the much-desired Kingdom of Shambhala could come into being. There was a great deal of disappointment among Aum's leadership, which included leading physical and biological scientists, over the way the police and the government were treating them. The movement saw itself as an avant garde spiritual group able to heal the pain of modernity, but it was considered by outsiders a deviant and criminal group.

The catastrophic apocalypse Aum sought to bring about was fueled by its resentment and theology but was made possible by its scientific know-how. Early in its development, the group began producing drugs and poisonous gases, using them as weapons against their enemies and as a way of keeping people from leaving the group. With the change to active apocalypticism, they turned to their scientists, for whom they provided well-funded labs, and asked them to develop sophisticated poisonous gases that could be used to kill and immobilize a large population. The plan was to begin the destruction of Japanese society, laying the groundwork for the apocalyptic transformation. On March 25, 1995, the potent nerve gas sarin was released by Aum followers in some twelve Tokyo subway stations, including the centrally located Kasumigaseki station, where governmental buildings were located. The attack injured over five thousand people and killed at least twelve. Japan was shocked by the attack and police began an investigation that ultimately discovered that this hitherto Buddhist-type religious group had not only launched a terror attack in a major city but had killed dozens of other individuals it considered enemies and had the capability to develop even more potent weapons of mass destruction in sophisticated research centers and warehouses. At the time of the attack Aum had also moved to the United States, where it had a small but well organized center. It was also particularly prominent in intellectual circles in the former Soviet Union.

Aum Shinrikyo members were a sophisticated group and attempts by some journalists to portray them as mere criminals or as having been brainwashed are entirely wrong. They were committed religionists, people who were disenchanted with modern Japanese society, and in their closed and sectarian world were acting in an entirely justified fashion to come to terms with the necessary end of the world. They believed that under the charismatic leadership of Shoko Ashara, they were unique in understanding what had to be done to save themselves and transform the planet. They had come to the conclusion that mass killings were "altruistic murder" committed to stop evil karma from increasing in the world and, in their interpretation, murder and destruction were the means to rid the world of evil so that truly spiritual values represented by the Aum communities could triumph.[13] In this strange amalgam of Buddhism and the biblical book of Revelation, with which Ashara was familiar, the intended killing of large numbers of people would cleanse the world, leaving an elite of superhumans who would have the character and training to create a superior world, the Kingdom of Shambhala. Aum was a small, sectarian group but it illustrates the central traits of catastrophic apocalypticism: how a group sees itself as central to the redemption of humanity and constructs a religious reality where violence and destruction are justified to transcend the evils and shortcomings of this unredeemed world.

It would be an error, however, to see apocalyptic violence as limited to new religions and cults. Elements of ultraconservative Christianity, as well, preach the legitimacy of violence in order to bring about the millennial return of Christ. Most evangelical Christians believe in the coming apocalypse, with years of tribulation and suffering before the forces of evil, led by the antichrist, will finally be defeated in the great battle of Armageddon, which will herald Christ's second coming and the establishment of the kingdom of God. Evangelicals and fundamentalist Christians are, by and large, premillenialists who believe in the rapture, whereby God will raise the faithful to heaven before the terrible events of the endtime and have them return to earth with him after the apocalyptic events at the end of time.[14] In this way faithful Christians will not have to undergo the terrible suffering that is part of the apocalyptic era. However, followers of Christian Identity movements are post-tribulationists, which means they do not accept Rapture theology and believe they as faithful Christians will have to stay on earth during the years of war and tribulation fighting for Christian truth and defending themselves against the forces of the antichrist. For some of these Identity groups, the current period is already the time of tribulation and, for them, there is a war in the United States between the forces of good, which they represent, and the forces of evil, represented by a "satanic" Jewish conspiracy which will bring the endtime.[15] These groups see themselves battling against the growing powers of the antichrist, which they identify with world Jewry, African Americans, and all other nonwhite ethnic groups, together with the U.S. federal government, which they claim is operating under the direction of a Jewish Zionist conspiracy to destroy American Christianity. Militant Christian identity groups see the coming apocalypse as a race war between Aryans, which includes all white northern Europeans, and the Jews and nonwhites who are in the grip of Satan and on the side of the antichrist.

In such a situation, beset by terrifying enemies, it is only reasonable, Christian identity groups argue, to organize militarily, store weapons, and use violence to protect themselves from their evil enemies. Some identity groups, like the Idaho-based The Order in the 1980s, went further and, as Michael Barkun, a perceptive student of identity, reports, seek "to stimulate what it saw as an inevitable, apocalyptic race war."[16] The Order, a very popular and important group, began a campaign of violence, including armed robbery, arson, and murder against those they considered the enemy. This included the murder of a radio talk show host in the Midwest who criticized the Identity movement.[17] Identity adherents also engaged in widespread counterfeiting, believing this would destroy the U.S. economy. Other groups sought armed confrontation with federal authorities in order to spark widespread rebellion. Some current groups engage in violence against the people they identify as the antichrist, shooting at Jews and Jewish institutions. Buford Furrow Jr., a member of the Aryan Nation and a follower of Christian Identity, was sentenced to life in prison for a 1999 California murder spree whose victims included children at a synagogue child care center and people who appeared to be Asian or African American. Whether they are protecting themselves or are actively engaged in violence, the Identity groups are convinced that they are in a war and are obligated to face a catastrophic struggle to defend Christian virtues, Christian culture, and the white Christian race.

Again it is important to emphasize the religious nature of this apocalyptic violence by adherents of Christian Identity movements.[18] For these people, their arms caches and weapons training, their murder of their enemies, and their violence in refusing to follow American law is a religious imperative. Their actions cannot be separated from religious belief and faith in their version of the Christian message. Some reporters and commentators want to reduce or explain away their actions as the result of psychological malfunctioning or social marginality, and still others, usually speaking from a Christian perspective, want to deny the legitimacy of the Identity version of the Christian faith. The perspective we are encouraging is to see all these groups as unique communities that have constructed their own version of a religious faith that is as sacred to them and ultimately true as the more normative and established versions of religious belief are to more conventional believers. Identity believers live in an apocalyptic war zone; their interpretations of everyday life confirm this experience as they live in enclosed communities with others who see things the same. Because of their deviant behavior, they come into conflict with law enforcement authorities and government officials, and this, too, reinforces their sense of being oppressed for their faith and gives additional validity to their sense of living in endtimes when those faithful to Christ will be persecuted. Finally, in viewing the adherents of Identity, we have to keep in mind that in spite of their unconventionality and deviance by established standards, they express, in a strange and exaggerated fashion, the inner core of biblical Christian faith in catastrophic apocalypticism. John Hall, the author of many studies of apocalypticism, points out that all these movements retrieve neglected or marginal—but still enduring—elements of normative religious culture which they refine to fit their apocalyptic worldview.[19] In other words, these movements do not create their apocalyptic scenario from scratch but use visions, myths, and legends of their own traditions to weave a new tapestry that speaks to their followers.

There is also a not-insignificant Jewish apocalyptic movement in Israel which receives strong moral and financial support from evangelical and fundamentalist Christian groups in the United States. The movement, known as the Temple Mount Faithful, sees the continued presence of the al-Aqsa mosque and the Dome of the Rock on the Jerusalem mount where the ancient Jewish temples stood as a desecration and the reason for the failure of the Messiah to come and redeem the Jewish people. The Temple Mount Faithful call for the destruction of these mosques, both central, sacred sites for Islam, and the immediate building of a new temple imitating the architecture and fittings of the ancient temples. The Temple Mount Faithful realize that the Muslim world would react militarily and a world war could follow as Islam fights to protect and maintain its sacred places, but in the worldview of the Temple Mount Faithful, it is appropriate for this to occur so that the final battles of Gog and Magog will take place as prophesized in Hebrew and Christian scriptures. The head of the movement, Gershon Salomon, a tenth-generation Jerusalemite and former Israeli army officer, explains that it is only through rebuilding the temple that messianic transformation can occur. In this view, the rebuilt temple is critical to the unfolding of the endtime.[20]

The Temple Faithful do not simply preach but have made several serious attempts to attack holy sites. The Israeli government takes the group very seriously and the Shin Bet, the Israeli secret service, infiltrates and regularly monitors its activities. So far the various attempts of the group to accomplish its goals have been stymied by technical difficulties or thwarted by intelligence received by the Jerusalem police enabling the police to stop the planned destruction. Elements of the group, together with other Jewish apocalyptic movements, have organized other attacks on Muslim targets in order to force violent confrontations which, in this view, will lead to a battle of Armageddon. They refuse to wait for God and his divine timing but want to speed up history and the endtime, and to do this, violent actions have become a justified tactic. Yehudah Etzion, one of the charismatic leaders allied with the group who took part in several bombing attempts and was imprisoned for the 1977 violence against civilian Arabs, told a packed 1998 Jerusalem Convention Center Temple Mount meeting, "We shouldn't wait for God but as it were, hurry him up. We should take up the burden first . . . and afterward He will agree and help us."[21] In this view, faithful human actors have a central and critical role in the coming world transformation.

Most fundamentalist Christian groups concur with critical elements of the Temple Mount program, but for their own Christian theological purposes. Fundamentalist Christians are biblical literalists who believe that according to the biblical scenario, the Jewish people must first return to the Holy Land and the temple must be rebuilt before Christ will return to earth. In this view, too, the Muslim holy places must be destroyed so that the biblical prophecies will be fulfilled. For fundamentalist Christians, after the temple is built and functioning, a time of suffering, war, and terror known as the "tribulation" will ensue, with the antichrist desecrating the temple. These events will lead to the eventual defeat of the antichrist, culminating in an awful apocalypse, after which Jesus, as king messiah, will return with the faithful to establish the kingdom of God as foretold in the New Testament narratives. The Jews have an important role to play in setting the stage for Christ's return. but if at some point they do not accept Jesus as lord savior, they will be with Satan and suffer all the torments of sinners removed from God. Chuck Missler, the former chairman of Western Digital Corporation and a leader in organizations helping the Temple Mount Faithful financially and politically, put it plainly and honestly: "So if we watch the Temple being positioned, on the one hand we're excited because God's plans are unfolding as he said they would. On the other hand if you have friends, if you have a heart for Israel you can't but feel pain because they have no idea what's coming."[22]

There has developed a very close and strange financial, moral, and emotional relationship between these two groups intent on initiating a catastrophic apocalypse so that the redemptive endtime will arrive. The Jewish militants fully expect history to end with the building of the temple and the arrival of their messiah, who will usher in the messianic age of love, peace, and prosperity. For their Christian supporters, the rebuilt temple is but a prelude to the final confrontation between Christ and antichrist in which the followers of Jesus, exclusively under his lordship, will emerge triumphant. Only genuine believing Christians will be saved from the terrors of the age of tribulation and the devastation of the apocalypse. Others—Jews, Muslims, ersatz Christians and nonbelievers—will not be spared and will be judged for their faithlessness. For the time being, however, these theological differences are put aside. From all reports there are hundreds of thousands of fundamentalist supporters of the Temple Mount Faithful in American fundamentalist churches. Newsletters are sent to several hundreds of thousands of Christians in the United States, and the bulk of funding for publications, rallies, travel, and other activities comes from the America fundamentalist community. Tens of thousands of American fundamentalist pastors have visited Israel under the guidance of Temple Mount leaders and there is a library of cassette, CDs, and books put out by the Christian supporters. Salomon is a welcome visitor to America churches, and he and his group's activities are hailed as worthy of the most intense support. Some of this activity is not public, which pleases both sides, and there exists a deep sense of mutual need, respect, and camaraderie between the groups.[23]

Unlike Aum Shinrikyo or Christian Identity, the Christian communities and the writers and thinkers who are supporters of the Temple Mount Faithful are part of the larger American religious mainstream. They cannot easily be written off as a fringe group or as a brainwashed cult. Bestselling writers like Tim LeHay with his Left Behind series, and Hal Lindsay with his *The Late Great Planet Earth*, describe futuristic apocalyptic scenarios in line with much of the thinking of the fervent Christian supporters of the Temple Mount Faithful.[24] None of the many Christian groups backing the Temple Mount organization avowedly supports violence against anyone and the leaders and pastors of these groups tend to be, in personal relations, kind and caring, expressing respect for other religions. Nonetheless, their financial resources, considerable political clout on the American scene, and well-organized churches support the catastrophic apocalyptic visions of their Israeli partners. Here we see a case of what might be called surrogate violence aimed at bringing about a Christian religious vision. The American Christian supporters themselves avow a catastrophic endtime which involves violence and destruction, but they need not actually involve themselves in violence. Instead they have a surrogate willing to perform the necessary preparations until the endtime when, as the true servants of Christ, they will be called to Jerusalem to welcome their lord and savior who will proclaim the True Kingdom.

Mystical Apocalypticism: The Solar Temple and Heaven's Gate

Mystical apocalyptic movements engage in violence by encouraging and committing religiously motivated suicide and self-mutilation in order to transcend this world, which they consider evil, corrupt, and, above all, without possibility of repair. Theirs is a particularly pessimistic view of the human condition. For those embracing mystical apocalypticism, there is no savior who can redeem humanity, no divine force which will transform life on the planet and no possibility for repentance or restitution. In one of the letters or "testaments" left by Solar Temple leaders after one of their group suicide/murder ceremonies in 1994, they talk about "the blissful illusion of those who believe that the world is improving and that man is progressing" and warn that the human race is "heading irreversibly toward its own destruction."[25] For them the world must and will be destroyed, the apocalyptic destruction must be total, and the only solution for enlightened souls is an ultimate and violent migration from this world and the evil human community which inhabits it. They believe that any perception that the world is improving or that human beings on this planet can change their insidious nature is dangerous because this only enslaves people into remaining on this doomed planet. Mystical apocalyptic groups like the Solar Temple and Heaven's Gate, among many others, believe they are possessors of gnostic enlightenment and are in mystical union with divine forces which enable them to transcend their human and earthly nature. They are convinced of the necessity of "transit" from this worldly reality to a another reality—purer, more advanced, and totally divine. This world is "rotten" and life here is, at best, lived in a "mammalian" and animalistic way, devoid of spirituality, soulfulness, and divinity. The suicides and murders carried out by these groups are presented as the most rational and sane response to a world mired in sin and materialism and awaiting an imminent catastrophe. One of the last messages before their group death sent by the elite that ran the Solar Temple group urged others, particularly sympathizers who were not fully committed members, to follow their example. It informed them "not to cry over our fate, but rather cry for your own. Ours is more enviable that yours."[26]

The Solar Temple is a dramatic example of mystical apocalypticism. The group began in French-speaking Switzerland in the late 1970s and early 1980s and grew to have a headquarters in Quebec, Canada, where it attracted members from other parts of the French-speaking world. John Hall and Philip Schuyler are two scholars who have carefully researched the group and its history, placing the Solar Temple's religious beliefs and philosophy in the context of Catholic mysticism.[27] Hall and Schuyler report that the leadership and followers of the group were generally well educated and middle class, with a background of involvement with Catholicism but an alienation from the church's move away from strong ritualism and the mystical and esoteric elements of Catholic traditionalism. The rituals of the Solar Temple, in contrast, were highly elaborate, with candles, robes, videos, and music all designed to create an otherworldly atmosphere. Indeed, the leadership claimed that the rituals actually put the members in touch with the great saints. Committed members were told about earlier lives they had lived—reincarnation was a fundamental belief of the group—and the movement's leaders were accepted as "secret masters" of the universe who had special knowledge of the past and future and could communicate with other worlds. The group modeled itself on the medieval Knights Templar, a somewhat mystical group that played a special role in the Crusades, and on certain nonconformist and heretical Catholic movements like the Rosicrucians and other rose-and-cross groups that, in different ways, sought to deny the reality of human death. Two important leaders of the group, Luc Jouret, a homeopathic doctor and a popular lecturer in French-speaking Europe and in Canada, and Joseph Dimambro, taught insiders that this world is a terrible illusion and illness and death are merely manifestations of the larger moral and ecological disasters which were about to destroy the world and cause great pain and suffering to those remaining on the earth.

Although the Solar Temple organization kept up respectable appearances in the 1980s and 1990s, holding their meetings in well-known hotels and sponsoring public lectures at colleges and universities, the group was evolving its own alternative reality and becoming a secret society with its own rules, values, and authority structure. When group members interacted with outsiders, they talked about things like the importance of spirituality in modern life, the value of preserving the environment, and the significance of prayer and ritual. These beliefs and values, in and of themselves, were not unusual in the cultural milieu of those attracted to new religions, from which the movement sought to gain new members and raise money. The reality of the matter was quite different. By the early 1990s the group had moved far from the countercultural world of new religious and social movements and considered itself to have broken the division between this sense world and other realities. Members believed they were a special elite who were literally beyond life and death. It was a commonly accepted belief among followers that they could, and did, communicate with great historical and religious figures of the past. In some of the Solar Temple's séances the Virgin Mary was believed to have appeared; this was a topic of great interest and reinforced belief in the group's doctrines and leadership. The conventional understanding of time and space was rejected, with members "knowing" they could migrate, at ease, from one time period to another. Past, present, and future, in the closed and mystical world of the temple community, could be collapsed. Conventional, earthly, and time bound rules had no meaning, no reason to be followed; laws were seen as irrelevant and social norms and restraints as unnecessarily limiting. In these conditions, the traditional bonds of marriage were negated and both male and female members were assigned "cosmic partners" by the masters. Relationships and identities were not fixed and a person with the proper mystical contemplation could be transported to another time and reality. Guns were purchased and could be used against defectors, and money was raised under false premises; all was permitted to the masters, the charismatic leaders who were endowed with special gnostic wisdom.

There were always elements of planned deception and manipulation in the rituals to convince followers and skeptics that reincarnated souls were indeed visiting the communal headquarters in Thierry, Switzerland, and rural Quebec. On occasion the police were informed of the group's activities, but no real action was taken against the group. In the early 1990s, the group came to greater notoriety after reports of gun smuggling had surfaced and one defector, Rose-Marie Klaus, furious over the breakup of her marriage in the movement, had brought a series of well-documented complaints of violence and financial improprieties to the Canadian police. At about this time, the group also experienced dissension about the future of the movement, with some apparently urging its continued operation as a mystical secret society while others were urging a distinctly activist apocalyptic path. The exact truth of the matter will probably never be known, but on October 5, 1994, twenty-three dead bodies were discovered in a fire in a Solar Temple farmhouse in Cheiry, a small hamlet near Fribourg, Switzerland. Shortly thereafter, the Swiss police found another twenty-five dead bodies in vacation villas owned by members of the group in the resort town of Granges-sur-Salvan. The next day, the Quebec police, hearing reports of fires in a resort town in the Laurentian mountains, found a number of bodies, including those of small children, in the remains of several luxury vacation homes owned by leaders of the Solar Temple.[28] The bodies, clothed in ceremonial robes, were ritually arranged in a circle like the spokes of a wheel. Some of the deaths were clear cases of suicide, while other people were shot at close range. The conclusion was that the group committed a mass murder-suicide. It appears that the killings were not haphazard but well-planned and carried out with ritual precision, though the possibility exists that some individuals might have wanted to leave at the last minute and were nevertheless murdered. It appears that the fires were set shortly before the mass killing. Still other group deaths were carried out in 1995 and in 1997, and there is strong possibility that the group has reconstituted itself in a different place under a different name.

The murder-suicides of Solar Temple members came as a great shock both in Europe and North America. Here were educated and generally successful people who had joined together in the belief that the endtime was imminent and, perhaps most amazing to commentators, thought that shooting themselves would not result in death but would magically catapult them to a superior and safer place. There were attempts in the press to explain the group deaths as the result of psychological brainwashing and coercion, but the background, religious fervor, and testaments, letters, and suicide notes left by the group for sympathizers and fellow travelers who did not participate in the violence showed this action to be more complex, rooted in a refusal to remain part of what these people felt was a hopeless world situation. One of the last messages sent to sympathizers said: "To you who are receptive to this last message, may our love and peace accompany you during the terrible tests of the apocalypse that await you. Know that from where we will be, we will always hold our arms open to receive those who are worthy of joining us."[29] Messages also informed those left behind that extraterrestrial forces had communicated with the group and urged members to leave the earth and enter a purer existence far removed from this worldly existence. They were also asked to burn their temples and dwellings so that these sites could not be contaminated by humans. The messages also reassured other Solar Temple faithful that the decision to make a "transit to the future" was made voluntarily and with full awareness of what was being done. The testaments also contained warnings for those remaining behind, letting them know that "the race is heading irreversibly toward its own destruction. All of Nature is turning against those who have abused it, who have corrupted and desecrated it on every level. Man will pay a heavy tribute for he remains no less than the one responsible for it."[30]

Scholars of religious apocalypticism are particularly perplexed by the apocalyptic violence of the Solar Temple movement. There appear to be two main approaches to the issue. The most sociologically minded analysts claim that the violent outcome was never an essential element of the group's program but was the result of, in Catherine Wessinger's words, "the failure of the millennial goal," the inability of the group to persuade modern society to adopt a spiritual approach to ecological issues and a more mystical and spiritual lifestyle.[31] Hall and Schuyler appear to consider the defections, the police surveillance, and, at times, the outright persecution of the group as pushing them over the line and actually moving to implement their program of mystical apocalypticism.[32] Certainly these social and psychological factors played an important role, in the movement's decision, but as students of religion we must insist on the centrality of the religious motifs in a group's decision to act violently against others or in mass suicides for their cause. Many religious and social movements face disappointment when they do not achieve their goals, but few engage in group murder and suicide. The Solar Temple was from the beginning a countercultural movement fighting secular rationality and the "disenchantment of the world," in Max Weber's words.[33] Adherents sought a world of mystery, enchantment, and miracles and an existence in which the limitations of the human condition could be transcended. These are age-old wishes and they are frequently unfulfilled within the boundaries of the finite human condition. In search of their transcendental goals and in fury at the recalcitrance of a society that remained deaf to their message, the group undertook a migration, a "transit" which held out for them the hope that their goals would finally be reached far from this world.

Interestingly, there was an English-speaking, American version of the Solar Temple known as Heaven's Gate. Heaven's Gate was a much more low-key, sober, and puritanical group, yet one whose mystical beliefs and collective suicide strongly parallels the story of the Solar Temple.[34] On March 27, 1997, some thirty-nine members of the group were found dead in a rented house in the upscale town of Rancho Santa Fe, outside San Diego, California. The suicides were carefully planned, with video recordings left by each member describing the motivations and teachings which brought them to end their lives in collective suicide. The dead bodies were all dressed identically in black pants, shirts, and running shoes; death came though the ingestion of a mixture of applesauce, Phenobarbital, and vodka. Days later, additional bodies were found. The media sought to interview as many surviving members and sympathizers as possible, and two members who were away from the compound when the suicides took place appeared on *60 Minutes*, a national news program, explaining the philosophy of the group and the motivations for the communal suicide. Shortly after their appearance, they were found unconscious in a California hotel room, having taken the same potions and dressed in the same outfit as their dead comrades.[35] Unlike some other groups, there were no children involved in Heaven's Gate, and there were no signs of coercion. The group was not under police investigation and members had lived quietly and rather anonymously in their community.

The tapes and documents left behind at the suicide site were clear. A flying saucer appearing in conjunction with the Hale-Bopp comet, the group believed, would take these liberated Heaven's Gate souls to a higher existence, to the "Evolutionary

Level above the Human," which their leaders had taught was the location of the kingdom of God described by Jesus in the New Testament. The higher level of existence was not a sense world and would not accept anyone who still had an animal or human nature. Group members had prepared themselves for their journey by living a Spartan life, with simple food and clothing, and had practiced a strict celibacy, with a significant proportion of the males undergoing castration to rid themselves of lower-level animal instincts and sensations. The Evolutionary Level above the Human to which they would be ascending was genderless and incorporeal. Bodies, emotions, and human attachments of any sort would hinder their entrance to the Kingdom to Come, a heaven of higher consciousness. The window of opportunity to join them, they said in their farewells, was short, but those with insight and the desire to transcend to a higher level would surrender their human forms and with good faith would be taken to the higher level. The farewell testaments and videotapes are striking for the sense of optimism and anticipation they convey; they raise intriguing questions about the definition of rational and normal behavior. Here were highly talented people—most worked in high-tech occupations like web page design—who had a history of voluntary commitment to the group, appeared to fully understand their coming suicides, and offered seemingly rational and reasonable motivations for their action. One woman said, "I think everyone in this class wanted something more than this human world has to offer." Another remarked about her unhappiness and said there was nothing in this world that attracted her. Yet another member said that this was the happiest day of his life. All insisted they were acting on their own free will and urged others to consider following them to the higher level of consciousness and existence.[36]

Heaven's Gate began in the 1970s under the leadership of Bonnie Lu Nettles, a registered nurse who was known as "Ti," and Marshall Herff Applewhite, a music teacher and church musician, known in the group as "Do." Both had strong Christian backgrounds—Applewhite was an accomplished church musician—but had become disenchanted with Christianity and had

read widely about mysticism, particularly theosophical doctrines and Hindu philosophy. When they first met, they found
they had much in common. and working together they blended
these interests with a belief in UFOs and extraterrestrial beings
to reinforce their conviction that human beings had to have a
way out of this difficult worldly existence. They were both attuned to apocalyptic elements from the Book of Revelation,
which they combined with a belief that a UFO from a higher civilization would come to earth to take enlightened beings to another reality.

Christian categories were an important part of Heaven's Gate
but were redefined by them to fit their New Age outlook. They
greatly cherished Christian values, stressing humility, modesty,
kindness, and gentleness. All who interacted with the group, including those who left the movement prior to the suicides, acknowledged their lack of rancor, and there was nothing similar
to the Solar Temple or Aum Shinrikyo's confrontation with political authority. After Bonnie Nettles died of cancer in 1985 and
Do became the "Father" and head of the movement, he was believed to be the Christ who had the divine message of liberation.
Do's teaching centered on the absolute necessity to minimize
human sense life and prepare to migrate from this mammalian,
inferior existence. The earth was on its last legs. Evolution could
go no further and the continued attachment to family, sexuality,
and physical place was a sin which kept humans from realizing
their true potential and would soon destroy the world. The
group's message was, "Join us, renounce sense life and attachment and prepare to be transferred to the higher realm." The
group arranged lectures and meetings at many colleges and universities and, it appears, large numbers of people interested in
space travel and mysticism came to their presentations. Few,
however, were willing to join so extreme a group that demanded
that bodily pleasures be renounced.

If Do and his message were divine truths, why did so many
turn a deaf ear to the message? Why did people, even those convinced of its truth, turn away from the group? One particular
event at a college campus where Do was shouted down was particularly galling and may have been the reason the group

stopped public proselytizing in the 1980s. The cause for this unwillingness to listen, for the hostility that confronted the group,
was the antichrist, which in Heaven's Gate teachings was "those
propagators of sustained faithfulness to mammalian humanism."[37] The cause of all suffering and the reason for the coming
apocalypse was the absolute refusal of humans to seek release
from their stultifying and crippling attachments to the body, to
sensory pleasures, and earthly thinking. There is a clear dichotomy in Heaven's Gate thinking between the forces of good, associated with a desire for the divine, nonearthly existence, and
perfect evil, associated with remaining earthbound and refusing
to recognize and act on what is so patently true, namely, the mis-
ery and meaninglessness that is this world and the glory and
kingdom that lie beyond the sensory realm.

A violent ending appears to have always been part of the
group's thinking. It is true that at an early stage, both leaders
held out the possibility that a spaceship would come to pick up
the faithful, but the value of human earthly life became so deval-
ued by the group that a decision to commit collective suicide
was not unexpected and was, perhaps, even welcome. The one
hope the group held out for the human race was interest in and
acceptance of their teachings. When it turned out that they were
unsuccessful and were actually ridiculed as they attempted to
spread their beliefs, suicide became more and more attractive. In
their final farewell message on their website, they explained
their actions:

> The loudest voices were those expressing ridicule, hostility or
> both—so quick to judge that which they could not compre-
> hend. This was the signal to us to begin our preparations to
> return "home." The weeds have taken over the garden and
> truly disturbed its usefulness beyond repair—it is time for the
> civilization to be recycled—"spaded under." [38]

Shortly after posting this message, Heaven's Gate members committed collective suicide or, in their understanding, exited the
self-destructive planet earth in "transit" to a higher evolutionary
level. There were no signs of coercion or struggle; all was neat

and orderly, with a small overnight bag next to each person ready for use during "transit." It is difficult to know just why the group opted for this apocalyptic ending when it did. Their belief system, with its strong emphasis on a literal afterlife and its denigration of earthly drives, certainly played an important role. But the theology of many religious groups includes a belief in a literal afterlife and their members do not make the same choice as the adherents of Heaven's Gate. The critical distinction in the case of Heaven's Gate was that this goal of transit to the higher level was not merely doctrinal and cognitive but involved very serious commitments and investments in behavior, money, lifestyle, and bodily transformation. Members lived communally for decades, suffered stigma and humiliation for their commitment to the group, and gave up families and friends, and many had undergone painful medical procedures. Rosabeth Moss Kanter, a sociologist who has studied the organization of communal communities, has shown that sacrifice for and investment in a communal group reinforces group belief and makes it very difficult to deny or leave the group. The great sacrifices and enormous commitments of Heaven's Gate members must have convinced them that their sense of truth and reality was, indeed, the ultimate truth. They had committed so much to the movement, to each other, and to the group's philosophy and had put so much trust in the charismatic Do, whom they called "father," that their collective act was, to them, rational and psychologically welcome and fulfilling. They would be greeted by earlier "masters" who had called them home and would finally find fulfillment in the Evolutionary Level above the Human.[39]

Utopian Communities and Apocalyptic Violence

Utopian groups frequently establish communities based on their teachings and beliefs that are, geographically and culturally, separated from mainstream society. Religiously inspired utopian communities see mainstream society as mired in sin, prone to criminality and immorality. These groups perceive the organization and well-being of mainstream society to be an illusion and that, very soon, the established social fabric will come apart and society as it now exists will be destroyed. There are strong endtime and apocalyptic themes in utopianism. Utopian movements believe they must retreat to their own separatist enclaves, where they will establish a society that will protect them from the corrupting influences of rampart materialism, acquisitiveness, and social inequality that are seen as endemic to contemporary culture. Utopians are aware that they are a minority, with strange and unconventional beliefs, and so they seek to establish their alternative societies in places away from the public eye where they can more easily live by their unconventional, countercultural beliefs and rules.

It is difficult for any group, particularly a countercultural utopian group, to extricate itself entirely from the grip of established social and legal institutions. These structures, as the sociologist Peter Berger demonstrates, have a very wide reach and place very considerable restraints on individuals and groups that would violate them. Work, family relations, and child care, just to cite a few examples, are all areas where society has established strict norms and procedures. The institutional rules are supported by both the legal apparatus of society and its moral codes. In other words, individuals and groups who do not follow socially approved forms and procedures in their work activity, family organization, religious behavior, or even dress and demeanor may not only be open to legal penalties but are also morally stigmatized as deviants who represent a dangerous threat to the social and political order.[40] This was certainly the case with the utopian groups we shall discuss, the Peoples Temple in Jonestown, Guyana, and the Branch Davidians in Waco, Texas.

This type of utopian community, self consciously and ideologically organized as an alternative society, in direct opposition to the values, norms, and goals of the established social order, inevitably comes into conflict with the established society and its definitions of normalcy, morality, and legality. What is deeply held as divine truth and charismatic prophecy within the

utopian community is often taken to be utter nonsense or, in extreme cases, as criminal behavior and mental illness, in the dominant society. Moreover, the labeling and stigmatization of these
alternative communities can be so severe that an assumption is
made by parents, educators, and mental heath specialists that
the people involved in these movements are not acting out of
their free will but have been kidnapped, coerced, or forcibly re-
socialized, or "brainwashed," to join the group. The assumption
is that no normal, rationally functioning person would freely
join a religious community that rejects the standards and behavior of the established normal society. This puts any utopian or
apocalyptic group in conflict with the dominant society.[41] It is a
case of realities in conflict, a kind of religious war over what is
ultimately right or wrong, what is truth and what is erroneous
belief, and finally what is the source of legitimate authority, the
charismatic leader or the traditions of the establishment. Some
apocalyptic and utopian groups seek to publicly deny their di-
vergence, presenting themselves as perfectly normal, like everyone else, and in this way "passing" in society without incurring
the negative consequences of membership in these alternative
worlds. To a degree, Solar Temple adherents and Aum Shinrikyo
in the organizations' early years did this with some success.
However, when the divergences between the utopian group and
general society are large and also when young children are involved, it becomes considerably more difficult to avoid confrontations which can lead to serious violence.

It is in the sociological and political context of being an alternative religious reality that the violence surrounding the Peoples
Temple in Jonestown and the Branch Davidian compound in
Waco, Texas, needs to be understood. There was, from the inception of these communities, a strong critique and rejection of
dominant American culture. Both movements adopted unconventional lifestyles involving sex with the charismatic leader,
communal child rearing, and unusual living arrangements and
were motivated by a powerful sense that American culture
would soon come to an apocalyptic end. The belief systems, in
both groups, emphasized the corruption and evilness of American society and each of these groups saw itself as holding out

the only hope for surviving the coming apocalypse. Like many religious apocalyptic movements, each of these groups was convinced that their leader was a divine messenger and that their group, and only their group, had the ability and divine inspiration to avoid the coming apocalypse. In the case of the Branch Davidians this view was rooted in biblical fundamentalism and particularly in the Seventh-day Adventist reading of the Book of Revelation. In the case of Jonestown, it was grounded in a socialist Christian critique of capitalism and in Rev. Jim Jones's conviction that a nuclear holocaust had to occur given the expansive and imperialistic nature of American capitalism.[42]

The violence at Jonestown was particularly gruesome. On November 18, 1978, followers of Jones's Peoples Temple died as a result of a mass suicide in Jonestown, Guyana, where the group had moved from its former headquarters in Oakland, California, to create a socialist, egalitarian community far from the dangers and intrusions of American culture. The mass deaths planned and directed by Jones shocked the entire world and put the issue of religious violence on the international agenda. Jonestown became, in Catherine Wessinger's apt phrasing, the "paradigmatic destructive cult."[43] It represented all that was evil and dangerous about utopian movements and was used to illustrate the dangers of unconventional religion and isolation from mainstream society. Early reports described the followers as "victims" and talked about their having been brainwashed and held against their will.

The actual events were more complex. The mass suicides—and later reports did indicate that some of the dead may have been murdered—took place after an investigative party from the United States consisting of California Congressman Leo Ryan and a group of news reporters and photographers came to Jonestown to investigate allegations of child abuse and kidnapping made by former members and a group which called itself the Concerned Relatives. Apparently, the investigative party had access to Jonestown and several people living in the compound took advantage of the visit and decided to return with Ryan and his party to the United States. At the airport, however, while boarding the plane, Ryan's party was ambushed by assassins from Jonestown and the visiting congressman and four others were killed. Following the assassinations, the residents of Jonestown gathered at the central pavilion in Jonestown and were instructed by Jones to commit mass suicide, a possibility they had discussed for years and had practiced ritually in "suicide drills" in preparation for the actual event. The Jonestown medical teams prepared a mixture of cyanide and tranquilizers which were injected or were taken in sugared juice drinks. Several people, including Jones, died of gunshot wounds, but there is evidence that more than a few were murdered against their will. The extant tapes—all was taped—record the discussions prior to the suicides, and though there is some disagreement, the consensus among group members was to go along with Jones. Some of the people are heard yelling that Jones took them to a promised land, gave them hope, provided for them, and if he asked for the ultimate show of faith, they were ready to oblige. Indeed, several members not at the compound during the mass suicide killed themselves and, in some cases, murdered their children as well, upon hearing of the group suicides. The most public of these events was the case of Mike Prokes, a former television news bureau chief and later the public relations officer for Jones, who four months after the mass suicide called a news conference in which he said, "I can't disassociate myself from the people who died, nor do I want to. The people weren't brainwashed fanatics or cultists: the Temple was not a cult."[44] After the news conference, Prokes went into the bathroom and killed himself.

The Peoples Temple was created as a Christian socialist commune by Jones, who had his roots in Pentecostal Christianity and its tradition of healing. It was also much influenced by Jones's Marxist politics. In the 1960s, Jones established Peoples Temple churches in various parts of California, where he led Pentecostal-type services and gained a reputation for advancing racial justice and equality. He and his wife Marcella adopted children from various racial and ethnic backgrounds and the movement quickly became popular with African Americans, who became his most fervent supporters and formed the bulk of his membership. Mary Maaga, who studied the composition of the Peoples Temple, estimates that about 85 percent of the population of Jonestown was African American, with the other members primarily from white, upper middle-class backgrounds.[45] The movement, then, was a curious amalgam of people from very different economic and social backgrounds who had a strong desire for the Marxist redistribution of wealth and the breakdown of racial barriers as well as a shared belief in the charismatic leadership of Jones. From all reports, the Peoples Temple was an open, interracial, interclass community whose members shared possessions and lived in relative harmony and cordiality. Jones himself was an important person in Northern California in the 1960s and 1970s whose help was sought by local politicians. Jones met with Rosalyn Carter during Jimmy Carter's presidential campaign and was invited for a personal meeting with vice presidential candidate Walter Mondale.[46]

There was another side to the movement. Jones also preached an apocalyptic socialist Christian message which foretold a coming nuclear holocaust which would bring about capitalist America's destruction. America, in his teachings, was the antichrist referred to in the Bible, and soon God would bring a massive apocalypse to eliminate this evil empire. He therefore urged that his followers move to Guyana, a Third World country uncontaminated by America's sins, and establish a workers' paradise where all could live in peace and harmony. As preparations for leaving the United States progressed, Jones demanded that those faithful to him sell all their possessions, leaving him in control of all money and properties. He presented himself as the savior—he referred to himself as in Christ's place—and his leadership grew more authoritarian and domineering. After the move to Guyana, Jones began using drugs heavily and established himself as the sole authority over all aspects of life in the commune. Gradually, Jones began having sex with various of the female members and fathering children out of wedlock. The rules of society, whether those demanding sexual restraint, financial accountability, or respect for human freedom, did not apply to him. He was divinely inspired and above earthly law and social boundaries. Still, Jonestown was a functioning religious community and Jones was considered the prophet and savior who would protect his people from the catastrophes to take place in the United States.

In the early 1970s, some defectors, mostly from among the white members, formed an anti–Peoples Temple organization, and with the help and guidance of the anticult movement began to lobby against Jones and his followers, claiming that there was no freedom in the movement and that Jones was taking drugs and abusing his followers and kidnapping their children. The most notorious situation was the case of the so called child god, John Victor Stoen. He was the son of a famous defector, Grace Stoen, who apparently had been Jones's lover but had left the commune and demanded that the child be returned to her. Jones claimed that he and not Stoen's husband, who continued to be a follower of Jones, was the biological father and that the child was to be Jones's special consort and share the divine qualities associated with Jones. It was this case and some others involving children that caught the public's attention and focused attention on the cultlike culture of Jonestown. Various government agencies began to investigate these charges and several court cases against the community were planned. It appears that the growing negative publicity and Jones's own theology came together and Jones began talking more and more about a coming apocalypse and the eventual need for "revolutionary suicide" so that the movement would not yield to the power of the antichrist—the society and government of the United States.[47]

In 1977 all the fears and suspicions appeared to come true as Ryan and his team arrived in Guyana to investigate, among other things, charges of kidnapping, abuse, and stockpiling of weapons. The fascinating thing about the charges was the question of definition. To a middle-class employed person from California, the goings-on at Jonestown were, indeed, criminal, but many people in Jonestown, it is fair to say, felt they had found a home and a life of dignity, with their needs being cared for, that they did not enjoy in the America they had left. In Jonestown, they lived in a multicultural community without the burden of penury and racism, and they had Jones and his vision to thank. The intrusions on privacy, the limitations on movement, and even Jones's strange personal practices were known to the inhabitants, but these very real problems were, it appears, a small price to pay for what many of the members felt they received in return.[48] Annie Layton, a nurse and part of the white hierarchy surrounding Jones and the last to die, wrote in a final statement that "Jim Jones showed us . . . that we could live together with our differences, that we are all the same human beings."[49]

Ryan was not entirely hostile to the group, and in some ways, he was impressed with what the group had managed to establish, but the defection of several prominent members who appealed to Ryan to help them leave and an altercation as the party was departing were traumatic for Jones and the community. Despite the civility of the visit, Jones and his associates saw it as heralding the end of the community. There was a sense that they were so different, that their ways so threatened the established American social and political world, that they would not be permitted to survive as a distinct community. Given the confluence of apocalyptic theology and rhetoric and the sense of the imminent destruction of their community, the group opted for mass suicide. As the members were ingesting the poison, Jones was heard on the tapes as saying over the loudspeaker, "This world is not our home." Finally, Jones yelled out, "We didn't commit suicide, we committed an act of revolutionary suicide protesting the conditions of an inhuman world."[50] Historians will never know exactly what happened, but Mary Maaga, who conducted lengthy interviews with many of the survivors and relatives, argues cogently that for the residents felt they faced a choice between loyalty to their vision and their charismatic savior and betrayal of this vision and of the many sacrifices they had personally made. Their choice was loyalty.[51]

The case of the Branch Davidians has many similarities to the story of Jonestown. Here, too, was a group living communally and following a charismatic leader, David Koresh, who had sexual relations with his female followers and had fathered almost two dozen children with them. The Branch Davidian compound in Waco was also a closed society—John Hall terms it a "state within a state," with its own rules and guidelines and with Koresh as the messiah.[52] Koresh engaged in all sorts of what to outsiders was bizarre behavior, and he was a virtual dictator in the compound. He demanded that men and women, with the exception of himself, live celibate lives, although he would sanction divine marriages between members he chose. He had relations with female Davidians as young as twelve and was arbitrary in his decisions, keeping all power to himself. Spankings and other physical punishment were not unusual and although this is not entirely unknown in extreme sects of Christianity, it was viewed as child abuse in the law enforcement community. Koresh's followers, however, accepted and understood his behavior as appropriate for someone of his divine standing: he was an incarnation of God and according to their reading of the Book of Revelation had the right to propagate special souls who "came from his loins." As strange as all this might seem to outsiders, there is considerable evidence that the families and the women themselves went along with this interpretation and lifestyle.[53] This issue of sexual and child abuse, however, would prove to be crucial in understanding the ensuing violence involving the Federal Bureau of Investigation, the Bureau of Alcohol, Tobacco and Firearms, and the Branch Davidian community at Waco.

The Branch Davidians are a sectarian outgrowth of the Seventh-day Adventist Church, which had its origins in the nineteenth-century Millerite millenialist movement which predicted the return of Christ and the end of the world in 1844. After the failure of the prediction, some Millerites established the Seventh Day of Advent Church, based on revelations from God to the leaders of the church about Christ's return to earth. These divine revelations were believed to have stopped in 1915 and the Seventh-day Adventist Church took its place as a more or less conventional denomination within American Christianity. In the 1930s, Victor Houteff, an Adventist, proclaimed himself a prophet of God and claimed he was receiving messages from God about the endtime. The established Adventist Church removed him from membership and he formed the Branch Davidian movement, with himself as the prophet.

From the beginning of the Branch Davidian movement, there was a sense among the group that they were God's chosen people and, through their prophets, had special insight into the divine will. Their theology is complex and based upon their particularistic reading of the Bible, particularly the Book of Revelation, but the central point is that God will reveal his apocalyptic plans to their prophets and it is only through this revealed teaching that salvation can occur. After several schisms within the Branch Davidian movement itself, Vernon Howell, a convert to the movement who took the name David Koresh to underline his connection to biblical kingship, assumed control of the Branch Davidian complex in Waco and established himself as the prophet of the movement. Koresh taught that God's return and the endtime were imminent and the faithful would have to withdraw from conventional society and prepare themselves for the end of the world. Again, differences in perceptions are critical. The Branch Davidians saw Koresh as the prophet who could unlock the secrets of the endtime through his specially given divine insights, while the government saw him as speaking gibberish and acting in an entirely irrational, uncontrollable, and even criminal fashion. The esoteric Davidian understanding of messiahship included the necessity for the messiah to engage in "sinfulness" as a means of purification and the Waco Davidians understood Koresh's behavior to be appropriate for his role as messiah and prophet, while the government saw these behaviors as criminal acts threatening the well-being of the residents and calling for police intervention.[54]

As was the case with Jonestown, Branch Davidian defectors and relatives angry at the movement brought charges, some of them accurate and others imaginary and concocted, like an intended series of child sacrifices, to the media and law enforcement officials. The group had begun purchasing weapons and this, too, was brought to the attention of the government. What motivated the police and the government to pay such careful attention to a rather unimportant sectarian group in Texas was its apocalyptic rhetoric. Koresh talked constantly about the coming battles between the forces of good and evil and the eventual need to offer one's life for God as the battle between Babylon, the world, and the people of God—the Branch Davidians—intensified. The Davidian theology was constantly evolving and was open to Koresh's changing interpretations, but what was indisputable in Davidian doctrine was a coming Armageddon in which massive death and destruction would occur and the Lamb of God, in this case, David Koresh, would be killed. As is the case in these narratives, the kingdom of God will follow the times of apocalyptic violence. This scenario certainly contained elements of violence and religious suicide but, as John Hall and Catherine Wessinger point out, much of this rhetoric may have been symbolic and not intended to be acted out in real time. The Davidians lived in a world of religious imagery and myth and it is uncertain whether the rhetoric was symbolic scriptural language or a planned attempt at war and violence.[55]

Waco survivors and sympathetic scholars argue that the Branch Davidians never presented any real threat of violence and it was the government's severe response that made the Waco community uncooperative and finally led members, at the end, to violence.[56] Perhaps we will never have any certainty on this matter. What is clear is that the apocalyptic language and the alternative culture and lifestyle in the Branch Davidian compound were successfully presented on television, in the newspapers, and to the government as proof that the Branch Davidians were a dangerous cult who were abusing their members, planning to kill their children in the compound, and arming themselves for an apocalyptic showdown. Comparisons were routinely made to Jonestown, although the cases were, in fact, quite different. For example, people in Waco were freely able to come and go and it is clear that the people who stayed with Koresh did so out of religious conviction to the very end. Nonetheless, the defectors and the antagonistic family members bombarded the government with dire predictions of coming violence within the compound. David Jewell, a leader of the opposition, clearly exaggerated the possible danger when, in 1992, he wrote a memorandum to Michigan Congressman Fred Upton stating, "Time is running out and I need to talk to the FBI or someone who can do something. If this does not happen, I believe that over 200 persons will be massacred next month."[57]

The government took this and many similar communications seriously and was able to obtain a search warrant to enter and search the compound, presumably for hidden and illegal weapons. However, as John Hall astutely points out, the fact that this was a utopian community, rumored to be arming itself and challenging, by its very existence, the official reality of the dominant society meant that all possible legal force would be brought against the group. The government welcomed the atrocity predictions, regardless of their accuracy, for they could be used to highlight the danger of unconventional religion. There was, as the sociologist and legal scholar James Richardson wrote after the event, a wholesale process of dehumanization of the Branch Davidians.[58] It was almost as if the government was saying that, despite evidence to the contrary, these people were coerced and dangerous and simply did not understand what they were doing. Additionally, David Koresh was entirely demonized and, despite the warnings of religious scholars who worked with the government for a time and attempted to show the religious logic and theological background of his pronouncements, the government insisted on criminalizing a religious conflict.[59] The disparity between the two perceptions became painfully clear when government spokespersons for the FBI and ATF described their goal as freeing hostages, while the members considered themselves freely and religiously committed to their community and charismatic leader.

The governmental probes continued and a kind of self-fulfilling prophecy was taking place, with each side believing the worst about the other. The Branch Davidian community, feeling unfairly persecuted, became more insular and increasingly emphasized its apocalyptic, violent endtime scenario; this served to reinforce the worst perceptions of the group by government investigators. Just what happened to bring about the violence and death is impossible to say, as there are completely conflicting reports from participants, eyewitnesses, and scholars. What is known is that on Sunday, February 28, 1993, after being denied access to the community buildings, seventy-six armed ATF agents raided the Branch Davidian compound in Waco. In the events that followed, four agents were killed and twenty wounded, while five Davidians were killed, and several, including David Koresh, were wounded. The ATF had bungled the assignment; the next day, the FBI took over and began a siege of the compound, stationing tanks around the perimeter and demanding that all in the Branch Davidian compound give themselves up to the FBI. The siege lasted approximately two months, during which negotiations continued. but the two sides were speaking an entirely different language and completely mistrusted one another. The government forces were convinced that this was a dangerous and criminal cult intent on violence. The Branch Davidians, as well as some religious scholars who were mediators in the dispute, defined it as a religious conflict which possibly could end peaceably if an appropriate theological understanding of the situation could be formulated. Things dragged on, but in the end on April 19, 1993, the FBI shot

> rounds of chlorobenzyilidene malononnitrilie gas into the building and used the tanks to punch holes in the walls and demolish parts of the building. At about noon the residence rapidly caught fire, producing an inferno. Nine Davidians escaped. Seventy-four died in the fire. Of these, twenty-three were children, including two infants who were born when their mothers expired.[60]

How did the fire which killed so many people start and who was responsible? Was the FBI right to consider the group a danger? Was there any evidence that children were harmed in the complex? And if the group was as peaceful as some say, why the violent rhetoric and the talk of suicide and apocalypse? Was Koresh a genuine religious thinker and leader or a crazed fanatic? These are questions that remain and still, in many ways, haunt the nation. After the violence, nothing seems changed. The Branch Davidians and their sympathizers have their own view of the events and their narrative is found in their websites and books. The government has its own story of heroism and courage as they tell of the officers who fought the dangerous forces of apocalyptical doom and cultural disobedience and died in support of law and social order. For those groups like the American militia groups, Christian Identity and others, who challenge the government with violence, the Branch Davidians are proof of the pernicious intentions of the federal authorities. The events at Waco have become a rallying cry for those who are convinced that the endtime is about to happen and that the American government and its leaders are determined to destroy any religious movement that offers an alternative to secular American society.[61]

Conventional Religion and Apocalyptic Violence

Apocalyptic groups are dismissed as dangerous and illegitimate by mainstream religions. Nonetheless, these groups often articulate the deepest longings of conventional religion. They, in their unconventionality, make manifest elements in the religious and cultural tradition which may have been repressed for generations by the more mainstream religious groups. It is for this reason that these apocalyptic groups are far more important than their official membership would indicate. Relatively few join such groups, and while they can wreak havoc in the society, they usually can be controlled in the short run by the vastly greater power of the government. Their potency and significance lie in what they tell us about the latent issues and hidden problems which face a society and religious culture. These groups are a kind of infantry which presages unresolved matters in religion and society.

The widespread secularization and the loss of sacred meanings in everyday life have left many people, in Peter Berger's formulation, feeling homeless in the universe and desirous of inculcating their lives with divine meaning.[62] The powerful emphasis on individualism and materialism in much of modern society is also unpalatable to large sectors of the population. Commitment to utopian groups stressing communal values and obedience to a leader felt to be endowed with divine powers is an attractive alternative for people disenchanted with the bureaucratic efficiency and rationality of modernity. Groups like

Heaven's Gate and the Branch Davidians have reenchanted the world of their followers and brought the sacred and mysterious back to human experience. Other groups we have studied refuse to abandon the supernatural elements in their traditions and are willing to challenge the secular consensus which has taken over many religious traditions. The Temple Mount Movement and their Christian supporters refuse to give up their literal biblical text. They refuse to compromise their traditions, to reinterpret them so they fit with secular and scientific understanding. If the Lord wills it, they say, it will occur, and it is our task to be obedient to the word and try as hard as we can to realize God's will. The Jewish temple must be built and the apocalypse and second coming will take place as described in the holy book. The Temple Mount organization has few active members who are willing to challenge the Israeli police, but large numbers of Jews in the Holy Land would like to see the temple built. Despite the Christian mainstream playing down the apocalyptic beliefs in Christianity, many Christians subscribe to beliefs about the war and terror surrounding the endtime. Again, not all are militant or public, but active Christian apocalypticism gives voice to views and desires of Christians throughout the world.

Rodney Stark and William Sims Bainbridge, distinguished sociologists of religion, explain that where conventional religions do not work, where they no longer meet the psychic and social needs of the populace, new religions, utopian movements, and innovative, charismatic religious teachers will emerge to replace the old traditions and teachers.[63] The unconventional groups we have studied are sometimes violent attempts at creating new religious understandings and organizations. It is therefore important that modern societies remain as tolerant of religious innovation and dissent as possible. Some types of religious violence are intrinsic to a religious conflict and some situations of religious competition always engender violent conflict and cannot be avoided. But a great deal of the violence associated with unconventional utopian movements can be limited with a social ethos of genuine tolerance and pluralism.

Notes

1. See Gershon Gorenberg, *The End of Days: Fundamentalism and the Struggle for the Temple Mount* (New York: Free Press, 2000) for a description and comparative analysis of apocalyptic visions in Judaism Christianity and Islam. See also Norman Cohn, *Cosmos, Chaos, and the World to Come: The Ancient Roots of Apocalyptic Faith* (New Haven: Yale University Press, 1993).

2. See David Bromley, "Constructing Apocalypticism: Social and Cultural Elements of Radical Organizations," in *Millennium, Messiahs, and Mayhem*, ed. Thomas Robbins and Susan J. Palmer (New York: Routledge, 1997).

3. Thomas Robbins, "Apocalypse, Persecution, and Self-Immolation: Mass Suicide Among the Old Believers in Late-Seventeenth-Century Russia," in *Millennialism, Persecution, and Violence: Historical Cases*, ed. Catherine Wessinger (Syracuse, N.Y.: Syracuse University Press, 2000).

4. See William Bainbridge, *The Sociology of Religious Movements* (New York: Routledge, 1997), chap. 5.

5. See Sydney E. Ahlstrom, *A Religious History of the American People* (New Haven: Yale University Press, 1972).

6. Tim LeHay and Jerry Jenkins, *Left Behind* (Carol Stream, Ill.: Tyndale House, 2000). See www.leftbehind.com for a listing of the many activities surrounding the apocalypse in contemporary Christian fundamentalism and a listing of the literature developed by the movement.

7. Quoted in "The Bible and the Apocalypse: Why More Americans Are Reading and Talking About the End of the World," *Time*, April 1, 2002, 49.

8. Thomas Robbins and Dick Anthony, "Sects and Violence: Factors Enhancing the Volatility of Marginal Religious Groups," in *Armageddon in Waco*, ed. Stuart Wright (Chicago: University of Chicago Press, 1995), 236–259.

9. Max Weber, "The General Character of Charisma," in *From Max Weber*, ed. Hans Gerth and C. Wright Mills (New York: Oxford, 1958), 245–248.

10. Catherine Wessinger, *How the Millennium Comes Violently: From Jonestown to Heaven's Gate* (New York: Seven Bridges, 2000), chap. 1, especially pp. 17–18. Wessinger discusses the social factors and theology promoting violence in a variety of apocalyptic and millennial groups, particularly the role of catastrophic themes.

11. See John R. Hall with Philip D. Schuyler and Sylvaine Trinh, *Apocalypse Observed: Religious Movements and Violence in North America, Europe, and Japan* (New York: Routledge, 2000), chap. 3. I am much indebted to the meticulous data and descriptive terminology presented in this volume. See also Mark S. Mullins, "Aum Shinrikyo," in Robbins and Palmer, *Millennium, Messiahs, and Mayhem*, 313–324, for help in understanding the movement's apocalyptic, catastrophic culture.

12. Quoted in Hall, *Apocalypse Observed*, 97.

13. Wessinger, *How the Millennium Comes Violently*, 143–151.

14. See Nancy Tatom Ammerman, *Bible Believers: Fundamentalists in the Modern World* (New Brunswick, N.J.: Rutgers University Press, 1987). Chapter 2 discusses the development of Rapture theology in evangelical and fundamentalist Christianity.

15. See Michael Barkun, "Millenarians and Violence," in Robbins and Palmer, *Millennium, Messiahs, and Mayhem*, 247–260.

16. Barkun, "Millenarians and Violence," 249.

17. Jack Levin and Jack McDevitt, *Hate Crimes* (New York: Plenum Press, 1993), 1–21, 46–64; Richard Abanes, *Rebellion, Racism, and Religion: America's Militias* (Dowers Grove, Ill.: Intervarsity Press, 1966). See also www.ajc.org/themedia/publication for a listing of reported incidences of violence.

18. Jeffrey Kaplan, *Radical Religion in America: Millenarian Movements From the Far Right to the Children of Noah* (Syracuse, N.Y.: Syracuse University Press, 1997), 47–68; Abanes, *Rebellion, Racism, and Religion*.

19. Hall, *Apocalypse Observed*, esp. chaps. 4 and 5.

20. See the Temple Mount website, www.templemountfaithful.org, for a statement. See also Gorenberg, *End of Days*, 157–180.

21. Quoted in Gorenberg, *End of Days*, 180.

22. Gorenberg, *End of Days*, 54.

23. See Jeffrey Goldberg, "Jerusalem End Games," *New York Times Magazine*, October 5, 1999, about the international ramifications of the group. Gershon Solomon also distributes a newsletter geared to his international Christian supporters.

24. LeHay and Jenkins, *Left Behind*; Hal Lindsay with C. C. Carlson, *The Late Great Planet Earth*, (New York: Bantam Doubleday Dell, 1999).

25. Quoted in Wessinger, *How the Millennium Comes Violently*, 226.

26. Wessinger, *How the Millennium Comes Violently*, 228.

27. Hall, *Apocalypse Observed*, 111–148, discusses the theological background of the group but also presents a great deal of information about the personalities of leaders and members of the group.

28. See Hall, *Apocalypse Observed*, 111–115, for the police record and

details. See Wessinger, *How the Millennium Comes Violently*, 225–228, for the social context of violence.

29. Wessinger, *How the Millennium Comes Violently*, 228.

30. Wessinger, *How the Millennium Comes Violently*, 226.

31. Wessinger, *How the Millennium Comes Violently*, 225.

32. Hall, *Apocalypse Observed*, 145–148.

33. See Max Weber, conclusion to *The Protestant Ethic and the Rise of Capitalism* (New York: Scribner's, 1958).

34. See Wessinger, *How the Millennium Comes Violently*, 229–246, for an insightful history and analysis. My analysis is indebted to Wessinger's careful documentation.

35. Wessinger, *How the Millennium Comes Violently*, 231.

36. See Hall, *Apocalypse Observed*, 172–175, for a description and testaments from the last days of the group before their suicide.

37. Wessinger, *How the Millennium Comes Violently*, 240.

38. The original Heaven's Gate website was *www.heavensgate.com*. There is now a website that has replicated much of the original content. See www.wave.net/vp9/gate, where the "farewell" and other extant documents can be found.

39. Rosabeth Moss Kanter, *Commitment and Community: Communes and Utopias in Sociological Perspective* (Cambridge: Harvard University Press, 1972).

40. Peter L. Berger and Thomas Luckman, *The Social Construction of Reality* (New York: Doubleday, 1967), pt. 2.

41. Charles Selengut, "Eschatology and the Construction of Alternative Realities: Towards a Social Conflict Perspective on Millennialism," in *The Return of the Millennium*, ed. J. Bettis and S. K. Johannesen (Barrytown, N.Y.: New Era Books, 1984).

42. See Hall, *Apocalypse Observed*, 15–43, for a report on Jonestown and 44–77 for a report on and history of the Branch Davidian community.

43. Wessinger, *How the Millennium Comes Violently*, 12–52, for a description of the events leading up to the mass suicide.

44. John Hall, *Gone From the Promised Land: Jonestown in American Cultural History* (New Brunswick, N.J.: Transaction Books, 1987), 291.

45. Mary McCormick Maaga, "Triple Erasure: Women and Power in People's Temple," (Ph.D. diss., Drew University, 1996).

46. Hall, *Gone From the Promised Land*, 168.

47. The catastrophic millennialism of Jones' worldview is explained in Wessinger, *How the Millennium Comes Violently*, 34–39.

48. See Judith Weightman, *Making Sense of the Jonestown Suicides: A*

Sociological History of People's Temple (New York: Edwin Mellon, 1983), who powerfully articulates this view.

49. Wessinger, *How the Millennium Comes Violently*, 51.

50. Quoted in Wessinger, *How the Millennium Comes Violently*, 51.

51. Maaga, "Triple Erasure."

52. Hall, *Apocalypse Observed*, 73–75.

53. See Wessinger, *How the Millennium Comes Violently*, 86–91. Also see J. Phillip Arnold, "The Davidian Dilemma—to Obey God or Not?" in *From the Ashes: Making Sense of Waco*, ed. James R. Lewis (Lanham, Md.: Rowman and Littlefield, 1994).

54. For an understanding of the role of David Koresh in Davidian thinking, see Wessinger, *How the Millennium Comes Violently*, 81–85.

55. Hall, *Apocalypse Observed*, 70–73.

56. See Lewis, *From the Ashes*, for a series of essays criticizing the government actions in this incident.

57. Quoted in Hall, *Apocalypse Observed*, 57.

58. James Richardson, "Manufacturing Consent About Koresh: A Structural Analysis of the Role of Media in the Waco Tragedy," in *Armageddon in Waco: Critical Perspectives on the Branch Davidian Conflict*, ed. Stuart A. Wright (Chicago: University of Chicago Press, 1995) 236–259.

59. See Michael Barkun, "Reflections After Waco: Millennialists and the State," in Lewis, *From the Ashes*, 41–49.

60. Wessinger, *When the Millennium Comes Violently*, 58. Wessinger offers a detailed view of the events, 102–108.

61. See James Richardson, "Lessons from Waco: When Will We Ever Learn," in Lewis, *From the Ashes*, 181–184.

62. See Peter L. Berger, *Facing Up to Modernity* (New York: Basic Books, 1977).

63. See Rodney Stark and William Sims Bainbridge, "Secularization, Revival, and Cult Formation," *Annual Review of the Social Sciences* 4 (1980): 85–119.

4

Civilizational Clashes, Culture Wars, and Religious Violence

The twenty-first century, in Samuel Huntington's pithy phrase, is the age of the "clash of civilizations" and a time of severe conflict between the world's religious communities. Huntington, in his widely read book, *The Clash of Civilizations and the Remaking of World Order*, argues that in the twenty-first century the major world conflicts are not between nation-states like the world wars of the twentieth century but are clashes and battles between the world's civilizations, each of which is composed of several nation-states sharing the same religion and historical identity. A civilization is a much larger entity than a nation-state, ethnic group, or linguistic category. A civilization is a transcultural entity combining people from various cultures, geographical regions, and political states into one civilizational grouping sharing a collective identity, history, and belief in their unique and common origin. For example, the people and culture in a Nile Delta village in Egypt will differ from a village culture in Jordan or Syria, but all would be an essential part of Islamic civilization. Similarly, the Germanic culture of a small town in Bavaria is different from an Italian small-town culture in Palermo or the Spanish culture of a seacoast village in Andalusia, but all identify with and are part of what we call Western civilization. A civilization, as Huntington explains, is "the highest cultural grouping of people and the broadest level of cultural identity people have short of that which distinguishes humans from other species."[1]

Huntington and others have listed seven major civilizational groupings in the world today, among them Western, Islamic, Sinic, and Hindu, but the concept of civilization as a mode of identity and camaraderie among different political or geographical units goes back to antiquity, when the rival Athenians and Spartans, as exemplars of Greek civilization, aligned themselves against the alien Persian civilization. Each civilization is anchored in its unique religious worldview, history, and moral system and has an attachment to land and territory it considers sacred and divinely set aside for it. Civilizational identities and commitments are not casual matters that can be freely or easily obtained or rejected but are matters of great significance for both individuals and societies, involving religious fate and historical identity. A civilization's claims to land, territory, or political power need not be, necessarily, legally or bureaucratically justified because these attachments and rights need no explanation or justification. The group's rights, in this view, are self-legitimating as they emanate from history, religious tradition, and collective identity. There is the sense, at least among civilizational loyalists, that civilizations reflect categories that mirror divine order in the universe.[2]

Each civilization constructs a historical narrative which describes its unique origins and its special and sacred mission for humanity. The events of the past, even seemingly pedestrian tales, become, in the group's telling, sacred history replete with tales of divine intervention on behalf of the group. These historical narratives, over time and through socialization and generational transmission, become the only acceptable view of history, akin to sacred texts and scriptures which cannot be questioned. Some of the most intractable conflicts all over the globe only make sense when viewed as sacred civilizational battles over religious promises and divine truth. The battles and struggles over territory, as well, are not ultimately fights about mundane issues of sovereignty or economics but about sacred history and religious authority. These narratives reinforce a prior sense of ethnocentrism and suspicion of outsiders and the seeds for civilizational misunderstanding and conflict are passed on from generation to generation.[3]

Faithful Hindus all over the world, for example, refer to the Indian subcontinent as "mother India," an area of sacred space and holy waters where the deities of the Hindu pantheon lived, taught, and interacted. India is sacred Hindu land and cannot be violated by those who do not share the Vedic traditions and destiny. The partition of this sacred inheritance in 1948 was and remains traumatic for orthodox Hindus. The continuing issue of Kashmir and the fight over what appears to be political authority is a civilizational struggle between Indian and Islamic civilization and is, therefore, impossible to resolve or even understand without a subtle and thoroughgoing comprehension of the religious issues. For its part, Jewish civilization claims divine rights to the land of Israel which centuries of exile and dispersion cannot undo. Islamic civilization has a very different view of the matter and in this regard the battles over the holy sites in Jerusalem and elsewhere are continuing religious battles over history and divine promise. Orthodox Serbians see the lands of the province of Kosovo as their Jerusalem, a sacred site where, acting on behalf of Christendom, they repelled invaders and built holy shrines to commemorate those sacred events. Changing demography and the influx of large numbers of Albanian Muslims who now make their homes in Kosovo can never sever Serbian rights to these lands and, for the Serbs, their civilizational claims remain as valid as ever.[4]

The civilizational perspective on religious conflict sees violence as a response to what a particular civilization understands as a threat to its religious culture, sacred lands, and historical identity. Violence, from this perspective, is a justifiable attempt to maintain the integrity of the group against real or imagined civilizational enemies who are out to destroy the group or deny them the possibility of fulfilling their historical and divine destiny. Consequently, what appears to outsiders, to those not sharing the civilizational identity, as small-mindedness or petty squabbling over holy sites without strategic value is, literally, a matter of life and death for those fully committed to their civilizational heritage. The civilizational perspective highlights the place of violence in a civilization's continuing struggle to insist on control of its sacred places, to insist that its religious culture, however unconventional or objectionable in the eyes of others, be respected and tolerated and that, ultimately, its view of human destiny triumph, and triumph over all others. For those faithful to their religious civilizational mandate, compromise is not readily possible and violence in the form of civilizational war or terrorism is appropriate and justified. The widespread secularization of Western civilization, particularly the removal of religion from the institutions of politics, mass media, and education, has resulted in an inability, particularly among governing elites, to recognize the religious nature and supernatural faith of other world civilizations. The West has assumed, erroneously, that people from all over the globe are essentially like secularized Westerners who desire economic growth and efficiency, business opportunities, and rational political compromise rather than commitment to religious goals. However, many people all over the world still maintain, as Max Weber put it, a politics of ultimate ends and an "ethic of absolute value" where civilizational goals are to be achieved no matter what the rational economic or military cost may be by Western standards. Put differently, the ends in many religious cultures do justify the means.[5]

This Western myopia has not infrequently resulted in a refusal to recognize the religious nature of much of the world's wars and violent confrontations. A popular and facile modern approach is to explain violence and conflict as a consequence of poverty and inequality. Newspapers, magazines, and television programs highlight the poverty and terrible living conditions of many of the world's peoples, which is an accurate picture, but then go on to explain their religious acts of violence as the result not of religious motivation but as an outgrowth of the poverty and enormous disparity between rich and poor societies. The underlying assumption is that people engage in assassinations, suicide bombings, and terrorism of all sorts because they are impoverished and lack education and a chance for economic improvement. The argument is that if you give people jobs, education, and economic hope, they will not engage in violence. This materialistic, Western elite view is incorrect. There are people all over the world, in various societies and civilizations, who are poor and oppressed and but who do not engage in religious violence. The extreme poverty in parts of Africa and Latin America has not produced any significant religious violence, although it has produced militant political and revolutionary movements. Poverty and inequality are evils, but they can result in either social passivity or aggression and violence. Religion can and has been used to legitimate both responses to human suffering, but there is no necessary connection between religious violence and economic deprivation. For the faithful of the world's religious civilizations, historical attachments and sacred rights matter more than economics or politics.

The centrality of religious commitment in the outbreak of religious violence and terrorism is seen perhaps most powerfully in the social background of the al-Qaeda suicide bombers who attacked the World Trade Center in New York City and the Pentagon in Washington, D.C., on September 11, 2001. Mohammed Atta, who piloted the first plane into the World Trade Center and was considered the ringleader of the operation, came from an upper-middle-class Egyptian family. His father is a respected attorney in Cairo and Atta studied architecture at Cairo University and received a master's degree in urban planning at the Technical University of Hamburg, where his professors thought him to be the most talented student ever to enroll in that university. Marwan al-Shehhi who piloted the second plane, was a student at the same university as Atta and was born into a distinguished family in the United Arab Emirates, where his father was a mosque official. Ziad Jarrah, who piloted the plane that crashed in Pennsylvania, was from the Bekáa Valley in Lebanon and also attended university in Germany. In fact the entire group, with few exceptions, was well educated and from middle-class families, making it possible for them to travel and live in respectable circumstances. The hijackers were no poverty-stricken group of mendicants without economic opportunities or political connections. Their motivation was religious and, under the guidance of militant Muslim preachers in Germany and Egypt, they came to see America as the Great Satan that had to be destroyed. In the great civilizational struggle, they saw themselves as martyrs for the future glory of Islam.[6]

The significance of religious motivation is not limited to the September 11 bombers or to militant Islam. The messianic Jewish settlers of the Gush Emmunim movement and their international supporters make no political claim to the lands of the West Bank, which they refer to with the biblical names Judea and Samaria. Their claim is religious, based on the books of the Bible and God's promises to ancient Israel. Daniella Weiss, the mayor of Kiddumin, the largest Jewish settlement in the Samaria region, explains that Jewish property rights are in the Bible. "History" she says, "is what puts us here," and she explains that it is religious conviction and fervor and not economics that keep the settlers in a dangerous and confrontational situation.[7] Similarly, the wars and conflicts between India and Pakistan and the wars and killings in Kosovo and Bosnia are, at their core, confrontations over religious and civilizational promises and goals. In both of these serious conflicts, which have resulted in many deaths and much suffering for all parties, there are political considerations for everyone, but it is religious motivation and the group's sense of history which fuel the conflict and gives it political salience.

The civilizational perspective on religious violence is a highly useful approach to contemporary conflict. It sensitizes us to the new religious alliances and configurations which now go beyond the traditional categories of religious and political conflict. The civilizational perspective argues that just as nation-states in the emerging modern era in the eighteenth and nineteenth centuries became the critical actors in intergroup conflict, replacing local feudal and regional entities, the twenty-first century is the age where civilizational groupings have become critical to understanding international affairs and interreligious relations in the twenty-first century.[8] In this age of globalization, to see religious conflict as limited to confrontations between specific countries or political entities is to miss the international religious unity that typifies civilizational. In this age of worldwide immigration, where the residents of nation-states no longer necessarily share a common religion, history, or identity, religious affiliation now provides an international form of identity where individuals feel a sense of peoplehood and destiny with their civilizational brethren, wherever they may live. It is surprising to a lot of people, but globalization and the new technologies of communication like e-mail and intercontinental travel have contributed to civilizational solidarity and have made virtually all religious conflicts a matter of global confrontation.

The new civilizational and international nature of religious clashes is seen with particular clarity in several current conflicts. The Bosnian Muslims, for example, have lived with Serbs for centuries, share common ancestry and racial features, and have not infrequently intermarried with Serbs. Still, when the conflict between Serbs and Muslims broke out in the former Yugoslavia, it emerged as part of a religious conflict between Islamic and Eastern Orthodox Christian civilization.[9] Muslims loyal to Islam supported their civilizational compatriots, while Russians and other Eastern Orthodox rallied around the Serbian cause. The internationalization of conflict is seen also in the wars between India and Pakistan over the status of Kashmir. These battles and ongoing clashes between the two sides are also intercivilizational struggles between Hindus and Muslims. Each side has its supporters throughout the world. This is also true for the Christian-Muslim confrontations in the Philippines and even for the intra-Christian battles between Protestants and Catholics in Northern Ireland.[10]

Religious terrorism is a particularly powerful illustration of the new international and civilizational nature of religious violence. Religious terrorists of all civilizational backgrounds are not loyal to a nation but to their religious civilization. The facts of birth, citizenship, language, or livelihood are less important—perhaps entirely insignificant—than religious affiliation and commitment to the civilizational agenda. The case of a relatively unknown American assassin who murdered what he considered a religious enemy illustrates the powerful interconnectedness between world religious civilizations and violence. On July 21, 1980, Dawud Salahuddin, an African-American convert to Islam who grew up in Long Island and attended Howard University in Washington, posed as a United States postal worker delivering mail to the home of Ali Akbar Tabatabai, an opponent of the Muslim leader of Iran, Ayatollah Khomeini, and shot him dead as he answered the doorbell. Salahuddin had never, at that time, been in Iran, nor did he have any relationship to Tabatabai. But Salahuddin undertook the mission to kill Tabatabai in defense of what he saw as genuine Islam. Salahuddin, who moved to Iran after the killing to escape prosecution, denies that his was an act of murder. It was "an act of war," he says, and part of a religious duty to save Islam from danger and contamination.[11]

Case Study: India and Pakistan

The wars and clashes between predominately Hindu India and Islamic Pakistan since their creation as nation-states in 1947 are a powerful illustration of religious civilizational conflict and violence in the contemporary world. Both nations were carved out of the British Raj, colonial India, in a partition plan to avoid civil war between the Hindu and Muslim populations in the subcontinent. The idea was that separating the two groups and establishing a political state for each would solve the internecine conflicts, but things did not quite work out that way. Tens of millions of Muslin Indians chose to stay in what was to become the Hindu state, India—they now number about 12 percent of the Indian population—and so a measure of contact and conflict was present from the beginning. The bulk of religious Hindus and a great many ordinary people saw the division of the motherland as a sacrilege, for the earth of India itself, to Hindu religious sensibilities, was a sacred site, a kind of deity in Hindu cosmology. Partition also resulted in Hindu India holding on to the Muslim majority state of Kashmir, which Pakistan insists is rightfully its territory. The more secular and internationally educated elites who negotiated with the British were less concerned with the religious aspects of partition than are those on both sides who hold strongly to the sacredness of their beliefs and traditions.[12]

The two peoples, despite serious religious differences, have much in common. Both societies are heirs to British rule and culture, the language of the educated elite in both countries is English, the educational systems are modeled on those of the West, and both societies have a cadre of well-educated and technologically skilled workers. The British left in 1948, but many public institutions, as well as forms of social interaction in both societies, are based on the British model. The personal appearance and style of the two peoples are so similar that it is fair to say that outsiders, people with little experience in interacting with Indians and Pakistanis, will not easily be able to distinguish between the two. Still, the two nations have fought several wars and hundreds of thousands of troops are poised to fight a battle that both sides consider essential to their national interest. Both sides have a proven nuclear capability, and given the religious, historical, and highly charged emotional climate, there is always the possibility that a confrontation could lead to nuclear war. General V. R. Raghavan, the highly respected former director general of Indian military operations, wrote that the enmity between the two sides is so serious that a nuclear war could break out between the two after a day or two of fighting. Both sides see the conflict as a war between right and wrong, good and evil, as each seeks to protect its sacred rights to land, resources, and sovereignty.[13]

Military battles and terrorist attacks have taken place between both sides throughout the years, but violent confrontations involving religious and national sites and ordinary citizens appear to have increased after 2000. A militant Islamic group demanding the ceding of the Kashmir state to Pakistan attacked the heavily guarded Indian parliament in Delhi on December 13, 2001, and ten people working in the government complex were killed. The terrorists were killed in the fighting but the fact that the parliament complex was breached was a blow to Indian pride.[14] This led to the massing of troops on the borders and very real threats of a major war. International pressure and the threat that international investors would leave the area cooled that confrontation, but serious civil violence between Muslims and Hindus in India followed. In February 2002, a train carrying a group of Hindus returning from attempting to build a temple on the site of a burned mosque at Ayodhya was attacked and several dozen Hindu pilgrims were killed. This was followed by attacks and the burning of hundreds of Muslims in their homes in a poor neighborhood in the city of Ahmedabad in Gujarat state in the following months.[15] There were accusations and threats from both sides, with Hindus claiming the Muslims were secretly helping their Pakistani Muslim brothers and Muslims complaining that the goal was to rid India of all Muslims. The confrontations continue, with people on both sides being killed and the threat of war still a concern for the international community. Several commentators, with some justification, see the increased Hindu concerns over holy sites and the increase in mass rioting as being encouraged by the ruling Hindu nationalist party, Bharatiya Janata, as a way of consolidating Hindu support for the nationalist movement. These commentators argue that it is contemporary politics which fuels the continuing clashes.

Surely there are issues of internal politics and international standing involved, but this conflict is much more than a political struggle between political adversaries. The Hindus see the Muslims as invaders who have conquered India in past centuries and defiled Hindu temples and holy places by building their mosques on sacred Hindu sites. Again, the partitioning of the Indian subcontinent, pushed by the Muslim leadership, was anathema to most Indians, who blamed the Muslims for this act of gross religious impropriety. In the classic Hindu view, Pakistan is Muslim India and all Muslims should go there. It is in this context that the struggle over Kashmir takes place. Kashmir is predominantly Muslim, though it is not certain that the Kashmiri Muslims want affiliation with Pakistan. The will of the people and the practicality of the entire issue appear to matter less than religious and historical claims as both sides demand the area as their rightful inheritance. For Islam, Kashmir is Muslim land, Dar al-Islam, which may not be ceded to infidels because it is allied with the Muslim world. The presence of Indian troops and the Hindu political rule over Kashmir violate the deepest beliefs of Islamic civilization regarding their obligations to maintain authority over Islamic places.[16]

Perhaps the cause célèbre of the entire conflict and the event which highlights the confluence of history, religion, and violence was the battle over a holy site, clamed by both Muslims and Hindus, in the north Indian city of Ayodhya. On December

6, 1992, Hindu militants destroyed the famous Babri mosque in Ayodhya, as well over 200,000 Hindus watched and cheered them on, shouting that the mosque was an abomination built on a temple holy site where the Hindu god Rama was born and ruled.[17] The mosque was successfully taken apart, stone by stone, and riots between the two sides erupted all over India, with some three thousand people being killed, some as far away as in the southern city of Bombay. The Hindus were responding to what they saw as a shameful and embarrassing period in their religious history, a history in Hindu civilizational terms of Muslim desecration of Hindu holy sites that were the dwelling place of a variety of divine beings, gods, goddesses, and sacred human/divine beings.

The Mughal invaders, Muslim and originally from Afghanistan, had conquered and ruled India for centuries, and in 1528 one of the Mughal leaders, Babar, chose the Hindu holy site Ayodhya as the location for a great mosque as a way, in the view of most historians, of demonstrating Mughal domination at a Hindu holy site. This affront to Hindu sensibilities remained part of their history, and as long ago as 1949, soon after Indian independence, there were riots at the Ayodhya mosque. It was claimed that the god Rama had made an appearance at the mosque, and calls were made to restore the site as a Hindu temple. The Indian government, at that time under the secularist Congress Party, closed the site, declaring it off-limits to both Muslims and Hindus. The events of 2002 are another chapter in this history of civilizational confrontation. For the Hindu nationalists, Ayodhya was one way of removing what they perceived to be the humiliations brought upon them by the past Muslim conquest and domination, humiliations that are seen as religious violations of sacred sites, sacred beings, and sacred history. Jack Hawley, the distinguished historian of religion at Columbia University, explains that "from the point of view of the Hindu militants who orchestrated the Ayodhya affair, it was an act that would make India whole again after the partition of 1947—whole in symbolic, if not political terms."[18]

In all of this we see that history, religion, and politics are closely interwoven and that, at least in some societies, sacred memories do not easily go away. Muslims were uncomfortable with a one-India solution in 1947 and many Muslims today feel themselves to be less than fully accepted in a Hindu India. The Hindu understanding of Indian history, religious space, and divine actions is so removed from Islamic approaches to these same matters that it is difficult for these groups to avoid religious and political strife.[19] Many people, including some scholars with great expertise, want to separate religion from violence, preferring to see religion as peaceful and politics as leading to violent confrontations, but the case of India shows that this is not so. Violence is part of religion, something that emerges from deeply experienced religious faith and living history. War and politics are the venues for religious battles.

Civilizational Contact and Religious Violence

The dispute between India and Pakistan is one of the most highly publicized religious disputes, but religious clashes occur all over the world. Some are also extremely violent but do not necessarily make the newspapers or television screens. Religious and civilizational identity and commitment hold strong in many parts of the world and tolerance and coexistence between religions proves difficult for many of the world's societies. Some Christian and Muslim communities have been engaged in violent confrontations in the Philippines for over a decade, and both foreign missionaries and local people have been killed. The militant Muslim extremist group, Abu Sayyaf, is particularly active in the southern Philippines and has carried out a series of murders and kidnappings of people they accuse of Christian proselytizing. An American couple, Martin and Gracia Burnham, representing an American church group, were kidnapped and held for several years in an Abu Sayyaf hideout; the husband was subsequently killed by the group in a rescue attempt by the Philippine army. In August 2001, two Philippine Jehovah's Witnesses missionaries were beheaded by the group, apparently for visiting people to talk about religion and encourage interest in Christianity. There were indications that the missionaries were interested in conversion activities, and this is indeed a critical aspect of the civilizational conflict. The Christians see their work as religious duty and Abu Sayyaf sees itself as both a military group protecting Islam and a missionary group encouraging conversion to Islam. Indeed, some kidnapped prisoners were told they could avoid death by converting to Islam.[20]

Religious tensions and violence have now emerged in places where earlier political repression appears to have also restrained religious conflicts. Armenia and Azerbaijan in the Caucasus have become a cauldron of religious and ethnic violence since the breakup of the Soviet Empire. Muslim groups are demanding greater legal standing and increased aid for their educational and religious institutions and have battled the Christian Orthodox communities. Christian communities claim the Muslims are not interested in help for their communities but want to take over the area and establish a Muslim theocratic society. Christian Armenians and Azerbaijani saboteurs have been well organized and throughout the 1990s were active in bombing Muslim communities, killing thousands and moving tens of thousands out of areas the militants consider Christian. Nigeria in West Africa has significant Christian and Muslim populations and conflict is ongoing over the degree of religious influence over the state. Some Muslim areas in Nigeria have made sharia the basis for both religious and civil law, and this is vigorously resisted by the Christian Nigerian community. One area of conflict is the Muslim insistence that the death penalty be given for violations of sharia law in marriage, particularly for adultery, while the Christian community sees this as discriminating against women, who can be more easily prosecuted for this offense, and against Christian attitudes toward the death penalty. Among the rising numbers of Christian-Muslim disputes are the continuing wars, persecutions, and acts of terrorism involving Orthodox Christian Russia and Muslim Chechnya. Thousands of lives have been lost on both sides, but the religious conflicts continue, despite some political compromise. The fact of the matter is that the Russian Orthodox see their homeland as a Christian entity and the

Chechnyan Muslims continue to deny the religious culture of the Christian community, demanding their religious and civilizational rights and privileges. This is a chronic clash that will not be easily resolved.[21]

Hindu-Buddhist violence has broken out with a particular ferocity in Sri Lanka over the religious nature of the government and society. Hindus feel themselves left out of this predominantly Buddhist nation and have turned to guerrilla tactics and assassinations in support of their demands. Civil wars, assassinations, and bombings involving various Hindu and Buddhist groups have become part of Sri Lankan society during most of the last decade. That country's Muslim population has also been attacked on occasion and mosques have been burned by Hindu militants, who claim that the Muslims are siding with and protecting Buddhists in Muslim homes and mosques. The long period of colonialization until World War II and the breakup of the Soviet empire have released long-simmering civilizational religious clashes in many parts of Africa and Asia, and we can expect increased religious violence in many of these regions.[22]

International migration and globalization have brought civilizational clashes to Western European society as well. The arrival of large numbers of Muslim immigrants in the 1970s and onward—Germany now has a population of 3.2 million Muslims, England has between four and five million Muslims, and France has in the vicinity of six million Muslims—has transformed religious relations in that part of the world. France and Germany, particularly, have seen the rise of anti-Muslim prejudice, and attacks on Muslims are not uncommon. Neither Germany nor France provide state-sponsored religious education for Muslim youth, while they do so for the Christian and Jewish communities. Right-wing politicians in Germany, France, and Austria, some with substantial followings, have called for moratoriums on Muslim migration, and some nationalist groups have called for population transfer. Great Britain has pursued a more integrationist policy, but socially and geographically the two communities remain separate. In England, as well, there are calls for the denial of Muslim rights and in English cities where there are a large number of unemployed, there have been an increasing number of attacks on Muslims and Muslim institutions.[23]

It is difficult to know the exact source of tension. Clearly the September 11 bombing of the World Trade Center and the worldwide fear generated by the al-Qaeda terrorist organization have brought Islam under suspicion, but the tensions and hostility predate these events. There appears to be a deep cultural and religious gap between Christian Europe, albeit a secularized Christian Europe, and the world of Islam. Some of the tensions, like those involving head coverings for women, beards for men, and the establishment of separate educational institutions might appear insignificant, but they have become important issues in the conflict. The observance and nature of Muslim holidays, fasting during the Muslim holy month of Ramadan, the modesty regulations in Muslim communities, and the strongly traditionalist faith held by most of the migrants are all sources of cultural discontinuity and tension with the modernity of European society. Each side is fearful that its way of life is being threatened. There is a sense that the European state cannot tolerate a traditionalist religion like Islam which does not only practice religion in the private realm of the family or mosque but seeks to influence government policy and international relations, competing with an indigenous European Christian civilization, even one far from its religious roots.

The West and the Rest: Globalization and Religious Conflict

Perhaps the most significant international struggle is the inter-civilizational clash between Western universalism and traditional religious cultures throughout the world. America is the leader and exemplar of Western modernity and believes it has an obligation to promote what it sees as the superior and universal culture of the West to the rest of the world. This proselytizing approach has always been part of the American ethos. From its inception, the United States has had a sense of manifest destiny, a belief in the uniqueness of America, and a religious conviction that the values, ideas, and social organization of America should become the enduring values of countries all over the globe. This sense of American uniqueness was glorified in song, myth, and popular culture and became an essential part of the American school curriculum. America was, in this view, free of the preju-dices and backwardness of other societies. In the words of the sociologist Seymour Lipset, it was the "first new nation," where equality and fairness could reign and where religious differ-ences did not matter, as they did in the old countries of Europe and Asia.[24] Whether this was ever the case is a question best left to historians, but the sense of American culture as needing to become the model for world culture remains to this day. It is this American sense of superiority and the view, in many parts of the world, that the United States wants all nations to imitate America, that motivates a good deal of the hostility to America all over the globe. Put simply, people in many parts of the world believe that the United States wants everyone to adopt American forms because these values and modes of social organization are superior. This attitude was summed up well by Samuel Hun-tington, who wrote, "What is universalism to the West is imperi-alism to the rest."[25]

The United States is the world's preeminent Western power but the unique complex of culture and social organization called Western civilization extends, of course, to the European nations and has its origins in Christian Europe and in the unique values of Christianity and in the Christian churches' relationship with the state. As globalization proceeds and cultural, economic, and religious barriers between nations fall, the values of Western mo-dernity, backed up by the enormous economic and international power of the West, have set the tone for all societies. The govern-ing elites in many non-Western societies, in efforts to compete with the West, have sought to imitate the West and have adopted many Western forms, values, styles, and attitudes. Everything from fashions in clothing to the relative status of men and women and the relationship between religion and political and economic institutions has been based in many parts of the non-Western world on the model of the West. In some cases this has worked fine, but in a great many situations this has put the Westernized elites in direct opposition to the masses of ordinary people in many parts of the globe who do not want to abandon their traditional ways.[26] The economic advantages of Westernization, it appears, do not outweigh the religious homelessness that many people experience when their societies follow the path of Westernization.

What is it about Western culture that is threatening to traditional religious cultures and in what ways does the West challenge "all the rest"? Scholars have described four basic areas in which Westernization comes into conflict with traditional religious cultures throughout the world: secularization, pluralism, individualism, and the status of women.[27] Western culture is predominately secular, which means that religion and religious values are removed from public life and replaced by secular and practical values and ideologies. Secularization means that the government and civil life of society are separated from religion and religious rules and operate on the basis of secular utilitarian principles in order to achieve desirable economic and political goals. Religion still has a place in modern societies but its role is limited to the private realm of personal faith and life-cycle events and celebrations. Mainstream Western religions understand and largely accept the reality that their dogmas and doctrines cannot serve as the basis for governmental and economic policy. Thus, secularization means that religion has lost the authority to dictate political policy or force people to conform to religious laws. Secularization inevitably challenges traditional religious belief as it encourages the pluralization of religions. Essentially, what Western secularization accomplishes is to cast doubt on the truth claims of any one religion and open the society to a variety of religions. Pluralism, as a central tenet of modernity, claims that no one religion or moral system is ultimately correct. Unlike traditional religious attitudes, which claim a particular religion to be the one and only God-given truth, pluralism views religion as a matter of choice.

Individualism is a natural consequence of secularization and pluralism and as a Western value argues that the self, the individual person, is free to pick and choose values, career, life style, and moral system. Unlike traditionalism's rules, which call for the individual to submit to religious law and custom, modernity encourages individual choice, even radical choice, in virtually all realms of life, including work, ethics, and sexuality. Western modernity has, therefore, challenged the traditional role of women. Whereas traditional religion, particularly the holy scriptures in Judaism, Christianity, and Islam, has viewed the status of men and women as distinctive, with men in the dominant position and women in a subordinate role, modernity rejects this generalization and leaves the definition of roles to the individual. Pluralism and individual free choice are to govern relationships between men and women, not the ancient texts of any particular religion.

It is not difficult to see the severe conflict and tension between Western modernity and traditional religion and how the West's insistence that traditional religious cultures adopt Western forms would cause anger and resentment and, in some cases, a war against the West. The separation of religion from the state means that the traditional social and moral order has disappeared. What to the West and to modern sensibility are freedom and democracy are to many others sinfulness and chaos. Opening up society to secular rule is to go against divine law and jeopardize the society's and the individual's well-being for eternal life. The result is that people can never feel religiously confident because they have abandoned the comforting truths and certainties of religious faith. To follow the West is to become spiritually and psychologically homeless, without a transcendental anchor to provide security and safety during life's journey. Traditional authority is compromised and the natural hierarchy of family, clan, and nation is destroyed. Bonds of reciprocity and loyalty are broken for passing political and materialistic gain. The Western abandonment of traditional roles for men and women and the rejection of the religious organization of family life have destroyed the moral basis of the West and have resulted, in this view, in widespread crime, immorality, and sexual deviance.

The universal value of secular modernity, held by the West but championed most prominently by the United States and often made a condition for international economic and military aid from the United States or from international organizations controlled by western interests like the World Bank, is fiercely resented by traditionally religious interests. These groups feel that the Western approach is one of religious and cultural genocide. The price for Western economic aid is capitulation to what traditionalists see as the abandonment of their indigenous religious faith and lifestyle. Traditionalists all over the world, including religious traditionalists in the United States, are, in the words of historians Martin Marty and R. Scott Appleby, "fighting back" and "fighting against" modernity, which they see as an attack on their way of life, their beliefs, and their God.[28] They fight back, sometimes with the ballot box, sometimes with legal challenges and noisy demonstrations, but also through violent confrontations with bombs and other weapons that Karen Armstrong describes in her popular book, *The Battle for God*. There is a battle raging worldwide over which civilizational values will prevail.[29]

Islam and The West

The most dramatic civilizational confrontation is between traditional Islam and Western culture. Militant traditionalists fight against the United States and against many of their own Muslim governments, which the traditionalists believe have permitted Western secularism to unduly affect Islamic society.[30] Islamic traditionalists are opposed to the separation of religion and state and believe that it is religiously required to have Islamic law, sharia, be an official and legal part of national life. Foreign policy and international relations, too, must be under the religious authority of religious scholars, and the truly Islamic state may not, even for national economic or political advantage, do anything that goes against Muslim teachings. In the Muslim view, morality, dress, and popular culture, including films, literature, and leisure activities, are not matters for individuals to decide but areas that come under religious legislation and custom. Islamic religion holds that sexuality, courtship, and marriage are not matters to be decided by the individual but to be directed by religious law and family tradition.

There are few, if any, governments, with the possible exception of Iran and Afghanistan when it was under Taliban rule, that have fully followed these strictures. Moreover, the ruling elites in many Muslim countries have been educated in Western universities and are themselves influenced by Western culture; they tolerate and, at times, encourage a politics and popular culture unencumbered by religious law. The leadership cadres in many Muslim countries see Westernization as a mode of economic development and are fearful that Islamic extremists will stymie economic development and prevent Western foreign aid. The case of Egypt is typical and demonstrates the issues facing Muslim governments throughout the Islamic world. Egypt is a solidly Muslim country and the prevailing social norms, public life, and legal system of that society are profoundly Islamic. However, Egyptian society also has a tradition of being hospitable to Western tourists, permitting mixed dancing, alcohol, and other adult entertainment. Politically, as well, Egypt has had significant relations with the United States and has cooperated with the West in military operations and cultural exchange. During the Gulf War against Iraq, Egyptian military and diplomatic forces were fully involved with the war effort, helped coordinate the cooperation of other Muslim states, and were very important in justifying the war as a war against a terrorist regime and not a war against Islam. The United States rewarded Egypt with considerable military and economic aid, though traditionalist elements saw this cooperation as a sellout to the evils of the West. Educational institutions, though Islamic, have maintained, even in the Islamic studies departments, a certain amount of academic freedom. The Coptic Christian Church, one of the oldest Christian communities in the world, has historically been tolerated and supported by successive Egyptian governments and has for a long time felt at home in Muslim Egypt.

This has been the character of Egyptian society. Militant traditionalists, however, reject these accommodations and compromises as capitulations to and imitations of the West.[31] For them, the absence of the full implementation of sharia is but the first step in the loss of Islamic identity and represents the pernicious growth of Western modernity within the precincts of their religious culture. Egypt is not a representative democracy and protests and public rallies staged by such anti–American groups as the Muslim Brotherhood and Islamic Jihad against Westernization are not permitted by the Egyptian government. Leaders of these movements have been arrested and imprisoned and the conflict with the government and its elite Western leadership has escalated to become a civilizational religious war between those who define themselves as the true defenders of Islam and the "infidel" Egyptian government, described as doing the bidding of its American supporters. These militant groups, feeling they have no say in government policy, have turned to violence and terrorism in support of their Islamic program. This was not difficult to justify, given their reading of Islamic law, which calls for violence against infidels and all others who challenge genuine Muslim faith. The most notorious killings took place at the pyramids and tombs at Luxor, between Aswan and Asyut, where Western European tourists were systematically ambushed by snipers and bombers.[32] While the victims of these attacks were tourists, the actual goal was to attack the government and to demonstrate that Egypt was unsafe to visit for Western tourists who do not respect Islamic law.

Anything that was related to Westernization in leisure, arts, or education was condemned.[33] Though long a part of Egyptian popular culture, belly-dancing establishments were bombed and the dancers and owners threatened with death. One Islamic weekly declared, "Belly dancing epitomizes the sickness of man's soul. By crushing it, we take the first step toward godliness." Naguib Mahfouz, a world-famous Egyptian author and the winner of the Nobel Prize for literature in 1988, was stabbed repeatedly in the face and seriously wounded in 1999 under orders of the militant Sheik Abdul Rahman. Mahfouz, an observant but not fundamentalist Muslim, was under a *fatwa*, a verdict demanding his death, for not treating Islamic holy figures with proper respect in his book *The Children of Gebelawi*. Mahfouz was eighty-three when the attack occurred; he survived, but the attack was just the first in a series of murderous assaults on authors and artists, all Muslim, who were thought to be violating Islamic law.[34] The militants saw artistic tolerance of non-Islamic art as an imitation of the West. They demanded that all art, literature, film, and entertainment be religious and that the government not permit any work which would challenge Islamic principles. The writer Faraq Fouda, who was knowledgeable about Muslim religious philosophy and challenged the militant traditionalist agenda as an imposition on historical Islam, was murdered. Mohammed al-Ghazali, a militant Islamic preacher testifying at the trail of Fouda's murderers, announced that it was appropriate to kill Fouda because he was a "secularist" bent on destroying Islam.[35] The universities and their faculties also came under attack. Academic freedom was shown by the traditionalists to be a Western import, alien to Islam, and those scholars questioning and seeking to reform central Islamic beliefs were persecuted as enemies of Islam.

The historic Egyptian tolerance of the Copts was also challenged by the traditionalists, who contended Islam must prevail in a Muslim land and that there was no place for non-Muslims to follow a culture which violated Muslim traditions. Coptic stores selling liquor, hairdressing parlors where men and women mixed, and churches were burned, and Copts were attacked in the street. Everything associated with the West was labeled immoral and to be avoided by pious Muslims. The *hijab*, the head covering for women, became a sign of Muslim authenticity, whereas going without head covering was a sign of aping the West. The male-dominated household was shown to be the approved Islamic form, while equality between men and women was termed "unnatural" and "un-Islamic" and an import from the West. Polygamy, permitted by Islamic law, gained new popularity as an example of a particularly Muslim form of marriage.[36] The greatest contempt was shown, however, for political leaders who followed a Western and American political agenda. These officials were considered traitors to Islam and deserving of death. This was the justification for the assassination of Anwar Sadat in 1982 for signing a peace treaty with Israel under the auspices of the United States and the justification for the many bombings of Egyptian governmental facilities in the 1990s and beyond. Hosni Mubarak, who succeeded Sadat as president, has attempted to play down his cooperation with the United States, but in critical ways he has continued the policy of Sadat and has been the target of dozens of assassination attempts. Egypt is in the midst of a religious civilizational war that Geneive Abdo, in her book *No God But God*, predicts will see "the triumph of Islam."[37] There is both a violent and educational struggle in Egyptian society to return, in all ways, to the values, laws, and lifestyle of Islamic civilization.

Jewish Traditionalism and Western Culture

Israel is often, and not without reason, seen as a Western bastion in the Middle East. This is true politically and socially for most of the population, but the traditionalists, known as *Haredim*, literally the ones who tremble before God, are fiercely and entirely opposed to Western modernity and will use all means to fight against this culture and value system, which they see as immoral and a danger to their Torah-based way of life. The Haredim are biblical literalists who meticulously follow the rabbinic laws. They are strict Sabbath observers and will not drive or do any work on that holy day; they eat only food supervised by their rabbis, Haredim men dress in black frocks, and women are segregated from men and dress in very modest clothes, with head coverings mandated for married women. They are opposed to secular education, limiting such studies to arithmetic and elementary language skills for young children; men spend the bulk of their time studying Torah texts and Talmud.[38]

The Haredim believe that Jews must live by Torah law alone. Although they desire and enjoy the protection and security given to them by the Jewish state of Israel, they consider the Israeli state and government to be a threat to Jewish religiosity because the state is based on Western values of individualism and secular democratic principles and permits freedom of artistic expression. They see the contemporary Jewish state as a place of immorality and sexual licentiousness for the way the state permits popular cultural expressions along Western lines. The Haredim live in their own neighborhoods, marry only within their group, and maintain their own school system to protect their children from what they regard as the atheism and coeducational immorality of Israeli public schools.

The Haredim also object theologically to the very existence of the state of Israel. Their position is that Jews are not permitted to create a state before the times of the messiah. They believe that war and military action by Jews against their enemies is forbidden. The Jewish task is to study the Torah and wait patiently for the miraculous coming of the messiah who will redeem the Jewish people. The Jewish state, based on the principles of European secular nationalism, is against Jewish tradition and an alien and dangerous import. Consequently, the Haredim will not serve in the Israeli army, salute the Star of David flag, or celebrate any state holidays or memorial days as this would be to honor a secular entity based on alien Western civilization. The great sin of the Zionist state, in their view, is that it has substituted secular nationalism for religious faith and observance of Jewish law.

Despite their avowal of nonviolence, the Haredim are ready to take on the state authorities and the secular public when they believe their religious interests are challenged. The most dramatic confrontations occur over Sabbath traffic in Haredi neighborhoods. Large crowds of Haredim gather at major intersections in Haredi neighborhoods in Jerusalem and in B'nai Brak, a Haredi town near Tel Aviv, and when a secular driver passes by on the Sabbath, stones are thrown at the driver with yells of "shabes, shabes," a Yiddish-Hebrew word used by Haredim in referring to the Jewish Sabbath. When the crowd grows strong toward evening, large groups of traditionalists block all traffic and engage in pushing and shoving with the police and secular Israelis. This is not a sporadic show of anger but a planned and coordinated traditionalist show of force to challenge the secular lifestyle of contemporary Israel. People on both sides are regularly injured, but the Haredim claim this is acceptable to protect the sanctity of the Sabbath. The Haredim believe they are the true remaining faithful Jews and these demonstrations and confrontations show that they will not be intimidated by the secular majority.[39]

Haredim are a minority in Israel, probably making up no more than 10 percent of the population, yet the number of violent activities carried out in the name of the group is not insignificant. There is a range of threatening behavior against secular enemies of the group that is considered justified, including harassment, arson, and vandalism. Although a central element of Haredi religiosity is religious passivity and waiting for supernatural salvation, the threats of secularism are so powerful and the allure of modernity so great that the Haredim have legitimated violent confrontation into their theological system. Large-scale confrontations also occur with Israeli archaeologists when they excavate ancient areas which Haredim claim are actually ancient Jewish cemeteries. The Haredim, appealing to rabbinic law, argue that even the remote possibility of violating the dignity of the dead makes any excavation work for historical or archeological purpose forbidden. Archaeology is secular nonsense imported from Western universities without any redeeming religious value, they assert. Archaeologists, of course, see things differently and argue for the advancement of knowledge and science. Haredim counter that all truth is available in scripture and archaeology gives a distorted view of the sacred history of the Jews. To outsiders, much of this wrangling appears trivial, but in the Israeli context serious violence has broken out between Haredim and other groups and governments have fallen because of these conflicts. Posters calling for mass demonstrations against archaeological excavations in Haredi neighborhoods frame the event as "a time to do battle for God." Archaeologists are portrayed as "godless secularists" who want to rob the Jewish people of their sacred sites and history. One Haredi organization put up signs critical of Western culture and its danger for Jews and Judaism, stating, "The secular Jews refuse to see that the triumph of secularism in the twentieth century led to the bloodiest war in human history, including the Nazi Holocaust."[40] In this religious view, Western culture must be opposed so that the authenticity of Jewish piety and faith is maintained.[41]

Christianity and Culture War

Traditionalist Christian groups in the United States, including fundamentalists and evangelical Christians and Catholic traditionalists, have their own unique rendezvous with Western modernity. In many ways, these groups are at home with modernity, with modern technology and communication and the social organization of modern societies. The rational and bureaucratic organization of the workplace, the intricacies of secular politics and international affairs, and the limited role of religion in the public sphere are familiar and understandable to these faithful Christians. Yet they remain outsiders and, in critical ways, hostile to the secular modernity of American culture. As James Davison Hunter puts it, traditional Christians are at war with their own Western culture.[42] Traditionalist Christians are angry; they are angry that the Bible is treated as literature and not the word of God, they are angry that evolution is taught as fact and the Bible as myth, they are angry that abortions are still legal, they are angry that pornography is acceptable, and they are appalled that Christian sexual morals are rejected by the society in favor of sexual modernism promoting consensual unions of any type, the increasing tolerance of homosexuality, and the widespread acceptance of sex outside the bonds of marriage. Traditionalist Christians see these changes as bringing on personal and societal disaster—as they say the AIDS epidemic demonstrates—and keeping people in a state of sin that will lead to eternal damnation. They see individualism, secularism, and the radically pluralistic ethic of modernity as entirely destructive of the human condition.

Traditionalist Christians want to "fight back," in the words of Martin Marty and R. Scott Appleby, by turning society back to God and Christian morality and values.[43] There is a deep schism in America between those who want to see Christian faith and values become part of the public and educational life of the society and those who opt for the individualistic expression of religion, limiting it to the private realm of family and voluntary association. Christian confrontations have been generally limited to political and verbal assaults against what traditionalists consider enemies of religion and, in the case of abortion providers, as murderers. Nonetheless, violence has been a part of the Christian traditionalist response to secular modernity. The story of the Christian confrontation with Western modernity is yet to be told. New movements are constantly forming and the Christian anger against what these groups see as a denial of the American heritage of Christian government and a full Christian public life is still in a state of incubation. There are large segments of the Christian world in the United States who believe that the government is hostile to traditional religion and criminal in its refusal to recognize the complaints and appeals of Christians throughout the land to return the United States to its Christian roots. These traditionalists are convinced that the American populace is behind them but are afraid to speak out for fear of reprisal. The talk in these circles is that an armed struggle between the forces of Christian good and the satanic forces of a secular federal government is coming. The forces of good, the faithful and traditional Christian community, will ultimately triumph, but much blood will be spilled and there will be much suffering. The Christian, in this view, must be ready to take up arms to defend Christian beliefs and Christian families.[44] Among the most extreme of these groups is the Aryan Nation movement, which preaches a blend of Christian fundamentalism, racism, and neo-Nazi anti-Semitism. This group and its affiliates, like the White Patriots Party, the White American Bastion, and the Silent Brotherhood, are also connected with the Christian Identity movement and actively pursue violence, including the murder of minorities and officials of the federal government. They believe that only the destruction of the modern democratic state and its culture will liberate Christian America from the satanic powers of the degenerate morality and values of modern Western civilization. There is a waiting game in America now and the confrontation that Huntington calls "the West and all the rest" is also on the American agenda.

Ethnic Conflict, Political Battles, and Religious Violence: Ireland, Serbia, and Bosnia

Religious differences, as we have seen, can be a source of considerable conflict and violence but religion itself can be used to foment political tensions and encourage ethnic confrontation and social change. Just when is a conflict truly religious in nature and when is it something else—ethnic, political, or economic—with religion being used to encourage the conflict? This is something that is never obvious and clear-cut. Not infrequently, a reporter or analyst will characterize a particular conflict so that it can be viewed through an ideological lens. In some cases, like explicit holy wars or clear-cut battles over specific religious issues, all will agree on the religious nature of the conflict. In other cases, like warfare over territory or civil wars over political issues, commentators will agree that religion is not a central component in the conflict. There are, however, a fair number of disputes all over the world in which the nature of the conflict is itself a matter of dispute between scholars and researchers.

Jonathan Fox, a political scientist specializing in the cross-cultural study of political and ethnic conflict, concludes that religion can strengthen and promote an otherwise political or secular conflict in three ways: (1) by making available the considerable institutional resources of a religious organization, like meeting space, money, and publicity; (2) by providing religious legitimation and moral justification for the conflict and in this way defining the actions of the group as fighting for God while the opposition is identified with the forces of evil; and (3) by involving the clergy and religious elite in the conflict to demonstrate publicly its importance and religious value.[45] Fox cites the involvement of the African American churches and the personal involvement of the clergy, particularly the charismatic preacher Dr. Martin Luther King Jr., in helping the civil rights movement achieve so many of its goals. Fox argues that by co-opting religion, political, national, and ethnic movements can gain popular support which would be unavailable without the religious imprimatur. In time the nexus between the two may be lost but the struggle will maintain its religious character.

The work of Fox and his associates surely does not apply to all cases of religious conflict. This school tends to downplay the significance of actual religious and theological differences, but it can be helpful in understanding the longstanding conflicts in Ireland and in the Balkans. In both Ireland, where the struggle is between two Christian groups, and in the former Yugoslavia, where it is an interreligious conflict between Orthodox Christian Serbs and Balkan Muslims, there are currently few explicit theological, scriptural, or ritual issues which are so serious that they would result in armed struggle. As the twenty-first century proceeds, all the parties in the conflicts are quite secularized and not very observant of their religious obligations. Birth control and living together before marriage are widespread among Catholics and Protestants in Northern Ireland and some of the largest and most famous Protestant churches are virtually empty on most Sundays.[46] The Muslims and Serbs, too, are relaxed about religious rules. Alcohol, forbidden by the Koran, is used by Muslims as well as Serbian groups and intermarriage and sociability between the groups were not unknown before the current outbreak of violence.[47] Like the Muslims and the Serbs, Irish Catholics and Protestants are ethnically and racially similar and outsiders cannot tell them apart. All the parties to the conflicts are long-time residents and recent migration and language are really not issues which divide them, as may be the case with other ethnic and racial conflicts.

Yet all these groups claim to be fighting religious battles and religion remains the marker which defines the struggle. The power of religious identity and religious legitimation is such that even people far from religious faith can be motivated to continue centuries-old battles in the name of religion. It appears that the very real historical, psychological, and economic grievances each of these groups experience are subsumed and expressed behind the banner of religion. The sacralization of the conflict has strongly inspired and motivated the partisans in the conflict but it has made a solution to many of the historical issues very difficult. What has occurred is that the very existence of the opposing group is experienced as so degrading, humiliating, and immoral that the enemy group must be fought and destroyed. Compromise, for many, has become the equivalent of surrender. It is true that the religious institutions in these conflicts have periodically condemned violence and killing as against religion, but by providing a sacred and institutional umbrella for the expression of grievance, religion remains a significant element in these struggles. These conflicts illustrate that a group's religion and history have continuing power to provide motivation for conflict and action even if the current points of contention are largely cultural and political.[48]

The Irish conflict did have its origins in religious prejudice and discrimination. In the seventeenth century, as part of an attempt to consolidate English rule, large tracts of land in Ulster were given to those, predominately Protestants from England, Scotland, and Wales, who were willing to settle the land and make it part of the English monarchy. The Planters, as these colonists came to be known, settled in formerly native Irish areas; the local residents were excluded from these areas and forced in many cases to settle on inferior land in the mountains or bogs. The Protestant community allied itself with English culture and nationality and by social custom and law discriminated against the native Irish. In the early years of English rule, Catholic worship was prohibited and Catholic priests were killed if they were found to be involved in religious activity. The local Irish saw the English as intruders, a foreign group that usurped their ancestral lands and treated them as inferiors in their own country. The Protestants, in the Irish view, were conquerors and colonialists who were out to destroy the indigenous religiosity of Irish Catholic culture.

There was a religious and theological element in the Protestant attitude toward Catholicism. The English were strongly influenced by the Reformation views of Christianity and particularly by the negative attitudes, popular in Protestant religiosity at that time, toward Catholicism. They saw their version of Christianity—Protestant and reformist and Reformationist—as superior, moral, and biblical. They identified Catholicism with narrowness, immoral practices, corruption, and the illegitimate authority of the pope. These negative stereotypes, coupled with the Protestants' higher social standing, led to long-term prejudice, discrimination, and stigmatization of the Catholic community. While these attitudes have disappeared in most parts of the contemporary Christian world, they still carry a certain weight in social and political interaction in Ireland despite several centuries and the transformation of both communities, and continue to contribute to the continuing conflict.

The centuries following the English colonization of Ulster saw the rise of much violence between the Catholic advocates of a separate state, known as Republicans, and the Protestant supporters of a continued alliance with England, known as Unionists. Some Catholic groups used electoral and parliamentary means to overthrow English rule, but several prominent and active Irish paramilitary forces like the Irish Republican Brotherhood used armed force against the Protestant powers. After one particularly bloody attack during Easter week, 1916, Irish Republican leaders were arrested and executed, bringing the Catholic militants increased sympathy and hardening attitudes on both sides. After much conflict, an independent Irish state was set up as part of a 1921 partition settlement in which the southern twenty-four Irish counties, predominately Catholic, would be under independent Irish rule and the six counties of Ulster in northern Ireland, having a majority of Protestants, would remain part of England.

Irish Republicans fought the plan, seeing it as a continuation of the Protestant takeover of three centuries before. Ireland was for the Irish only, meaning the Irish Catholics whose land was taken away and whose religious culture was denigrated and persecuted. The Protestants saw Ulster as their land; after all, they had been there for centuries, they constituted a majority, they were part of England, and they retained a sense of being a dominant and superior group. The Irish Republican Army continued the armed Catholic struggle in Northern Ireland against English rule with military strikes on Protestant targets, while the Protestant community used the almost exclusively Protestant police force and social and discriminatory economic legislation to reign in Catholic protest. Some movement in social and economic equality occurred in the aftermath of World War II, when some of the earlier discriminatory legislation was overturned, but it appears that it was a case of too late and too little. In the 1960s, Catholic civil rights groups, borrowing techniques from the American civil rights movement, began a program of civil disobedience involving massive protests and sit-ins which the government could not control. The government called in the British army in 1969 to restore order, and this eventually resulted in armed confrontations between the IRA and other armed groups with the British forces. The rise in violent confrontations led to the establishment of Protestant militia groups that attacked Catholic targets and communities.

By the 1970s, the situation had become extremely bleak, with confrontations and killings almost every week. Car bombings, drive-by shootings, and arson were almost routine events. Catholics and Protestants were segregated into separate neighborhoods and a Catholic venturing into a Protestant neighborhood or a Protestant into a Catholic neighborhood risked being killed. In 1972, over 460 people were killed in violent confrontations. In the 1980s the number of incidents decreased, although in 1985, there were still hundreds of incidents and hundreds were wounded and murdered on both sides. Serious and frequent violence continued into the 1990s, when promising negotiations between the two sides and the British government had a limiting effect on the violence.[49] The major groups active on both sides appeared to want a compromise and in the opening years of the twenty-first century, there was an official armistice, with all sides calling for a renunciation of violence. The British troops left Ireland, leaving the Irish to settle their differences. However, as with such other agreements and armistices in the past, the two sides fought over the provisions of the agreement and very serious violence again broke out, with the British army returning to maintain a very difficult armistice yet again.

Despite continuing negotiations and occasional optimistic reports, there are signs that the "troubles," as locals refer to the centuries-old conflict, are not over. The religious and cultural elements of historical feuds are not so easily resolved by signed agreements and handshakes. In July 2001, like every July, members of the militantly Protestant Orange Order in Portadown, Northern Ireland, a historic and religious citadel for Protestants, marched in their bowler hats and black suits, carrying banners commemorating centuries-old Protestant victories over Catholics. The tradition is to march along a route which includes Catholic neighborhoods, and this usually leads to rioting and confrontation. In 2001, as part of the peace negotiations, the police permitted the march but rerouted it so that it would not pass through Catholic sections of the town and provoke an incident. Catholics see these marches as reminders of their subjugation under Protestant rule. Protestants claim the marches are an expression of their culture and history and, in the words of one marcher, rerouting the parade shows that Catholics "are taking away the rights of the majority." The marcher added, "That's what you get when you bother with Rome." On the same day in July that the police had to keep the marchers separate, the *New York Times* reported that a dissident IRA faction had been uncovered and was planning a bomb attack. [50] The conflict continues.

Northern Ireland is on the road toward secularization, but some of the old stereotypes and fears persist. Most children still attend separate religious schools, either Catholic or Protestant, and live in separate neighborhoods; particularly among the working classes, there is little socializing between the two groups. History, so important in shaping a common identity and outlook, is still taught differently in the different religious systems and this, too, contributes to the generational transmission of suspicion. Moderates and those less attached to the churches are now seeking to break down these barriers. One new approach has been the attempt to establish one school system where all children would attend, with a common curriculum for all, regardless of religion. These attempts have not been very successful so far because each of the religions wants to maintain its own school system, with its sectarian curriculum. The militant religious leaders on both sides still appear to want separation. Catholic priest and educators often deride what in their view is the weaker moral basis of Protestant society and education and some Protestant leaders still proclaim Catholicism as an inferior and papist religion.[51]

The future of Northern Ireland remains a conundrum. Some commentators blame all its troubles on religion. "If today's Ulster residents," claims one writer, "weren't Catholic or Protestant, they would have no reason to belong to one camp and hate each other."[52] Those in this camp remain deeply pessimistic about any solution as long as religion remains a core Irish identity. John Ardagh, in his book, *Ireland and the Irish,* deals with Ireland as a changing society and sees the current problem as a matter of political will.[53] If all the parties in the conflict—the British government, the government of the Republic of Ireland, and the political leaders of the religious communities in Northern Ireland—come to an equitable solution for all sides, which Ardagh sees as currently happening, the religious factor will fade away. The future will tell.

The violence in the former Yugoslavia has its own unique dynamics, but there, too, we see a confluence of history, religion, and ethnic grievance.[54] In the Yugoslavian case, as well, there is disagreement over whether it is a religious conflict or a nationalist struggle hiding behind religious history and symbols. The Western powers that ultimately ordered the armistice arrangements between the parties considered it a political dispute and dealt with it as such, using political pressure and military power to stop the continuing violence. Many historians and writers, however, describe this age-old Balkan conflict as a religious war. Anthony Lewis, writing in the *New York Times* on January 1, 1993, explains: "It is really religion that identifies the Serbs, Croats, and Muslims of former Yugoslavia: Eastern Orthodox, Roman Catholic and Muslim. They are all of the same South Slav stock and speak the same language, Serbo-Croatian. But to religion has been added nationalist emotions."

Yugoslavia was created after World War I as a confederation of Orthodox Serbs, Catholic Croatians, and Muslims in the province of Bosnia-Herzegovina. Originally, as Lewis rightly indicated, all these groups were Slav in origin and even today they look alike, speak the same language, and, despite their denials, have much in common culturally as well. Their differences are religious, Croats having become Catholic and the Serbs Eastern Orthodox after the schism between Rome and Constantinople in the eleventh century. A more serious division occurred in the 1400s, when Muslim Turks invaded the Balkans and numbers of Slavs converted to Islam and were rewarded with special privileges. The invasion and victory of the Muslim Turks and their political rule over the region for hundreds of years was never forgotten and remains vivid in the Serbian religious and historical imagination to this day. The Muslim converts were not foreigners or outsider invaders but fellow Slavs who, in the view of the Christian Serbs, abandoned their religion and joined in the persecution of their Serbian brothers and sisters in those bygone times which are, nonetheless, powerfully real and immediate even today in Serbian consciousness.[55]

World War II saw the breakdown of this uneasy confederation. The Croats sided with the Nazis and were rewarded with their own independent state of Croatia, which they saw as a sign of God's blessing of their Catholic faith and proceeded to torture and murder hundreds of thousands of Serbs as Christian heretics. The Bosnian Muslims, though not Christian, cooperated with the Croats, seeing the Serbs as their historical enemy. Serbs joined various underground forces and fought Yugoslav Catholics and Muslims throughout the war. The civil wars and killings during the war were particularly brutal—some historians report that German military commanders themselves were shocked by the brutality between the Slavic groups—but the rise of a totalitarian Communist regime under Marshal Tito, with the support of the then–Soviet Union, worked to suppress the intergroup tensions. Tito permitted no real dissent and under his "iron fist" policy, Yugoslavia functioned, at least outwardly, as a tolerant society with little expression of religious or ethnic conflict.[56]

The death of Tito and the fall of Communism all over Europe spelled the end of the unwieldy Yugoslav state. Without totalitarian repression, the old tensions reappeared and, in 1991, the Catholic Croatians declared their secession from Yugoslavia and established the independent state of Croatia, an act encouraged by the Vatican as an exercise in Catholic rights to self-determination. The Serbs saw this as a betrayal and serious loss of national power and a civil war again ensued in which thousands were killed and displaced before an armistice was reached. In 1992, the Muslims in Bosnia-Herzegovina followed the Croatian example and declared their own state, precipitating another and more fierce civil war. The Orthodox Christian Serbs, through their historical lens, saw the Muslim move to independence as the recapitulation of their past humiliations at the hands of the Muslim Turks in the fourteenth and fifteenth centuries. For the Serbs, this was not a straightforward political challenge but a Muslim drive against Orthodox Christianity. The Bosnian Muslims were attempting, warned the Serb leaders, to spread Islam all over Europe, and although there was no evidence for this, the Serbs claimed that the Muslims were planning a Muslim theocracy in the region with women forced to wear head coverings, Christianity outlawed, and Christian churches destroyed. The Serbs protested that European civilization was in danger if the Muslim state was permitted to continue.[57]

Serbs in Bosnia formed militias to fight the Muslims and the soldiers defined the battle as a war not only to win back Bosnia for Serbia but also to finally teach the Muslims a lesson and avenge their defeat at the hands of the advancing Muslim forces in 1389. Slobodan Milosevic, the president of Serbia, called for "ethnic cleansing," a planned campaign to rid Serbian areas of all non-Serbs, Muslims, Croats, and other Catholic minorities. The campaign was horrific; rape, torture, and murder of civilians were commonplace. Hundreds of mosques were destroyed and bombings and sniper attacks on Muslim and Catholic neighborhoods were not uncommon. One particularly grim incident occurred in the Bosnian town of Prijedor, where Muslim prisoners were forced to bow as if in prayer to the holy city of Mecca and then clubbed to death. Over one thousand Muslim fighters, calling themselves *mujahadin*, fighters for God, came from various countries to help their religious brethren. With casualties growing every day and under enormous international pressure, NATO forces attacked Serbian positions in April 1994, forcing a cessation of most of the fighting and leading to a cease-fire.[58]

The fighting between Serbs and Muslims, however, continued in the Serbian province of Kosovo, the site of many ancient churches, the burial ground of saints, and the place where the decisive battles with the Muslim Turks occurred.[59] Kosovo is the

Serbian holy land, the Jerusalem, Rome, and Mecca of the Serbian Church, sanctified in Serbian telling by the heroic defense and sacrifice of life by the Orthodox Serbian Christian defenders of the province against the attack on Christian Europe in the never-to-be-forgotten battle of 1389. The bulk of the population of Kosovo now, however, is Muslim, mainly Albanian Muslims who have moved to Kosovo over the last decades as the Serbs have left this poor and undeveloped area for the more cosmopolitan areas of the country. The Serbs wanted to expel the Albanian Muslims from what they consider their holy land and fighting broke out between Serb militias and the Albanians fighting under the banner of the Kosovo Liberation Army. This war, too, caused much suffering on both sides and a fragile peace now is in place under the auspices of United Nations forces that patrol the area.

The tensions, grievances, and prejudices, however, continue. The Serbs believe the international community, particularly the European community and the United States, has let them down by refusing to recognize their just cause and considerable sacrifices on behalf of the Christian West. Muslims and Croats see the Serbs as aggressors who refuse to recognize the political realities of the twenty-first century and base their worldview on dubious myths of the past. There is relative peace in the region now, but none of the parties believes the conflict is over. Each side is convinced of its utter righteousness and the iniquity of the others. The "Balkan ghosts," in Robert Kaplan's apt words, are waiting for another day.

The question, however, remains: Are these conflicts religious or something else? Some commentators insist that the Yugoslavian wars are pure examples of the violence which religion breeds. Most reports in the American press, even in journals sympathetic to religion, reported the conflict and violence as, at best, a case of religion gone wrong. One commentator in a Texas newspaper, in shock at the carnage of the war, concluded: "The Slavs are of the same race. They look alike, live alike, talk the same language, bleed the same color. Only their religion divides them. And that may be history's greatest irony. We hate in the name of what should teach us to love."[60] Paul Mojzes, in his useful book, *Yugoslav Inferno: Ethnoreligious Warfare in the Balkans*, makes the point that the wars are both ethnic and religious.[61] Each church or religion in the conflict links itself with the political state and with ethnic history, and this reinforces the ancestral enmities. The historian Peter Black agrees, explaining that in the Balkan situation, unlike the situation in the United States, "religious identification becomes part of national identity expressed through language and communication of national myth. Thus being Orthodox is part of being Serbian."[62] Clearly, any analysis of these types of violence requires an understanding of the religious dimensions of national and societal life. The civilizational perspective on violence and conflict calls for greater sensitivity to the continuing hold of religious sensibilities, traditions, and memories in the worldview of societies, governments, and civilizations throughout the world. Politicians, diplomats, and statesmen who fail to recognize the continuing force of civilizational and religious loyalty will woefully misinterpret many issues of war and peace.

Notes

1. Samuel P. Huntington, *The Clash of Civilizations and the Remaking of World Order* (New York: Simon and Schuster, 1996), 43.
2. Huntington, *Clash of Civilizations*, 40–48.
3. See Huntington, *Clash of Civilizations*, 267–298, for a consideration of the dynamics of civilizational conflict.
4. See Jasminka Udovicki and James Ridgeway, eds., *Yugoslavia's Ethnic Nightmare: The Inside Story of Europe's Unfolding Nightmare* (New York: Lawrence Hill Books, 1995). Also see Mark Mizower, *The Balkans: A Short History* (New York: Random House, 2000).
5. Hans Gerth and C. Wright Mills, eds., *From Max Weber* (New York: Oxford University Press, 1958), 77–128.
6. See the extensive investigative report on the September 11 hijackers in *Frontline: Inside The Terrorist Network*, prod. and dir. Ben Loeterman, 60 min., PBS Video, 2002. See also Peter L. Berger, *Holy War, Inc.: Inside the Secret World of Osama bin Laden* (New York: Free Press, 2001), 24–40.
7. Interview with Daniella Weiss in PBS film series PBS film, *The*

Glory and Power, Part 2: This Is My Land, prod. Jane Treays, 58 min., PBS Video, 1992.

8. Huntington, *Clash of Civilizations*, 19–39.

9. Robert D. Kaplan, *Balkan Ghosts: A Journey Through History* (New York: Vintage, 1994). See also Huntington, *Clash of Civilizations*, particularly 270–272.

10. James A. Haught, *Holy Hatred* (Amherst, N.Y.: Prometheus, 1995), 61–71, 166–167.

11. Ira Silverman, "An American Terrorist," *New Yorker*, August 5, 2002, 26.

12. See Isabel Hilton, "Letter from Kashmir," *New Yorker*, March 11, 2002, 64–75. See also Ved Vehta, *Portrait of India* (New Haven: Yale University Press, 1970), 123–160.

13. "India and Pakistan: Dicing With Armageddon," *Economist*, May 18–24, 2002, 39–40.

14. Jack Hawley, "Pakistan's Longer Border" (paper presented at the conference, "Understanding Religious Violence," St. Bartholomew's Church, New York, N.Y., February 2002).

15. Somini Sengupta, "After Riots, Some Muslims Fear for Their Future in India," *New York Times*, March 21, 2002, sec. A, p. 10.

16. Hilton, "Letter From Kashmir."

17. Christopher Jaffrelot, *The Hindi Nationalist Movement in India* (New York: Columbia University Press, 1996). See also "Ayodhya: India's Religious Flashpoint," http://edition.cnn.com/2002/world/asiapcf/south/12/06/ayodhya.background [accessed June 30, 2003].

18. Hawley, "Pakistan's Longer Border." Hawley explains the confrontation as a religious battle as a larger religious civilizational confrontation which has no neat political solution.

19. See Ron Hassner, "Charismatic Authority and the Management of Religious Conflict" (paper, presented at the Society for the Scientific Study of Religion, Salt Lake City, November 2002).

20. Ted Olsen, "Two Hostages Die in Attempted Missionary Rescue in Mindanao," www.christianitytoday.com/ct/2002/122/51.0.html [accessed June 29, 2003]; "Jehovah's Witnesses Beheaded in Philippines," Guardian Unlimited, August 22, 2002, www.guaradian.co.uk. Also see the report on Abu Sayyaf prepared by the Council of Foreign Relations on www.terrorismanswers.com/groups/abusayyaf.html.

21. Huntington, *Clash of Civilizations*, 252–258.

22. Haught, *Holy Hatred*, 107–115.

23. See "Muslims in Western Europe," *Economist*, August 10, 2002, 21–22, for a report on the situation on conflict in Western Europe.

24. Seymour Martin Lipset, *The First New Nation: The United States in Historical and Comparative Perspective* (New York: Norton, 1979).

25. Huntington, *Clash of Civilizations*, 184.

26. Huntington, *Clash of Civilizations*, 183–206.

27. Peter L. Berger, *Facing Up to Modernity: Excursions in Society, Politics, and Religion* (New York: Basic Books, 1977). See also Bruce Lawrence, *Defenders of the Faith: The Fundamentalist Revolt against the Modern Age* (Columbia: University of South Carolina Press, 1995), chap. 1; Karen Armstrong, *The Battle for God* (New York: Alfred A. Knopf, 2000), 135–232.

28. Martin E. Marty and R. Scott Appleby, "Conclusion: An Interim Report on a Hypothetical Family" in *Fundamentalism Observed*, ed. Martin E. Marty and R. Scott Appleby (Chicago: University of Chicago, 1991), 814–842.

29. Armstrong, *The Battle for God*, particularly 317–372.

30. Huntington, *Clash of Civilizations*, 254–258. See also Bernard Lewis, *What Went Wrong? Western Impact and Middle Eastern Response* (New York: Oxford University Press, 2000); Geneive Abdo, *No God but Allah: Egypt and the Triumph of Islam* (New York: Oxford University Press, 2000), chaps. 1 and 2.

31. Haught, *Holy Hatred*, 81–94.

32. Haught, *Holy Hatred*.

33. See Abdo, *No God but Allah*, 41–70, for a portrait of the process of Islamic traditionalization in Egypt.

34. Abdo, *No God but Allah*, 47.

35. Abdo, *No God but Allah*, 94.

36. Abdo, *No God but Allah*, esp. chap. 1; Khurshid Ahmad, "The Nature of Islamic Resurgence" in *Voices of Resurgent Islam*, ed. John L. Esposito (Oxford University Press, 1983).

37. Abdo, *No God but Allah*, chap. 1.

38. Samuel Heilman, *Defenders of the Faith* (Berkeley and Los Angeles: University of California Press, 2000) for an ethnograhic report on the Haredi community.

39. Ehud Sprinzak, *Brother Against Brother: Violence and Extremism in Israeli Politics From Altalena to the Rabin Assassination* (New York: Free Press, 1999), 87–113.

40. Posters in Haredi neighborhoods are a way of communicating rabbinical edicts to the population.

41. Armstrong, *Battle For God*, 202–214.

42. James Davison Hunter, *Culture Wars: The Struggle to Define America* (New York: Basic Books, 1992).

43. Nancy Tatom Ammerman, *Bible Believers: Fundamentalists in the Modern World* (New Brunswick, N.J.: Rutgers University Press, 1987), 72–102. Marty and Appleby, "Conclusion," 814–842.

44. Morris Dees with James Corcoran, *Gathering Storm: America's Militia Threat* (New York: Harper Collins, 1996); Kerry Noble, *Tabernacle of Hate: Why They Bombed Oklahoma City* (Prescott, Canada: Voyageur, 1998); Mark Juergensmeyer, *Terror in The Mind of God: The Global Rise of Religious Violence* (Berkeley and Los Angeles: University of California Press, 2000), 19–35.

45. Jonathan Fox, "The Ethnic-Religious Nexus: The Impact of Religion on Ethnic Conflict," *Civil Wars* 3, no. 3 (2000): 1–22.

46. John Ardagh, *Ireland and the Irish: Portrait of a Changing Society* (London: Hamish Hamilton, 1994).

47. Huntington, *Clash of Civilizations*, 268–272; Kaplan, *Balkan Ghosts*, 3–48.

48. See Padraig O'Malley, *The Uncivil Wars: Ireland Today* (Boston: Beacon Press, 1997) for an informative history of the Irish question in a sociological and political context.

49. Haught, *Holy Hatred*, 61–71.

50. "Army and Police Keep Order at Protestant March," *New York Times*, July 8, 2000, sec. A, p. 6; "Weapons Cache Found," *New York Times*, July 8, 2000, sec. A, p. 6.

51. Ardagh, *Ireland and the Irish*, 157–234.

52. Haught, *Holy Hatred*, 70.

53. Ardagh, *Ireland and the Irish*, 345–436.

54. Haught, *Holy Hatred*, 25–28.

55. Udovicki and Ridgeway, *Yugoslavia's Ethnic Nightmare*. This book contains a series of insightful essays analyzing the conflict in historical perspective.

56. See Denis Denitch Bogdan, *Ethnic Nationalism: The Tragic Death of Yugoslavia* (Minneapolis: University of Minnesota Press, 1994).

57. See Paul Mojzes, *Yugoslavian Inferno: Ethnoreligious Warfare in the Balkans* (New York: Continuum, 1994).

58. Haught, *Holy Hatred*, 31–39.

59. Noel Malcolm, *Bosnia: A Short History* (New York: New York University Press, 1994), 234–252.

60. Former Rep. Jim Wright quoted in Haught, *Holy Hatred*, 73.

61. Mojzes, *Yugoslavian Inferno*.

62. Quoted in www.religioustolerance.org/curr_war.htm [accessed July 27, 2002].

5

Religious Suffering, Martyrdom, and Sexual Violence

Religion is an imperialistic institution. It not only demands the conventional loyalties and commitments of mind and soul, but it also claims proprietorship over the physical being of the faithful. The physical body, in religious thinking, is not something over which the individual has final authority but is subject to the rules and regulations of religion. The idea that body, which in modern society is considered the unique property of the individual over which only the individual has jurisdiction, is rejected by religious theology. The physical body, like everything else in creation, is ultimately a religious matter and is to be used and even abused in the interest of the religious community. All religions insist on what can be called the "corporeality of faith," on the right and duty of religion to call upon the faithful to show religious obedience by enacting their faith in physical acts of commitment, self-sacrifice, and violence. Central to understanding this genre of violence is what we shall term the perspective of the corporeality of religious violence.

The central liturgical statement in Judaism, the *Shema Yisrael*, contains an affirmation of the absolute oneness of God followed by a commitment to love God and be willing to offer one's body, soul, and property to the Lord.[1] The offering of the body and the acknowledgment that the body is but a divine property and rightfully to be directed by religious goals is powerfully expressed during the high holiday services when the Jewish worshipers appeal for mercy and blessing for the coming year by proclaiming that "body and soul" they belong to God.[2] The Islamic tradition, too, calls for the dedication of all one's faculties and physical being to the Muslim faith and community. The Muslim faithful acknowledge the right of the religious community to impose physical punishment and to call upon believers, in exceptional circumstances, to offer their very life in defense of Islamic truth, faith, and society. Christianity encourages greatly the life of the spirit and imposes prohibitions on sensual and bodily pleasures, urging followers to minimize and transcend carnal expressiveness. This is not to say that Christianity demands asceticism, but it places great value upon avoiding bodily temptations and accepting pain and suffering as sacred activity and promises religious rewards to those who do so. God, in Christian thinking, is best known and served through transcending the material and earthly. In Christianity, too, self-sacrifice for God and the community is exalted. Some Eastern religions like Hinduism and certain movements in Buddhism actively encourage asceticism and violence against the body as a means of purification and as the distinct means to enlightenment. In these Eastern traditions, there is a great dichotomy between the inferior nature of the body and the moral superiority of the purely spiritual and nonmaterial. Death is frequently portrayed as a release from a corrupting physicality to an elevated level of being.[3]

Religious institutions are uniquely suited to demand rights over the bodies of the faithful and to inflict pain and impose violence upon their followers. Religions are the ultimate definers of reality—what religion claims as truth is truth for the genuine believer—and they can, therefore, define their regulations, limitations, and expectations regarding the body, severe and horrific as outsiders might view them, as appropriate and fully justified. This is so because religion need not appeal to any other authority for legitimating their rules, for they are, at least for the faithful, the final and ultimate authority acting with divine sanction. Consequently, religion can insist on relatively minor bodily pain like fasting or rightfully demand bodily mutilation; finally, it can ordain murder, death, and suicide in pursuit of religious goals. Religions promise salvation and claim that it is their singular regimen of religious prescription that will ensure the benefits of salvation and eternal life. Max Weber, the great sociologist of comparative religion, explained that the monopolistic claim to provide religious benefits exercises a "psychic coercion" on believers, leading them to undertake acts of self-denial and self-mortification that they would ordinarily never consider.[4] The promises of salvation are so desirable and the power of religious socialization so extensive that believers will do hurtful things to their bodies, in the belief that the pain and violence will lead to eternal salvation. Put differently, faithful believers will accept all sorts of pain, abuse, and violence in the religious realm that they would not tolerate in the ordinary secular, workaday world. Therefore, our entire discussion in this chapter must be undertaken with the awareness that what may be seen as abuse or criminal violence in a secular setting or in a contemporary academic study could be seen from a particular religious believer's point of view as religious duty having beneficent consequences not understood by outsiders. John Hall, following Max Weber's analysis of rationality, explains that there is a "cultural logic" to religious violence, meaning that for believers the violence and pain will lead to the desirable and, for them, "rational" goal of salvation and union with the divine.[5]

Routine Violence, Sacred Pain, and Religious Masochism

We often think of religious violence as extraordinary, something unusual, brought about by collective religious or political tensions and stresses. Frequently, this is the context of violence. There is also a great deal of self-inflicted "pain and suffering" in religious life that is ordinary and habitual. This self-inflicted pain and suffering is an essential part of the prescribed ritual life incumbent upon members. Fasting, for example, is an essential element in many of the world's religions. Islam calls for a fast during daylight during the Islamic holy month of Ramadan. While special dispensations are made for the ill, elderly, and others whose life would be endangered by the fast, the month-long daylight fast, particularly during the years when Ramadan, calculated by the lunar calendar, occurs in summer, is difficult and physically painful. For the extremely pious and for members of mystical sects of Sufism, there are longer periods of retreats and fasting—some versions with minimal food intake lasting as long as forty days—involving complete isolation from normal society and absolutely no contact with any other person. These retreats, as the German Muslim psychologist Michaela Ozelsel shows in her wonderfully insightful book, *Forty Days*, are extremely physically demanding and full of pain and suffering. They are days of near starvation, nausea, hallucinations, and fainting, but for the believer these days are also days of transcendent joy, union with the divine, and quantum spiritual and psychological growth. On the twenty-sixth day of her forty-day *halvet*, or period of absolute isolation and stringent fasting, Ozelsel is, in her words, "near bottom." She is barely conscious, weak from lack of food, unable to read or even concentrate on her prayers, but, being the believer she is, she welcomes the suffering as an opportunity for authentic awareness and insight. Ozelsel speaks in the idiom of Sufi Islam, but the experience she describes is typical for all rituals of religious self-affliction.

> Suddenly at the height of my despair, I realize with absolute certainty that all my strivings, which has taken so many different forms over the course of my life, was nothing but striving for Allah. The forms were nothing but veils. Although this sudden knowledge is unmistakably firm within me, it is still only *ilm al-yaqin* or rational knowledge. Oh, if I could become *ayn al-yaqin!* If I could feel in my heart what I now know so surely in my head. Let this be my only prayer.[6]

Judaism similarly has a host of fast days. While exemptions for the ill are available, the religious norm is to persist in completing the fast despite physical pain. Contemporary Christianity has a more attenuated repertoire of fast days, but the tradition of fasting continues in monasteries and in intentional Christian communities throughout the world. Mourning practices in many religions also prescribe severe limitation on food intake, sexual interaction, and other bodily pleasures, including bathing or changing clothes. For the pious in many religions there are special pilgrimage regimens to sacred sites which include physical pain and suffering, which are seen as necessary to further religious understanding and commitment. Trips in the desert, to difficult-to-reach mountain sites, or to deserted areas where holy events are alleged to have taken place are essential aspects of religion. Believers often describe these journeys as life giving, as something they have waited for all their lives. Their accounts, such as that of an American Muslim on his hadj to Mecca, show that although the events are inspiring to the faithful, they can also be fraught with physical danger.[7]

Hinduism particularly has a full regimen of pilgrimages which involve routine and continuing pain and suffering. One of the famous Hindu pilgrimages is that to Sabari Malai marking the path of the god Lord Ayyappan, son of Shiva, in his encounter with a beautiful demon. The pilgrims follow Ayyappan's forty-mile journey, during which they promise to be celibate, eat or drink little, and, most arduous of all, walk on the heated ground all forty miles barefoot. Most of the pilgrims end up having lacerated feet, severe blisters, and foot and leg sprains. Again, this suffering and assault on the body are not seen as a violation of the body but as *bhakti*, service and devotion and mystical union with Lord Ayyappan.[8]

Many of these devotional acts of self-deprivation and self-inflicted pain do not involve serious danger or violence, but in some religious settings, the rituals and celebrations take on more extreme forms and become increasingly violent. Ariel Glucklich, a psychologist who studied the variety of painful and dangerous religious rituals all over the world, describes a Catholic Easter ritual practice in the Philippines in which pious volunteers are nailed to crosses and lifted above the crowd in an enactment of the death of Jesus. In Shia Islam, as practiced in Iran, for example, the faithful enact the martyrdom of Hussein at Karbala by beating themselves until they bleed to honor their sacred version of Muslim history. Medieval Christians would sometimes commit suicide through ritual fasting, which they undertook as a mode of self-purification to avoid falling sway to the temptations of Satan. Christian Scientists and some other Christian groups refuse to allow certain medical procedures to be performed, preferring to die or even to let their children die—often against civil law—in order to remain faithful to their religious teachings.[9]

Simon Weil, a French Jewish Catholic convert and philosopher who endorsed self-mutilation and engaged in extensive ritual fasting and self-denial, referred lovingly to these types of self-inflicted suffering as "affliction," as acts of serving and glorifying God, as "imitatio dei," participating with Christ in his Crucifixion on the cross.[10] Weil may have been unusually welcoming of suffering and pain, but all religions share this sense of the desirability and worthiness of pain and suffering. Pope John Paul II, in a commentary on the epistles of Saint Paul where Paul talks about the Christian's joy in suffering, remarks that "suffering seems to belong to man's transcendence."[11] Pain to the body, in this view, is not something to be avoided or that needs justification, it is a way of serving and participating in God's work. Judaism, though opposed to ascetic denial, also speaks of the power of pain and suffering as a way of expiating past sins and as a means of purification. Collective suffering of the Jewish people is not to be seen as arbitrary or accidental but is to be viewed as *yesurim shel ahavah*, literally, afflictions of love brought by God for the spiritual improvement of the community of Israel.[12] Pain and suffering, terrible as it might appear, is also, for Judaism, an occasion for service, dedication, and even happiness. Some religions, such as Hinduism and some types of Buddhism, see the routine denial of the body as a higher form of consciousness and accord special and honorable status to those who most forthrightly take up practices and lifestyles which result in self-denial and self-affliction. The religious virtuosi in Hinduism and Buddhism who live highly ascetic lives, almost completely removed from human contact and physical pleasures, who allow their bodies to undergo consistent and routine pain and self-mutilation, are the exemplars to be honored, adored, and followed.

Rite-of-passage rituals are, par excellence, the arena where religion demonstrates its rights over the body, demanding pain, suffering, and occasionally acts of violence. In much of modern religion, earlier rituals involving pain or torture have been dropped or made almost entirely symbolic. However, Judaism and Islam still retain circumcision as a central element in forming a Jewish or Muslim identity. Although female circumcision is not an essential element of Islam, some Asian and African Muslim communities similarly insist on some form of this practice. These rituals, although not intended to be brutal, do involve cutting, bloodletting, and severe pain. Religion freely demands this pain as the price of being initiated into the group and showing commitment to the demands of group ritual. Religion has a great deal to offer—a divine message and eternal life—but an exchange is demanded from the young initiates, and that is to offer their physical being, their bodies, to be violently acted upon by the religious authorities. The religiously grounded pain and violence are intended to be transformative, to create a new religious being. To become full members of the religious community, adherents must make some sacrifice, suffer some violation of the body, to demonstrate the power and value of religious commitment. The significance of these rituals, as the anthropologist Roy Rappaport points out, is not the pain, hurt, or physical changes per se but the meanings attached to them. Faith and religious commitment are frequently abstract but, as Rappaport tells us, "When that sign is carved on the body the abstract is not only made substantial but immediate: Nothing can be experienced more immediately than the sensations of one's body—and if that mark is indelible, as in the case of the subincision . . . it is ever-present." The body becomes the physical exemplar of divine truth.[13]

The willingness to accept pain and violence in the name of religion and for the sake of God is part of a larger religious surrender to God and religious teachings. Peter Berger explains that all religions, in seeking to provide a theodicy, an answer and religious interpretation for human suffering, ask believers to acknowledge all human suffering as divinely ordained and to be willing to accept the routine and extraordinary pain and suffering inherent in human existence as the will of God. The essential message of religion, in this view, is that suffering and human tragedy are not random or haphazard but are rather elements in a just and benevolent divine plan whose ultimate meanings elude human beings.[14] Bodily suffering, pain, and the experience of violence and terror are indeed all in God's plan. The faithful follower of tradition, the genuine believer, the truly religious person not only does not deny God's decrees for human suffering and tragedy but actually welcomes the evil as an occasion to serve and praise God. There are, in Berger's terms, strong elements of masochism in the religious response to suffering and pain. In order to give ultimate meaning and a sacred order to life, its disappointments and tragedies as well as its joys and satisfactions, the religious faithful deny their individuality and freedom and attribute everything to the all-powerful deity. This is, as Berger argues, the typical characteristic of masochism in which the "intoxication of surrender"[15] to the all-powerful "other" reduces confusion and ambivalence as the believers, by their radical self-denial and claim to nothingness, appear to transcend their own suffering and torment.

> The masochistic surrender is an attempt to escape aloneness by absorption in an other, who at the same time is posited as the absolute and only meaning, at least in the instant when the surrender occurs. Masochism thus constitutes a curious convulsion both of man's sociality and of his need for meaning. Not being able to stand aloneness, man denies his separateness, and not being able to stand meaninglessness, he finds a paradoxical meaning in self-annihilation. "I am nothing—and therefore nothing can hurt me" or even more sharply: "I have died—and therefore I shall not die," and then: "come, sweet pain; come, sweet death"—these are the formulas of masochistic liberation.[16]

The costs are clear: the denigration of self and the willingness to suffer without complaint and the refusal to blame God for any evil or suffering. The gains, however, are considerable. In exchange for submission, the believer's life is infused with meaning and sacredness; all of life, including physical pains, mental torments, and the terrors of death, is invested with holiness and is seen as part of a continuous relationship with the all-powerful deity. Life, as Berger puts it, is invested with *nomos*, divine meaning, law, and order, and the threat of human aloneness and meaninglessness is avoided. The psychological and religious retreat into inferiority and submission is rewarded with divine union.

The religiously grounded masochistic response to the terrors and violence of the universe is enshrined in Jewish theology and is seen vividly in the biblical story of Job. God tests the faithfulness of Job, a pious, wealthy, and highly esteemed patriarch. Job is made to suffer greatly and is forced to endure a series of tragedies, losing his health, family, possessions, and social standing; but when urged to denounce or reject God for his fate, he utterly refuses. Instead, he pronounces himself to be a faithful servant of God no matter what his fate. Nothing can deter Job from his faithfulness, for even the torments which befall him only make him cling to God. At a particularly low point, he is again urged to reject God, but he announces his continuing faith and relationship. "Naked I came from my mother's womb," Job cries out, "and naked I shall return. . . . May the name of God be blessed forever" (Job 1:20). Job is the biblical hero and the prototype of the faithful believer who epitomizes religion's demand to tolerate, sometimes even welcome, pain and torture as appropriate, legitimate, and justified. Job, as the biblical hero, refuses to accept the explanations of his "friends" that God is evil and unjust. He is forever the faithful servant, obedient and trusting in the wisdom and righteousness of God and his decrees. Job's suffering is ultimately not the issue. What really matters is recognizing the majesty, glory, and legitimacy of all of God's commands.

Christianity has elaborated these biblical themes in the gospel narratives. In the Gospels, human suffering and acceptance of violent death are given the highest religious standing. God, the omnipotent and omniscient divine being, becomes human and suffers cruelty and torment, as a human person, on the cross. The suffering of Jesus on the cross is entirely unwarranted and underserved. Jesus, in the Christian narrative, is without sin and wrongdoing—he is blameless and pure—and suffers not for his sins but as an atonement for all humanity. In this way, Christianity has profoundly affected the Western understanding of human pain and suffering. If God himself surrenders his divine nature and suffers physical torture and death, does this not demonstrate the great value of suffering and relativize the meaning of suffering for ordinary mortals? In having God suffer in a human and carnal way, Christianity, perhaps more power- fully than any other religion, reclaimed human corporeality for the service of religion. Albert Camus, who deeply understands the intriguing power and psychology of the Crucifixion, ex- plains it this way:

> In that Christ had suffered, and had suffered voluntarily, suf- fering was no longer unjust and all pain was necessary. In one sense, Christianity's bitter intuition and legitimate pessimism concerning human behavior is based on the assumption that over-all injustice is as satisfying to man as total justice. Only the sacrifice of an innocent god could justify the endless tor- ture of innocence.[17]

Islam, as the most recent of the Abrahamic religions, contin- ued this biblical tradition of willing surrender and the full accep- tance of pain and suffering for the sake of religion. The very name Islam comes from the Arabic 'aslama, to submit, and Islam has a profound theology of submission and bodily offering for the sake of religion. The Koran urges believers to undertake ac- tion which they initially would not want to do because of the psychic or physical pain involved, but the Koran tells believers that no matter what the cost, following God's instructions will always result in greater reward. The key in Islam, as in the other monotheistic traditions, is not to focus on mundane reality, on secular interpretations, but to follow religious commands with- out question in the assurance that ultimate reward will come to the truly faithful. The experience of pain, the call to violence, and the experience of psychic despair—experiences which ordi- narily would be seen as negative, unwarranted, or hurtful and dangerous—are, through the prism of religious interpretation, considered to be acceptable, even desirable, and a sign of God's love and grace.

Religious Martyrdom

The apotheosis of religion's claim on the body is seen in the phenomenon of religious martyrdom. The term "martyr" was first used in connection with the early Christians in the Roman Empire who, at the threat and verdict of death, would proudly announce their Christian faith to Roman officials.[18] The early Christian martyrs would, in the words of an ancient Roman historian, "deliberately" rush forward in the presence of Roman governors and state officials announcing their fidelity to the new Christian faith—and conversely demonstrating their disloyalty to the official Roman cult—which resulted in these early Christians being beaten, tortured, and killed. The word martyr is itself of Greek origin and originally meant witness, and indeed the early Christians were engaged in witnessing to the truth of their religion, a truth they believed entirely worth dying for.[19] These early martyrs were much admired and imitated in early Roman Christendom, and the belief existed that those willing to offer "witness" would be granted a special place in the heavenly kingdom. They were dying a physical death but would be rewarded with something greater and everlasting. By the second century, the word martyr had gone beyond its original meaning of witness and had begun to be used to describe, in more general terms, an individual's willingness to sacrifice his or her life for a religious cause. From the very beginning of the phenomenon, the idea of forgiveness of sin and great eternal reward in an afterlife was attached to martyrdom. The term has been extended from its original use in early Christianity and is now used to refer to all who offer their life and well-being for the cause of God and religion. Martyrdom began as a specific Christian religious act but, in contemporary usage, also describes all religious—and sometimes even secular—individuals who are willing to suffer and die for their faith and community of believers.

Martyrdom asserts that genuine religious commitment is ultimately about honoring and glorifying God and religious truth and not about self-preservation. The martyr proudly proclaims that the human body is to used in the service of religion. An early Christian leader in Asia Minor exhorted his followers, "Desire not to die in bed, in miscarriages, or in soft fevers, but in martyrdoms, to glorify Him who suffered for you."[20] The Jewish rabbis speak of *kavod hatorah*, maintaining the honor of God's teachings, as a reason to offer one's life. Life is precious, teaches the Talmud, but at a certain point it is to be surrendered for the higher value of transcendental truth. In the case of Islam, as well, life is greatly valued and is to be enjoyed and cherished, but the call to martyrdom is present when the community of Muslim faithful is threatened or when God's revealed word is denied. Martyrdom, then, is never an individual act and is to be fully differentiated from suicide. The martyr offers his individual corporeal existence for God, but his or her action is enmeshed in an elaborate theological and sociological framework of meaning and expectations. There is an implicit expectation in martyrdom that God will respond to the great sacrifice and offering of one's life for religion by revenging the martyr's death and heavily punish the enemies who caused the martyr's death. Martyrdom is seen as an act so religiously potent that it calls upon God to intercede for his faithful followers and to grant special privileges to the martyr in the everlasting life after death. In this way, the martyr remains a living part of the community. His or her death is a testament to religious truth, an inspiration, and a means to effect a divine response to the dangers facing the religious community.[21]

Those outside the precincts of the religious community are frequently totally uncomprehending of the nature and motivation for martyrdom. One approach used by those outside the martyr's community to make sense of this seemingly incomprehensible act is to see the martyr as "brainwashed," as acting in a programmed fashion as a consequence of psychological conditioning.[22] In this view, the martyr is not choosing, out of free will, to be a martyr but is being psychologically and sometimes physically coerced by religious fanatics to undertake an act of martyrdom. The model of brainwashing is taken from the treatment of prisoners of war in the Korean and Vietnam Wars, where all sorts of psychological techniques were used to extract information with the result that even the most patriotic officers would break down under duress and give vital information to the enemy. The martyr, in this view, is put under such stress that he or she consents to die. The consent is really a function of torture and torment and is not freely given. Another view is to acknowledge that the person is consciously offering his or her life but to deny any genuine religious motivation for the act of martyrdom. The martyr, in this view, is using religion to advance his family's social and economic status—the families of contemporary martyrs being handsomely compensated—or the act of martyrdom is really a suicide undertaken out of despair but acted out for religion to make it more acceptable. When properly analyzed, argue many secular critics, the martyr will turn out to be a maladjusted and clinically depressed person. Religious martyrdom, in this view, is just a psychological rationalization for suicide. Secular writers attempt to play down the religious motivations because, in many cases, they themselves are far removed from religious sentiment and cannot imagine that educated and rational individuals would offer their lives for religion. Labeling martyrs as emotionally ill or psychologically weak also works to play down the continuing power of religion in the modern world, something many secular commentators do not want to acknowledge.

The fact of the matter is that martyrdom cannot be reduced to an act in response to brainwashing or coercion or to gain financial advantage. Surely some of these motivations may be present in certain cases, but most martyrs act out of genuine religious motivations fueled by the belief in an afterlife with wonderful rewards for their willingness to sacrifice themselves for religious ends. Martyrs are both young and old, single and married, with children or without children, highly educated or school dropouts, and there is absolutely no evidence showing any general characteristics of martyrs. Some martyrs have difficulties in life adjustment or may come from a background of poverty, but others are extremely high achievers from well-to-do, high-status families in their societies. The lead plane hijacker martyr in the World Trade Center bombing, Mohammed Atta, came from a solidly middle-class Egyptian family, as did a number of his fellow plane hijackers, and he had recently received a master's degree in urban architecture from the Hamburg Technical University in Germany where his thesis professor described him to be the best student in the program.[23] The failed English hijacker, Richard Reid, who attempted to blow up an Air France plane in 2001, on the other hand, was an unemployed school dropout.[24] Among Christian martyrs, as well, are highly educated, prominent individuals, simple peasants, and uneducated converts who, though new to the faith, are willing to martyr themselves. Jewish history is replete with the record of the martyrdom of the most distinguished Talmudic rabbis in the community, but Jewish martyrs also include those who were far removed from scholarship and a number of people and movements who martyred themselves against the will of the official religious leadership.

R. Scott Appleby, in his book *The Ambivalence of the Sacred*, draws attention to the complexity, ambivalence, and continuing attraction of martyrdom in pious religious communities.[25] The martyr acts out, in some critical ways, the deepest truths held by the group: the belief in the afterlife, in the ultimate sacredness of the group's goals, and in violence and martyrdom as legitimate means to serve and glorify God and destroy God's opponents. Martyrdom is, however, a unique form of violence seeking purely religious goals. The martyr who kills himself in a suicide mission against school children and civilians, as in the case of Hamas martyrs, or in murdering civilians praying in a mosque, as was the case with Dr. Baruch Goldstein of the Kach movement, is engaged in ritual killing and not in a personal vendetta.[26] The same Hamas movement which calls for volunteers to martyr themselves in the killing of Israeli civilians also has a highly regarded system of medical clinics and welfare organizations that help Muslims throughout large sections of the Middle East.[27] The same Dr. Goldstein who, in a self-understood act of religious martyrdom, killed twenty-nine worshipers during prayers and was then killed himself was noted for his medical compassion and his willingness to treat Muslims and Jewish patients in the West Bank city of Hebron where he lived. Martyrdom is a unique social and religious phenomenon and can be treated only in the context of religious history and theology.

Martyrdom in Christianity

Martyrdom is an important part of Christian history and theology. The early Christians, it is reported, in efforts to challenge what they took to be a pagan Roman government would regularly announce their opposition to the government, declaring their faith in the truth of the Gospels and announcing to the magistrates, "I wish to die, for I am a Christian."[28] Historians report that this voluntary martyrdom brought on by antagonism to the government was not idiosyncratic but continued for centuries with large numbers of Christians dying as martyrs. Famous early Christian martyrs include Justin Martyr, executed in the second century by Marcus Aurelius, and Saint Sebastian, killed in the third century in the Roman campaign to destroy Christianity; but historians insist that martyrdom was not at all unusual. Some ancient accounts describe scores of Christians lining up on particular days waiting to be killed as they proclaimed their Christian faith. The historian G. W. Bowersock reports that early Christian writers, even those who had reservations about martyrdom, claimed that "such conduct was widespread and, in many quarters, admired."[29]

Martyrdom continued throughout Christian history. As Christian missionaries evangelized in hostile settings, they were sometimes killed as the bearers of an alien and antagonistic religion which the indigenous peoples saw, often correctly, as an attempt to invalidate and destroy the native religions. Many narratives tell of Christian missionaries who were murdered in their desire to convert the Native Americans. Other accounts tell of Christian missionaries in India and China and among primitive tribes who died from starvation and disease or were murdered by natives who resented the missionaries' attempt to convert the natives to Christianity. The coming of the Protestant Reformation saw the emergence of a new type of Christian martyrdom in which Protestant reformers killed by the Roman Catholic Church and government authorities for their heretical beliefs were accorded martyr status by the growing Protestant denominations. Jan Hus, burned at the stake in Prague in 1415, and Michael Servetus, Heinrich Vos, and Johannes Esch were all murdered for their allegiance to innovative and reformationist religion and were considered by the Protestant reformers to be religious martyrs. There are also Catholic martyrs who were killed by fervent Protestants for their refusal to accept Protestant truth. Both traditions still maintain and teach stories of the martyrs killed by other Christians.[30]

The contemporary period still celebrates Christian martyrdom. The Second Vatican Council reiterated the continuing significance of martyrdom and proclaimed contemporary Christian martyrs as exemplifying the highest form of love and Christian witness. There can be, said the Vatican statement, no greater demonstration and Christian commitment than the martyr's willingness to sacrifice his life.[31] Perhaps the most famous recent Christian martyr was the German Pastor Dietrich Bonhoeffer, the head of an underground Christian seminary who led the Christian resistance to the Nazi regime and was executed in Flossenberg prison in April 1945.[32] Bonhoeffer was an intensely serious and pious Christian. He had deep roots in Germany but took some graduate education in the United States and was working as church pastor in England when hostilities broke out between the two countries. He was a fervent foe of Nazism and very much aware of the totalitarian, despotic, and murderous nature of the regime. He was torn between remaining in England where he was a successful pastor and returning to Germany and fighting a regime of terror in which he knew he might lose his life. This was not, for Bonhoeffer, a political or even a practical question but a religious quandary as to where his Christian duty was calling him. He wrote to the great theologian Karl Barth, who advised him, using biblical references and allusions, to return immediately to Germany. "Under no circumstances," Barth wrote to him, "should you play Elijah under the juniper tree or Jonah under the gourd and in fact you should return to your post on the next ship."[33] Bonhoeffer did immediately return to Germany where he organized virtually the only Christian resistance movement to Nazism. The critical importance of Bonhoeffer's mission was that it was a German Christian witness against Nazism and could not be viewed as a foreign or communist opposition. The German government attempted to negotiate with Bonhoeffer, to stop his speeches and opposition, and to have him join the establishment German Christian churches who were not in opposition to the Nazi regime. Bonhoeffer refused and, under the threat of imprisonment and death, continued to preach and in his words "be a Christian witness" to the evils of Nazism. He encouraged German officers to resist the regime on Christian principles and was a pastor and adviser to the small but not insignificant German opposition which tried to topple the regime. After his arrest, he wrote important works about the duty of Christians to resist evil and be willing to be martyrs as they witness to the Christian opposition to evil. The German authorities ordered him killed just days before the end of the war. An SS doctor who examined him before his execution described him as devout to the very end, "brave and composed. I have never seen a man die so actively submissive to the will of God."[34]

Contemporary Christian martyrdom still involves witnessing to the truth of Christian doctrine, but, in modern times, it has involved a willingness to identify with and serve the poor, the suffering, and the persecuted even in the face of danger to one's life. A powerful example is the case of El Salvador's Archbishop Oscar Romero, who was slain in 1980 for his public support of peasant rebels who fought against the government-backed forces that sought to stop the popular revolt. Romero knew of the danger he faced because of this support, but he spoke forcefully as the country's foremost Christian representative in support of greater economic equality. The church, he maintained, opposed the repression of the poor and powerless peasants and stood with them in their struggle. This was a Christian duty and witness, and Romero understood that this involved challenging the powerful elites in his country who finally took his life. Romero's martyrdom fused political, sociological, and religious motifs as he sought to offer his life for the betterment of the poor and underprivileged.[35]

Similar cases of Christian martyrdom occur all over the

world as missionaries working in hostile environments as relief workers, nurses, doctors, teachers, educators, or simple laborers are killed or tortured for teaching about Christianity and encouraging people to convert. These worker missionaries are aware of the dangers but are called to do their work knowing that local hostility to Christianity could result in their death. In 2002, for example, the American evangelical community mourned the death of a young American missionary nurse, Bonnie Penner, who worked in a Christian-affiliated prenatal clinic in Sidon, Lebanon, which provided care for needy local residents. The clinic was attacked by Muslim militants who objected to the missionary activity at the center, and Bonnie Penner and other Christian workers were shot as they were working in the clinic office. One local official told journalists that "the killing was the result of a hostile Muslim reaction in Sidon to the preaching" that Penner was doing to attract local youth groups to hear lectures and participate in Christian activities.[36] In spite of her good relations with the community and her work as a nurse, Penner was seen as a dangerous influence on the local community in her attempts at evangelism. Similar cases involving the murder of Christian missionaries and parishioners in Pakistan and the Philippines and other places in Asia and Africa have taken place. The attacks against Christians appear to increase when missionary efforts are successful and more local people begin attending and identifying with the Christian churches. These events are not entirely unforeseen—the missionary workers know the terrain—but their calling is to spread the gospel and bring as many people as possible to Christianity despite the personal dangers involved. In their willingness to sacrifice their lives, these modern missionaries are martyrs following in the historical tradition of martyrdom from the times of the early church.

Martyrdom is, of course, a relative concept. What one community considers legitimate martyrdom can be seen as dangerous, illegal, and criminal behavior by other groups. This is the case with some antiabortion activists who consider those who kill doctors who provide abortions as martyrs because, at the risk of their own lives and imprisonment, the gunmen "martyrs" are defending the rights and life of the unborn child. In their willingness to kill and be killed on behalf of the unborn, they uphold and defend the Christian message of the sacredness of life. They are witnesses, in this view, to the call of the gospel to sacrifice oneself for Christian truth. For example, James Kopp, the antiabortion activist who killed Dr. Barnett Slepian, a Buffalo, New York, gynecologist who provided abortions at a local clinic, as he was preparing dinner in his family home in October 1998 was considered a religious martyr by elements in the antiabortion movement. These activists provided Kopp with money and documents that enabled him to escape capture for several years. After his capture in an international FBI manhunt in France in 2001, Kopp acknowledged doing the shooting but claimed that his motives were pure and genuinely religious; as he explained, it was indeed a terrible act to shoot another human being in the privacy of his home. Kopp, however, was unrepentant about the legitimacy of his deed. "The only thing that would be worse to me," he explained, "would be to do nothing, and to allow abortions to continue."[37] Kopp and the other militant gunmen in the movement who kill abortion providers have a clarity of purpose, and they freely admit that they are ready to die for their religious convictions.

Martyrdom in Judaism

Martyrdom and the willingness to offer one's life for God has deep biblical roots in Judaism. The Hebrew Bible records the story of the patriarch Abraham, who is commanded, as a show of faith, to offer his much beloved son Isaac as a sacrifice. Both father and son willingly go along with God's directives and are ready to complete the sacrificial offering, when, at the last moment, a heavenly voice saves Isaac, substituting an animal offering. This biblical narrative, referred to in Jewish theology as *Akadath Yitzchak*, the binding of Isaac, serves as the quintessential example of true faith and has became the model for Jewish martyrdom through the ages. The binding of Isaac has come to mean that God, in his mystery and grandeur, can demand the death of the innocent and that God, at times, will desire that the faithful sacrifice their lives in honor of God's name and sacred teachings. The lesson learned from Abraham's willingness to sacrifice his beloved son is that life is not an ultimate value; rather, obedience and complete unquestioning faith in divine Providence are demanded of the faithful Jew.[38]

The message of Isaac's offering has had enormous effects on Jewish culture, history, and jurisprudence. It has set up a psychological and religious worldview in which martyrdom is readily accepted in times of crises and communal tragedies. Jewish theology has greatly admired life and has encouraged the pleasures and physical gratifications of earthly existence, but it has also made an important place for martyrdom when the Jewish community is threatened. Throughout history, Jews have seen martyrdom as a legitimate response to forced conversion or to any restrictions of their cultic and religious life. Each era in Jewish history has had its own experience with martyrdom, and all are seen as part of the unique relationship between God and the Jewish people in which Jews are continually challenged to prove their unyielding fidelity to God. Martyrdom is seen throughout the Hebrew Bible as biblical personalities like Samson offer themselves in defense of the Jewish community. The message of the biblical stories is that it is appropriate and worthy to sacrifice oneself in defense of God and his teachings.

Perhaps the most prominent example of Jewish martyrdom is the story of the mass suicides in 70 c.e. at Masada, a mountain fortification in the Judean desert. There 960 Jews—men, women, and children—were surrounded for three years by Roman soldiers during the Judean revolt. As the Romans finally breached the walls of Masada, all the inhabitants committed suicide rather than be taken prisoners. The Jewish Zealots at Masada believed that it was preferable to die as proud Jews than be the victims of rape, slavery, and conversion to Roman idolatry. The details of the final days at Masada are not entirely known, but as reported by the historian Josephus, each man was responsible for killing his own wife and children. Lots were to determine the order in which the men were killed, and the last two survivors simultaneously killed each other. The Jews at Masada also burned all the remaining food, so that when the Romans came to the mountaintop, they were greeted by the bodies of the martyrs and the fires burning all over the encampment. Josephus, who was not sympathetic to the Masada martyrs, nonetheless called attention to their religious fervor and willingness to die for religious purposes. Most peoples defeated in war with the Roman armies accepted the religion and domination of the empire, but the Jews, as Josephus explained, preferred death as martyrs to abandoning their identity and religious heritage.[39]

The Masada narrative continues to animate Jewish martyrdom, self-sacrifice, and religious nationalism. Elite units of the Israeli Defense Forces are inducted during candlelight ceremonies at Masada, where they take their oath of office in what is considered the sacred site of the Masada martyrs. The two-thousand-year-old events at Masada are used to socialize the new recruits to identify with the sacrifices made on behalf of the Jewish people so long ago and to urge that this model of self-sacrifice continue. In earlier eras, as well, Masada was the model for Jewish resistance against powerful enemies and overwhelming odds. When many Jewish communities came under attack during the Crusades the Spanish Inquisition, and the many medieval pogroms, European Jews took Masada as the ultimate model of resistance. Martyrdom, while always a minority response, gradually became the preferred rabbinical reaction to threats to religious belief and practice. Throughout the long period of medieval and early modern anti-Semitism, the martyr who refused to eat unkosher meat, violate the Sabbath, or convert to Christianity under threat of death was the religious ideal. The martyr was the Jew who demonstrated to all that death in loyalty to divine commands was preferable to a life of apostasy. Martyrdom received new meaning and potency in the European Holocaust in which millions of Jews were murdered as part of the Nazi program of genocide.[40] The view of the Jewish community is that all who were killed as Jews are to be accorded martyr status, for their deaths are ultimately religious sacrifices in loyalty to their Jewish heritage. In Jewish theological thinking they are referred to as *korbanot*, sacrifices to God, who died in honor and in "sanctification of God's name." Specially mentioned in this connection are those who took their own lives rather than compromise their religious obligation.

Religious martyrdom continues in the state of Israel, where individuals who are killed in terrorists attacks are regarded as martyrs. By living in the state of Israel in fulfillment of God's commandment to settle the Holy Land and putting themselves in danger by going about their routine activities, these people are witnesses to God's plans. These deaths are terrible and tragic, but for the believers they are a necessary element in the divine drama for the apocalypse which is fast approaching. Each of these martyrs is a sacred warrior in a battle for God and his faithful. The director of a large school in an isolated Jewish settlement in the Judean hills where several teenagers were killed or severely wounded by a Muslim gunmen explained that these children were martyrs who by their suffering will liberate the Jewish people. When asked when he would close the school because of its dangerous location, he emphasized that each student had the right to drop out but that ultimately Jewish history and destiny will be decided by the willingness of the faithful to offer themselves for their religious convictions.[41] For Judaism, both Jewish history and religious nationalism fuel the continuing emphasis on martyrdom.

Martyrdom in Islam

Religious martyrdom has a long and glorious history in Islamic theology and culture. The Islamic martyr is known as a *shahid*, literally an eyewitness who testifies to his faith in Allah by fighting and dying in religious battles against enemies of Islam. The shahid is honored for his purity of faith and is rewarded in the afterlife with eternal bliss, including all types of sensual and materialistic pleasures. The Muslim martyr by his death bestows honor upon his community and family, and they are rewarded with increased communal standing, religious prestige, and economic compensation. The shahid is willing to die for his beliefs, but his motives are to be based upon communal concerns and religious faith and never on personal distress or psychological illness. Islamic theologians, while encouraging death and religious martyrdom for religious purposes, are totally opposed to personal suicide, which they considerer a serious sin contrary to Islamic law.[42]

Throughout Muslim history, martyrs have been honored in memorial celebrations and in holy sites erected in their honor. Perhaps more than among Christians and Jews, religious martyrdom has been an essential element in Islamic religious culture. Islam sees martyrdom as a strategy to be used in religious conflict. The martyr not only resists religious coercion and apostasy but also is ready to destroy the enemies of Islam by consciously taking his or her own life. The martyr, in Islamic thinking, is related to the warrior hero who protects his community on the battlefield. The actions and death of the martyr are not only a demonstration of Muslim faith but also can serve the practical goals of attacking or destroying Islam's enemies. The martyr who gives his life in a "suicide attack" is actually an Islamic warrior, worthy of the label shahid, who is furthering religious goals that cannot be achieved by conventional means.[43] In Islamic thinking, civilians as well as military combatants may be killed in suicide missions which religious authorities have sanctioned as actions in defense of Islam. A martyr has the Muslim right and duty to attack all targets which violate the legitimate rights of the Muslim community. From the Muslim perspective, the suicide bomber who blows himself up with dynamite attached to his body to kill as many diners in an Israeli restaurant as possible, the highjacker who tries to bomb a passenger plane or the assassin who plans an attack on an enemy of Islam and is aware that he will be executed, are not guilty of suicide but are engaged in the fulfillment of the highest religious duty.

Sheik Ahmed Yassim, the charismatic leader of the Muslim fundamentalist Hamas movement, which supports suicide martyrs, explained that Muslim martyrdom is incomprehensible to Westerners because it is uniquely related to Islamic faith in the afterlife. The martyr does not think of himself or his earthly life, the sheik explained, but is focused on eternity. "The only aim is to win Allah's satisfaction. That can be done in the simplest and speediest manner by dying in the cause of Allah."[44] One would-be martyr who volunteered for a suicide mission but was unsuccessful because his bomb failed to go off explained that by "pressing the detonator you can immediately open to the door to Paradise—it is the shortest path to heaven."[45] Suicide martyrdom is not an individualistic or idiosyncratic action but a community event surrounded by religious and communal rituals. Just before the martyr leaves on his mission, he performs a series of bodily absolutions, recites prayers in the mosque asking for success in his mission, and is bid farewell by his teachers with the prayer "Allah be you with you, may Allah give you success so that you achieve Paradise." The martyr responds with the ritual *"Inshallah,* we will meet in Paradise." Later, as the martyr sets off the bomb, he intones, *"Allahu akbar,* Allah is great, all praise to him." When news of the martyr's death reaches his family and community, "the bomber's family and the sponsoring organization celebrate his martyrdom as if it were a wedding. Hundreds of guests congregate at the house to offer congratulations. The hosts serve the juices and sweets that the young man specified in his will. Often the mother will ululate in joy over the honor Allah has bestowed on her family," according to Muslim commentator Nasra Hassan.[46] Similarly, Thomas Friedman of the *New York Times* reported that Azimi Abu Hilayel, upon learning that his son Na'el had died in a suicide martyrdom operation, said, "I thanked God when I learned that my son had died in an operation for the sake of god and the homeland."[47] The mother of another suicide martyr interviewed on al-Jazeera television, the international Arabic-language news channel, said that despite her great affection for her son, she encouraged him in his martyr activities. "Our purpose is not to live. Our purpose is to seek Allah, this is our highest and most precious purpose from the day we are born to the day we leave this life." The mother acknowledged her sorrow and loss but concluded that our "lives would not be happy without the jihad—the jihad is our life."[48] Martyrdom by suicide bombing has become an integral part of contemporary Islam, and dozens of Islamic martyrdom brigades are attached to Islamic movements all over the world. One very influential and active group is the Al-Aqsa martyrs brigade affiliated with the Palestinian Fatah movement, which actively supports martyrdom attacks on civilian targets. After a complex action involving two suicide bombers who killed some thirty people at a bus station in central Tel Aviv, Israel's largest city, the al-Aqsa brigade explained that the bombers' actions had the approval of religious authorities and called the young bombers "martyrs" who blew up their "pure bodies" on behalf of Islam.[49]

Not all Islamic religious authorities are in agreement with the current emphasis on suicide martyrdom. The chief mufti of Saudi Arabia, Sheik Abd al-Aziz bin Abdallah, is opposed to suicide missions, labeling them "not jihad for the sake of Allah but pure murder." The Muslim legal scholars at al-Azhar University, perhaps the most influential center for Islamic scholarship, had previously also been opposed to suicide missions but by the year 2000 had begun to give them limited approval as a legitimate form of martyrdom. The increasingly influential *fatwas*, or religious proclamations, issued by Osama bin Laden and al-Qaeda in their quest for a worldwide jihad against the West have had considerable influence on Islamic thinkers. Much of the sentiment in Islam, has moved toward permitting suicide martyrdom. Increasingly, suicide martyrdom is permitted not only against infidels and "enemies" of Islam like Israel and America but also now are approved against Muslims like Hosni Mubarak of Egypt and Anwar Sadat before him, who are defined as infidels and therefore appropriate targets for assassination.[50] Yet despite the evidence for the ecclesiastical and popular support for suicide martyrdom missions, occasionally objections from even the most faithful Muslims appear in the Muslim press. One such objection was expressed in a letter to the editor in the influential London Arabic newspaper *Al-Hayat*. In the letter M. G. Saber, a pious Muslim and the father of a suicide bomber who carried out an attack on an Israeli city, acknowledged the significance of the shahid in Muslim religious battles but argued that suicide martyrdom as currently practiced is actually closer to suicide than martyrdom. In a stirring close to his letter, he accused the Islamic leaders of using his son and others like him as human weapons in religious struggles while the children of the leadership evade martyrdom operations. "But what tears at the soul, pains the heart, brings tears to the eyes more than anything is the sight of these sheiks and leaders evading sending their sons into the fray—such as Mahmoud Al-Zahar, Isma'il Abu Shanab and Aziz Al-Rantisi [all militant leaders of martyrdom operations]. . . . Al-Zahar sent his son Khaled to America, Abu Shanad his son to Britain, Rantisi's wife has refrained from sending her son Muhammad to blow himself up. Instead she sent him to Iraq to complete his studies there."[51]

Religious martyrdom of any type is perhaps the most difficult form of religious violence for modern secular societies to comprehend. Why die what appears to modern sensibilities to be an absurd and irrational death? Why should a believer put himself in a life-threatening situation? The martyr, in contrast, sees his or her death as immensely meaningful and fully expects a divine reward. Martyrdom also has very practical social and psychological consequences for the religious community. Acts of martyrdom demonstrate to the martyr's community, as perhaps nothing else, the validity and ultimate truth of their faith. In some unspoken way, the martyr energizes the community to remain faithful, for otherwise they betray the martyr's sacrifice. The martyr, by a powerful appeal to religious motivation, converts what may be secular, economic, or ethnic conflicts into sacred battles over truth. Martyrdom by its very nature is not open to compromise and negotiation. There are many conflicts all over the globe—Israel and Palestine, Northern Ireland, India and Pakistan, to name a few—where rational political solutions may be brokered, but the continuation of religious martyrdom casts the conflict as a search for absolute goals where compromise and political solutions are impossible. Religious martyrs, then, are much more important than their numbers would indicate because their deaths encourage and prolong conflict and violence.

Religion, Sexual Abuse, and Violence

Substantial evidence now exists of widespread sexual abuse and violence in religious communities and institutions, including the abuse of children by religious functionaries including priests, rabbis, and ministers. American media have reported that hun-

dreds of Catholic priests, some with the knowledge of their ecclesiastical superiors, have been involved for decades in the
systematic abuse and rape of minors in their church care.[52] The
scandal extended from local parish priests to bishops and cardi-
nals with international reputations. Even so prominent and distinguished a churchman as Cardinal Bernard Law of Boston was
forced to resign for transferring recidivist offenders from one
parish to another without revealing their past sexual abuse and
engaging in legal cover operations for some of the incidents.[53]
One of the most notorious cases involved the Reverend Paul R.
Shanley, an apparently popular priest in Boston who is reputed
to have seriously abused over thirty people in his church career.[54] He is now in prison, but the Boston archdiocese is accused
of permitting him to continue to have contact with children after
knowing of his misdeeds. The abuse was spread across the country and involved major urban centers as well as rural parishes.
By most estimates the church will end up paying $1 billion to
victims in legal settlements.[55]

The Catholic Church, as the nation's most visible religious
hierarchy, received the most publicity from the media, and
many commentators viewed the sex scandals as a "Catholic crisis." As the investigations and reporting of religious abuse wid-
ened to other communities, however, it became clear that other
religious institutions and organizations faced many of the same
problems. The leading national Orthodox Jewish community organization, the Union of Orthodox Jewish Congregations, was
reported to have participated in a coverup of abuse in their
youth organization for decades. A charismatic rabbi from New
Jersey, Baruch Lanner, had abused large numbers of teenagers,
both boys and girls, who were part of the youth movement he
supervised. The same rabbi was also found to have molested
teenage girls in a high school in which he was the principal.[56]
Additionally, just as the Catholic crisis was unfolding in the
media, allegations were brought to the police that the leading
cantor and teacher in New York City's most prestigious Reform
synagogue, Temple Emmanuel, was arrested on charges of
molesting students during his tutorial bar mitzvah lessons.[57]
Both liberal and conservative Christian congregations as well as

Muslim groups and new religious movements were shown to be similarly involved in sex scandals. As more and more reports were publicized, virtually every religious group was accused of some form of sexual abuse and violence. While some reports in the media overestimated the degree of abuse, mounting evidence makes it clear that sexual abuse, violence, and subsequent coverups were, and remain, a serious problem for religious communities.

The relationship between religion and sexual violence is complex and requires analysis and interpretation of the unique link between theology and social organization. However, while most analysts and commentators are shocked and pained by the prevalence of reports of religious sexual abuse—particularly, of children and young people—most view the abuse as the result of psychological malfunctioning or mental illness on the part of the adult perpetrator. The abuse, in this view, is not a problem of religion per se but of the actions carried out by mentally ill individuals. Another version of this understanding sees the problem as a lack of supervision and a failure to properly train religious officials in how to deal responsibly with the children or young adults in their care. Better training, formal procedures, psychological testing, and better supervision, according to this approach, will effectively deal with the epidemic of abuse in religious life. There is merit in these understandings, but they fail to take into account the unique nature of religious institutional life, which operates according to its own rationales and normative patterns based on a religion's understanding of its sacred missions and obligations, which are different from those outside the religious community.

To understand the nature of the relationship between religion and sexual violence, one must appreciate religion's understanding of its special place in human societies. As discussed earlier in this chapter, the individual's worldly existence and well-being are not central to religious goals. Religion places what it asserts are divine goals over and above individual happiness and well-being. In this theological understanding, it is the church and the ecclesiastical leadership, flawed as they may be, that must be protected, for the church and its representatives ultimately will ensure that God's will is done. Put simply, in the larger scheme of things, while religious authorities are not unsympathetic to, or unconcerned about, victims of abuse, the protection and standing of religion and the clergy must take precedence over such concerns and allegations of abuse.

Consequently, scholars of religion have argued that the prevalence of sexual abuse in religious life is not incidental or merely the result of individual deviance but can be traced to certain structural realities of religious institutions. Chief among these factors: (1) the religious leadership cadre as a sacred elite, (2) religion and secrecy, (3) religious ideology, and (4) religious socialization.

A Sacred Elite

The ecclesiastical leadership in all religious systems sees itself as a specially constituted spiritual cadre who are called to be God's representatives on earth, and it is they who are entrusted to carry out the divine mandate. These groups, in their understanding, constitute a sacred elite with esoteric knowledge of the divine will and a unique and intimate relationship with God as result of their special study, ordination, or charismatic leadership. In their roles as ministers, priests, rabbis, imams, or gurus, they conduct rituals such as masses and prayer meetings; their expertise enables to them to render religious decisions and verdicts; and it is they who pass on the tradition to the next generation, making religious life and continuity possible. Their mission is so important and central to religious life, in their self-understanding, that the normal rules governing everyday life do not necessarily apply to them. They can be forgiven their misdeeds because of their contribution to religion. Their exalted status places them, particularly for the young and innocent, beyond suspicion; the assumption is that what they do is probably appropriate. It is psychologically difficult for the faithful laity and even for religious officialdom to question the activities of the religious elite.

The events surrounding the trial and conviction of Rabbi Baruch Lanner highlighted years of abusive practices that the teenagers in his organization refused to report. The event also demonstrated the refusal of many in the rabbinate and in his organization to dismiss him or even to acknowledge the problem when it was reported to them. Lanner had been accused of impropriety for years and evidence of his activities was mounting, but religious authorities had regularly exonerated him, sometimes with knowledge of the offending behavior, or minimized the nefariousness of the behavior. It was only through the activities of a prominent investigative journalist, Gary Rosenblatt, that he was dismissed and charges brought against him. Many of those interviewed by Rosenblatt conceded Lanner might have been doing these things but more or less exonerated him because he was a distinguished scholar of Talmudic law who had a gift for working with children and brought many of them to affiliate with Orthodox Judaism. He was also a charismatic and successful fund-raiser. Lanner was so valuable and such an insider member of the Orthodox Jewish clerical elite that he could get away with the abuse. In other words, he was treated and evaluated according to the norms reserved for the sacred elite, whose religious status matters more than their deviant behavior.[58]

Such treatment also occurs in other religious communities. Father Bruce Ritter, for example, the charismatic founder of the successful Catholic Convent House organization for drug rehabilitation and runaway teens, was an immensely popular priest and administrator but during his tenure routinely abused young males in his charge.[59] The charges were for a long time not accepted and were explained as stemming from the psychological problems of disturbed youth who were homeless or abused from childhood. It took an investigation, again by outside sources, and reports of financial improprieties to get Ritter fired. He never entirely admitted his guilt and was finally sent for rest and meditation to a Catholic retreat center. His accomplishments were lauded and his problems explained away when he resigned and left the center. This same situation occurs in many cases of clerical abuse in other religions; a protective wall of silence and clerical camaraderie denies accusers the right to be taken seriously and permits a double standard to exist, one for the laity and another for the religious elite.

A Secret Society

A consequence of the religious hierarchy's view of itself as a sacred elite is its organization and functioning as a secret society. In this view, the decisions and deliberations of ordained, anointed, or charismatic leaders who are responsible for the reputation and financial well-being of the institution are rightfully to be kept out of the public eye. Outsiders, including the laity and governmental officials, have no real legitimacy to pass judgment or make policy. Religious policy and decisions related to religious personnel can be decided only by an inner group of elite leaders who can be trusted to place the concerns of the religious community above all else, including individual rights, the legal system, or even the lower clergy. Sexual abuse and violence within religious institutions, abhorrent and sinful as they may be, are not necessarily to be reported to secular authorities. This does not mean that the particular religion approves of these nefarious activities but, rather, that the punishments for, and the publicity about, them need to be controlled by religious authorities to protect the institution's larger spiritual goals and social activities.

Again, the religious hierarchy acts as a secret society not in support of the sinner but in full consciousness of the need to fulfill what it takes to be the mission of religion. Traditional Judaism, for example, condemns homosexuality. Yet cases of homosexual abuse in Jewish seminaries and elementary school yeshivas, while condemned, are rarely reported. Even in cases of parental and community protests, the rabbinical hierarchy has dealt with the problem internally, refusing to report the abuse. Both in the United States and in Israel, the rabbis argued that while the actions should be condemned, the fragile standing of traditionalism in these societies made it necessary not to publicize the cases. In one celebrated case, the teenage child of a prominent family was abused, but the world's leading traditionalist rabbi at the time ordered them not to press charges "so that the words and teaching of the Torah not be sullied." The position of the rabbinical leadership was that when the honor of the Torah community, *kavod hatorah*, is threatened by such disclosures, individual concerns and grievances must be set aside.[60] Catholic bishops first responded in a similar way to the revelation of abuse in their institutions. This was to be a matter for the church elders to decide according to internal religious policies. Only when the crisis appeared to become uncontrollable did the policy shift to require that the secular authorities be immediately informed. Church conservatives, to this time, disagree with this policy on the theological ground that the church is a society apart from civil law.[61]

Secrecy is also to be used to protect those values and sexual mores which are just and appropriate theologically in the group's religious universe of meaning but are inappropriate, disapproved, or illegal in secular civil society. The details of ecclesiastical laws related to sexual practices and norms are sometimes not shared with outsiders in the belief that they will be met with ridicule or recognized as a form of abuse or violation of law. The specific religious guidelines regarding marital relations between husbands and wives in fundamentalist movements, for instance, are so male oriented by contemporary standards that fundamentalist churchgoers do not want to share their religious understanding of marriage, lest they be accused of abuse. Islam, as well, has norms and understandings regarding male-female interaction that are considered inappropriate or even abusive by secular standards. Several authors report that from a Muslim point of view, as prescribed in sharia, it is very difficult for a woman to prove a case of rape. Rape is clearly proscribed by Islam, but Islamic law and culture have made it difficult to prove in Islamic court. The author V. S. Naipaul reports a case in Pakistan, which is not unique, in which a Muslim holy man, a *pir*, could not be convicted for raping the fourteen-year-old daughter of one of his followers, because under Islamic law four eyewitnesses to the crime are required.[62]

Religious Ideology

A significant element in understanding the persistence of abuse in religious contexts is the role of religious belief and ideology.

Carolyn Holderread Heggen, a Christian therapist, in her essay "Religious Beliefs and Abuse" argues that strongly held religious beliefs concerning men and women could create an environment of abuse and function to justify abuse on religious grounds. Heggen argued that the biblical creation narrative in Genesis 2 is used not only by Christians but also by Islam and Judaism to justify male dominance and "women's secondary and subordinate nature to man because she was created after and from him."[63] Heggen and other scholars claim that patriarchy emerges directly from the biblical account and that "the inherent logic of patriarchy says that since men have the right to dominate and control, they also have the right to enforce that control. It is this overall component of patriarchy and its assumptions of ownership of women and children by men that make it vulnerable to violence and abuse." She concludes that the implication of the biblical view is that "God intends men to dominate and women submit."[64] Indeed, in all the traditional biblical religions, this view of men and women remains dominant. Some liberal or post-Christian groups reinterpret the Bible as a narrative of equality between the genders, but Heggen is correct in describing the prevalent view as justifying male authority, domination, and power over women. This theologically based attitude does not mean, of course, that all the faithful are abusers, but the biblical story of Eve as the bearer of sin does serve to foster relationships and attitudes which result in abuse and violence. To those outside the religious community, these narratives do not carry the gravity and immediacy they have for believers who take these events as guidelines for current behavior. For the faithful, these biblical events are not merely tales and parables but instructions on how to live the good life.

There are also other theological themes regarding suffering, sin, and the afterlife that make sexual abuse, however painful and traumatic, tolerable and meaningful for those living in religious societies which encourage great piety and religious commitment. Religions of all types function primarily as institutions which provide succor for people in distress, help societies create meaning, and justify the inequities and pain inherent in human existence. In this regard, theological explanations of sin, suffering, and the afterlife all function to make the human experience of disappointment, pain, and ultimate death more acceptable by giving religious and ultimate meaning to human life. Suffering, therefore, is transmuted from a merely human experience to service in religious dedication and faith. Sexual abuse as well can be, incorrectly, made acceptable both to the victim and to others as another form of legitimate religious suffering and expiation.[65] Women, particularly, in religious history have been encouraged to endure suffering as a sign of religious devotion, and this has included the persistence of the toleration of abuse. One pious Christian woman who suffered thirty years of abuse in her marriage put it this way: "The one advantage of my husband's abuse is that I don't expect to spend long in purgatory after I die; I am already refined and prepared for heaven by my years of hell on earth."[66]

Some religious ideologies are somewhat tolerant of some types of abuse while prohibiting others. In some religions, sexual violence against enemy women, prostitutes, and other women who are defined as immoral, or even unattached, is not met with serious objection. Some Catholic researchers, for example, studying sexual offenders explain the high incidence of child and male molestation among the Catholic clergy as a consequence of the theological distinction between being "unchaste" and not actually violating priestly vows of chastity, which would be the case in an adult heterosexual interaction. The *New York Times* on November 12, 2002, reported that "some priests relied on this distinction to rationalize to their victims, the authorities or church superiors that mutual masturbation, fellatio or touching of children's bodies, however wrong, left their celibacy vow intact."[67]

Religious Socialization

Donald Capps, a professor at Princeton Theological Seminary, in his essay "Religion and Child Abuse: Perfect Together" argues that the religious socialization of children leads to child abuse.[68] Capps's position is that religion demands, above all, behavioral conformity, and religious parents coerce children, sometimes with abuse and violence, to obediently follow the path of religious conformity, frequently to their own detriment. Capps's essay has been criticized for its indictment of religious socialization as excessively focused on punishment, guilt, and repression, which Capps sees as leading to character maladjustment and faulty interpersonal relationships. Be that as it may, Capps calls important attention to the role of the religious factor in mediating and continuing sexual prejudice, abuse, and violence. The socialization to obedience, so valued in religious society, while it produces respectful and well-behaved children who do not question adult authority, also encourages repression, fear, and anxiety when they are faced with the decision to stand up to or possibly report a clerical abuser. The court records are full of children who waited decades before reporting their abuse to their parents or to the legal authorities. The consequence of religious socialization can be a loss of personal autonomy where the individual refuses to question even the most nefarious activities of religious officials. Therapists working with people who were abused, particularly in religious settings, in the 1970s and 1980s, before the scandals became public, report that the victims knew what was happening was not right but frequently could not fault so special and exalted a personage as a religious teacher or clergyman.

Religious communities which base their religious culture on the literalist reading of sacred texts in spite of good intentions often encourage traditionalist forms of abuse and violence. Western biblical traditions, for example, all trace their teachings about homosexuality to the biblical passages in Leviticus that severely condemn homosexuality as an "abomination" worthy of the most extreme punishment.[69] In traditionalist settings of family, home, and religious school these passages create a climate of prejudice which can and does involve attitudes of violence and discrimination toward such groups. In Islam, a significant passage in the Koran permits occasional physical violence against recalcitrant wives, while in Judaism and Islam divorce is readily available to men but can be difficult to obtain for women.[70] In traditionalist settings, the hierarchical organization of society means that parents frequently have the right to discipline and punish adolescent children. In some communities murder of children, usually of daughters, for reasons of "family honor" due usually to sexual misdeeds like premarital sex or adultery is not, strictly speaking, a religious obligation, but this type of violence, not that uncommon, is abetted by the need to maintain religious obedience and conformity.

This chapter has discussed the role of religion in various forms of violence against the self and in the relationship between religion and different types of sexual abuse. Though religion has been a force for the protection of human life and has promulgated a host of laws and injunctions against suicide and abuse, it nonetheless contains elements which continue to permit and encourage acts of personal violence and abuse. Religion is not a one-dimensional institution, and it would be incorrect to see religion per se as responsible for the abuse and violence in contemporary society. The relevance of biography, biology, and the uniqueness of each case is not to be ignored in coming to understand these instances of violence. Any examination of violence must take into consideration the complex of factors which go into producing the phenomenon. This chapter has illustrated how religious teaching and socialization contribute to our growing understanding of sexual abuse and personal violence.

Notes

1. Nosson Scherman and Meir Zlotowitz, eds., *The Complete Artscroll Machzor: Yom Kippur* (Brooklyn, N.Y.: Mesorah, 1993), 37.

2. Scherman and Zlotowitz, *Complete Art Scroll Machzor*, 75.

3. Robert Elwood, *Many Peoples, Many Faiths: An Introduction to the Religious Life of Mankind* (Englewood, N.J.: Prentice Hall, 1976), see particularly 59–136.

4. See John R. Hall, "Religion and Violence: Social Processes in Comparative Perspective," in *Handbook for the Sociology of Religion*, ed. Michele Dillon (Cambridge: Cambridge University, forthcoming). Hall insightfully interprets the Weberian position.

5. Hall, "Religion and Violence."

6. Michaela M. Ozelsel, *Forty Days: The Diary of a Traditional Solitary Sufi Retreat* (Brattleboro, Vt.: Threshold Books, 1996), 88.

7. Michael Wolfe, *The Hadj: An American's Journey to Mecca* (New York: Atlantic Monthly Press, 1999).

8. Ariel Glucklich, *Sacred Pain: Hurting the Body for the Sake of the Soul* (New York: Oxford University Press, 2001), 37–38.

9. Glucklich, *Sacred Pain*, 11–39, for a discussion of these various practices.

10. See Simone Weil, *Gravity and Grace* (New York: Octagon, 1983).

11. Quoted in Glucklich, *Sacred Pain*, 4.

12. See an analysis and critique of this concept in Jewish theology, see Eliezer Berkovits, *Faith After the Holocaust* (New York: Ktav, 1973), 124–128.

13. Roy Rappaport, *Ritual and Religion in the Making of Humanity* (Cambridge: Cambridge University Press, 1999), 112.

14. Peter L. Berger, *The Sacred Canopy: Elements of a Sociological Theory of Religion* (New York: Doubleday, 1969), 53–80.

15. Berger, *Sacred Canopy*, 54.

16. Berger, *Sacred Canopy*, 56.

17. Quoted in Berger, *Sacred Canopy*, 77.

18. See G.W. Bowersock, *Martyrdom and Rome* (Cambridge: Cambridge University Press, 1995), 3–17.

19. Bowersock, *Martyrdom and Rome*, 5.

20. Bowersock, *Martyrdom and Rome*, 9.

21. Samuel Z. Klausner, "Martyrdom," in *The Encyclopedia of Politics and Religion*, ed. Robert Wuthnow, 2 vols. (Washington, D.C.: Congressional Quarterly, 1998), 494–497.

22. See Eileen Barker, *New Religious Movements: A Practical Introduction* (London: HMSO, 1992), 17–24.

23. See *Frontline: Inside The Terrorist Network*, prod. and dir. Ben Loeterman, 60 min., PBS Video, 2002.

24. *New York Times*, January 1, 2003.

25. R. Scott Appleby, *The Ambivalence of The Sacred: Religion, Violence, and Reconciliation* (Lanham, Md.: Rowman & Littlefield, 2000), 81–120.

26. Ehud Sprinzak, *Brother Against Brother: Violence and Extremism in Israeli Politics From Altalena to the Rabin Assassination* (New York: Free Press, 1999), 1–4, 239–243. See also Michael Ben-Horin, ed., *Boruch Hagever* (Jerusalem: Special Publication, 1995).

27. Ziad Abu-Amr, *Islamic Fundamentalism in the West Bank and Gaza: Muslim Brotherhood and Islamic Jihad* (Bloomington: Indiana University Press, 1994).

28. Bowersock, *Martyrdom and Rome*, 3.

29. Bowersock, *Martyrdom and Rome*.

30. Klausner, "Martyrdom."

31. Quoted in Robert Royal, *The Catholic Martyrs of the Twentieth Century* (New York: Crossroad, 2000), 27.

32. See William Kuhs, *In Pursuit of Dietrich Bonhoeffer* (Garden City, N.Y.: Doubleday, 1969).

33. Quoted in sermon-essay by Mark Styker reprinted on www.mupctoday.org/seminars.

34. See Judith Quarles, "Dietrich Bonhoeffer," www.dmon.net/uuso.

35. Anna Peterson, *Martyrdom and the Politics of Religion: Progressive Catholicism in El Salvador's Civil War* (Albany: State University of New York, 1997).

36. Associated Press, November 25, 2002.

37. See www.cnn.com/2002/law/11/20/abortion.doctor.ap for a full report.

38. See Elchanan Wasserman, *Yalkut Mamimorim and Mictoovim* (Brooklyn, N.Y.: n.p., 1986).

39. Chaim Potok, *Wanderings* (New York: Ballantine, 1978), 273–294.

40. Eliezer Berkovits, *Faith after the Holocaust* (New York: Ktav, 1973), 70–76.

41. Interview with author, April 14, 2001.

42. H. A. R. Gibb and J. H. Kramers, *Shorter Encyclopedia of Islam* (Ithaca, N.Y.: Cornell University Press, 1965), 515–518.

43. Jeffrey Goldberg, "The Martyr Strategy," *New Yorker*, July 9, 2001, 34–39.

44. Nasra Hassan, "An Arsenal of Believers," *New Yorker*, November 19, 2001, 36–41.

45. Hassan, "Arsenal of Believers."

46. Hassan, "Arsenal of Believers."

47. Thomas Friedman, "To Leaders of the Muslim World," *New York Times*, November 27, 2002, sec. A, p. 3.

48. Reported in www.memri.org [accessed September 24, 2002].

49. *Ha'aretz* www.haaretz.com, [accessed January 6, 2003].

50. For a report on Palestinian suicide see Kahaled Abutomeh, "Judge Permits Suicide Attacks," www.jerusalempost.com [accessed October 2, 2002].

51. See "Letter from Father of Suicide Bomber," www.memri.org [accessed October 8, 2002].

52. The Investigative Staff of the *Boston Globe*, *The Crisis in the Catholic Church* (Boston: Little, Brown, 2002).

53. J. Ashe Readon, "The Cardinal and the *Globe*," *Religion in the News*, Spring 2002, 5–10.

54. Fox Butterfield with Jenny Hontz, "A Priest's Two Faces: Protector, Predator," *New York Times*, May 24, 2002, sec. A, p. 1.

55. Andrew Walsh, "Bishops Against the Wall," *Religion in the News*, Spring 2002, 30.

56. Gary Rosenblatt, "Lanner Charged in Sex Abuse," *Jewish Week*, p. 1.

57. See also reports on www.theawareness.org.

58. Gary Rosenblatt, "Stolen Innocence," *Jewish Week*, June 23, 2000, 1.

59. Charles Sennett, *Broken Covenant: The Story of Father Bruce Ritter* (New York: Simon & Shuster, 1992).

60. Personal communication and interview by the author with the parents.

61. Andrew Walsh, "The Scandal of Secrecy," *Religion in the News*, Spring 2002, 3–31.

62. One version of this narrative is found on www.longcreek.com.

63. Carolyn Holderread Heggen, "Religious Beliefs and Abuse," in *Women, Abuse, and the Bible*, ed. Catherine Clark Kroeger and James Beck (Grand Rapids, Mich.: Baker Books, 1996), 16–18.

64. Heggen, "Religious Beliefs and Abuse," 22–24.

65. Berger, *Sacred Canopy*, 61–77.

66. Berger, *Sacred Canopy*, 23.

67. *New York Times*, November 12, 2002, sec. A, p. 20.

68. Donald Capps, "Religion and Child Abuse," *Journal For the Scientific Study of Religion* 31 (1992): 1–14.

69. See the traditionalist biblical Judeo-Christian position restated in Maurice Lamm, *The Jewish Way in Love and Marriage* (New York: Jonathan David, 1980), 65–70.

70. Andrew Rippin, *The Contemporary Period*, Vol. 2 of *Muslims: Their Religious Beliefs and Practices* (London: Routledge, 1993), 101–103.

Conclusion: Toward a Holistic Approach to Religious Violence

This book has described and analyzed the seemingly never-ending cycle of religious conflicts, clashes, and wars across the globe: the wars and terrorism in the Middle East, the Hindu-Muslim struggles in the Indian subcontinent, the emerging violence between the West and militant Islam after September 11 and the bombing of the World Trade Center. Even after periods of relative peace in Ireland and the former Yugoslavia, these religious battles persist in inflicting pain and suffering. Religious violence and terrorism continue in the Philippines, Australia, Yemen, and Sudan. In many parts of the former Soviet empire, particularly in Chechnya and in the Caucasus, there are ominous signs of growing religious and civil strife over religious identity.[1] There does not appear to be any region in the globe immune to religious violence. A critical question, however, is just how *religious* are many of these religious conflicts and outbreaks of religious violence. Are they truly examples of religious violence or, as some have argued, merely attempts to use religion as a vehicle to justify secular political or nationalist goals, seek economic improvement, or express ethnic resentment over mistreatment or minority status?[2] Religion is such a powerful tool to motivate people to action and provide resources for social movements that it is highly useful in battling for nationalist and secular goals. Leaders of national, ethnic, and linguistic movements are aware of the ability of religious belief to motivate collective action, and they often seek to use religious language and symbols to foster and justify continuing ethnic conflict even in situations where religion was not initially an element in the conflict.[3]

The bulk of cases involving religious violence are, however, motivated by religious doctrine, faith, and sacred fury. Fury to champion God's will, to oppose one's religious enemies, and to insist upon the imposition of God's law for humanity is the key motivation underlying religious violence. Most journalists, social scientists, and diplomats, operating in a highly secular framework, refuse to recognize the religious motivation for religious violence even when those engaging in this behavior acknowledge religion to be the reason for their violent activities and sacred fury.[4] There is, in many sectors of the Western media, academia, and the diplomatic corps, the sense that the religious violence of ordinary believers is being manipulated by social elites for their own economic and political gain. The religious wars, the violent demonstrations, even the dramatic suicide bombings, argue the Western intelligentsia, are not authentically religious events but attempts to use the pious masses to force competing ethnic groups or powerful states to make political concessions or to gain economic advantage for the governing elites. There is certainly truth, in some cases, in these claims, but the fact remains that religious violence is not, ultimately, about economics, political power, or even territory. It is about conflicting sacred visions, prophetic pronouncements, and eschatological expectations. Each religious community is convinced of the truth and legitimacy of its theological claims and is, on occasion, ready to wage war and engage in violence in support of what it takes to be an absolute religious truth.[5]

In such cases of outright religious violence, there are no necessary practical goals or objectives that are sought, no economic gain that is to be gotten. The goal of the violence is religious and spiritual and the rewards are based upon divine promise and eternal life. For example, the Jewish militant Temple Mount activists and their American Christian supporters, who seek to build a third Jewish holy temple in the precincts of the al-Aqsa mosque in Jerusalem, are willing to conduct illegal activities, risk arrest, and engage in violent clashes with the Muslim faith-

ful in order to build an edifice on contested land that they believe will usher in the messianic age. Their motivations are truly
eschatological, as there is really no political or economic advantage to their work.[6] From all available data, it appears that the
young suicide bombers of the militant Hamas and al-Jihad organizations, as well, are motivated by religious fervor and fury and
give their lives for Islam without attention to practical political
objectives.[7] Similarly, the large number of recent assassinations
in the Middle East among both Jews and Muslims, including the
killings of Anwar Sadat of Egypt and Yitzchak Rabin of Israel,
had little effect on the political policies of these countries but
were committed by passionate believers who where doing battle
for God. The goal was religious revenge and the assassins saw
themselves as instruments of the divine will.[8] The important
fatwa, religious verdict, never carried out and now rescinded,
calling for the murder of the Muslim-born though nonpractic-
ing, British writer Salman Rushdie for writing in his book *The
Satanic Verses* what many Muslims considered irreverent and
disrespectful passages about the prophet Muhammad is an example of the power of religion to sanction violence for purely
religious purposes.[9]

The violence and murders committed by members of radical
Christian antiabortion movements are also powerful examples
of religious violence carried out for transcendental religious purposes without regard for utilitarian concerns or political goals.[10]
For these religious militants, as Bruce Hoffman reports, violence
"is a sacramental act or divine duty executed in direct response
to some theological demand or imperative."[11] There are no politically articulated goals in their activities and the point of their
violence is to punish those they label "sinners and child killers."
In this regard, these religious radicals differ greatly from secular
terrorists—or mainstream abortion opponents—who generally
have a political program and are limited in their actions, to some
extent, by the public's response. The secular terrorist must always measure the utility of his activity and see whether the violence will help achieve his political or nationalist goals. Sacred
terrorism fueled by sacred fury can be more destructive because
the only goal is religious revenge. This is also the case with the

apocalyptic movements we have studied. There are no secular, practical, this-worldly limitations on their violent and suicidal behavior. The death and destruction they cause are the religious ends they espouse. The goal of their religious commitment, to put it bluntly, is violent death.

The conflict between Muslims and Hindus in India and between Muslim Pakistan and Hindu India over Kashmir is somewhat is more complex, involving both political and economic issues. Here, as well, however, the underlying issues are not diplomatic or matters of international trade but a contest over religious history, sacred places, and religious honor. To Hindu India, Muslim invaders violated sacred sites by building mosques over the abodes of the Hindu deities, and Pakistan is still, in pious Hindu eyes, a nation that truncated the sacred oneness of the Indian subcontinent. The Hindu religious regimen of deity prayer and temple worship is considered problematic by the strongly monotheistic Muslim community and the violence and killing that still go on between the two communities are about religious truth and what is rightly to be seen as sacred space. The riots and killings at Ayodhya, a place considered sacred by both traditions brought all these issues to the international stage. Here was a site, unusable and in disrepair, that was claimed by both religious communities. The violence was really not over real estate but religious honor, the ephemeral motivation for many outbreaks of religious violence. Similarly, the problem of Kashmir, now controlled by India but claimed by Pakistan as Muslim land, has elements of a political territorial dispute, but the religious fervor and history of the dispute do not permit a political, diplomatic solution. The violence in this civilizational conflict is, in the final analysis, religious.[12]

This is not to say that all religious violence is exclusively and inherently religious. Religious issues can become enmeshed in nationalist or ethnic disputes when the competing parties share a common religious identity.[13] For example, the disputes in Ireland and in Bosnia and the former Yugoslavia have significant nationalist and ethnic elements, but the collective religious identity of each side has encouraged a strong element of religious violence. Religious leaders and religious ideology have contributed much to making religion a critical element in the clashes. The Basques in Spain and the Corsicans in France are two European ethnic groups that similarly have engaged in violence in pursuit of their nationalist goals, but because all parties in these disputes share a common Catholicism, religious violence has not occurred. However, in the Irish and Yugoslavian cases, one can argue that religious violence has become a salient feature of the struggles because of the collective nature of the religious identities of the parties. In Lebanon in the 1970s and 1980s, under conditions of economic distress and civil war, serious religious wars, with hundreds being killed on both sides, broke out between the Christian and Muslim communities, which had lived well together in more serene times. Was this a truly religious war or a religious conflict caused by political or economic turmoil? Similarly, was the "ethnic cleansing" in the former Yugoslavia motivated by religion or was it an ethnic dispute gone awry?[14]

In some instances, however, religious rhetoric and appeals to religious violence have been manufactured by political or ideological groups to gain support for a particular political platform or secular movement. The power of religion to motivate participants and to legitimate violence is so great that many movements seek support for violence in religious scripture and tradition. The Ku Klux Klan is a powerful American example of the use of religion in support of racial oppression and violence. The Klan claimed to be doing God's work in furthering the interests of the "superior" white race, and the violence in which it engaged was religiously sanctioned. There are contemporary heirs to the Klan like the Christian Identity movement, which similarly has appropriated religion and religious violence in support of its racist agenda. Some extreme and violent environmental and animal rights groups, with distinctly secular platforms, have become progressively more "religious" as they seek to legitimate their violent activities with appeals to religious scripture. This is a sensitive and problematic issue in religious studies, for on what clear-cut basis and criteria can scholars and social scientists legitimately evaluate the religious motivations of a social movement? The legitimacy and authenticity of religious claims are not easily given over to empirical examination.

The nature of religious faith and commitment always remains personal, idiosyncratic, and, in the final analysis, beyond scientific understanding. The fact of the matter is that even in situations where religious motivations may be manipulated to create group solidarity and commitment, the religious emotions eventually come to be experienced as genuine and the violence is carried out for what is seen to be a sacred purpose.[15] The potency of religious motivation is such that even when manipulated for secular ideological purposes, the conflict and violence take on the characteristics of a sacred struggle, making it more difficult to resolve.

Analyzing Religious Violence: A Holistic Case-Study Approach

The most fruitful way to understand religious violence is to analyze each case from a variety of perspectives, taking into account the unique theological, historical, economic, and social-psychological factors operative in each specific event. This comprehensive, holistic approach means that each particular case will present a unique set of religious, historical, and sociological conditions that set off and, possibly, continue the violence. For example, a particular religious tradition may encourage a doctrine of holy war and violent religious conflict, but in the absence of other factors like widespread poverty, grievances, and resentment against governmental authority or strong charismatic leaders, the call to holy war may be dormant, only to be resurrected as immediately relevant in the presence of other situational factors. Many fundamentalist movements all over the world have, at times, successfully used widespread resentment against the government as a strategy to attract people to their movement. There is some evidence that the violence among several militant Islamic groups in Egypt and Algeria, as well as the violence among some American Christian militia groups, has been able to tap earlier social and political resentment.[16] Again, this is not always the case. Many cases of doctrinal violence and religious war are simply religious battles fought for reasons of faith. What a holistic approach provides is an opportunity to investigate all the variables operative in a specific case.

A holistic approach is particularly helpful in cases of civil war and ethnic conflict where religion figures prominently in the conflict. Religious factors can be the essential reason for violence in an ethnic and civil conflict, or ethnic factors themselves can draw out the religious issues dividing the groups. Each case has its own unique conditions. The religious violence in the Sudan between the predominately Muslim population in the north and the Christian population in the south is both religious war and a conflict over the nature of religious authority over state institutions. The outbreaks of violence between the Christian Copt community in Egypt and some Muslim groups, similarly, are religious battles but have elements of cultural conflict and historical resentment. The growing violence between radical religious nationalists and secular Jews in Israel is a battle over legitimate political compromise involving boundaries and settlements, but it is, at the same time, a religious battle over the nature of Jewish identity and the religious nature of the state of Israel. Growing civil unrest and the potential for significant religious violence exists in many parts of the former Soviet Union, where Muslim communities, long repressed by the atheistic Soviet regime, find themselves in conflict with the government and the leadership of the establishment Russian Orthodox Church, who view them as both a religious and political threat.[17]

Some cases of religious violence are predictable. A violation of a sacred site may make it impossible for a religious community to practice their rites, or the mass arrest or religious murder of members will provoke a violent response.[18] There are other cases in which people are caught by utter surprise by the outbreak of religious violence because of the spontaneous, often shocking and scandalous, pronouncements of religious charismatic leaders. Charisma, as Max Weber pointed out almost a century ago, is a special gift of authority and leadership possessed by some individuals that permits them to have their followers obey their orders without question.[19] One follows the charismatic figure not because the requests are logical, ethical, or politically sound but because the charismatic person represents divine truth. Religious violence often finds legitimation and encouragement in the pronouncements of charismatic leaders. These leaders can offer interpretations of doctrine and scripture which, in their view, demand religious violence against those they define as enemies of God. Charismatic leaders are frequently unpredictable; they do not have to play by conventional religious rules and do not need approval from religious peers or official religious bodies. What they say is truth to their followers and if what is asked is murder, violence, and mayhem, the followers are ready to obey. Nonetheless, even charismatic leaders do not operate in a religious vacuum and their calls for violence often resonate with the traditional theology and world view of their followers.

The call to violence by charismatic leaders—not all demand violence—is an important element in understanding certain cases of religious violence The most shocking recent case of a charismatic leader calling for religious violence is Osama bin Laden's call for a holy war against America and the suicide bombings of the Pentagon and the World Trade Center. Again, bin Laden's call for sacred terrorism, as charismatic and extreme as it was, must be seen in the context of militant Islamic theology and its doctrine of holy war, but the figure of Bin Laden is still central to the level of violence and the deep hatred of the religious enemy.[20] Bin Laden is probably the best known of this genre, but all traditions have such leaders who by their piety, personality, and acumen inspire compliance and adoration among their followers. The Branch Davidian followers of David Koresh were,[21] similarly, ready to die for their leader, and the Jewish Defense League followers of Meir Kahane were also inspired in their tactics by Kahane's teaching.[22]

Some ethicists, scholars, and commentators seek to discount the significance of religious violence, arguing that violence never really accomplishes any positive goals but merely results in more violence and destruction.[23] A holistic approach, however, investigates the unique functions and purposes of violence in the social organization of religious groups and argues that, contrary to some of these assumptions, religious violence, as ethically problematic as it may appear to secular and modernistic thinkers, may have important sociological functions for religious groups.[24] For some groups, being involved in religious violence against religious antagonists serves to encourage greater social solidarity and group cohesiveness among members. There is a sense that despite any disagreements which may exist, as René Girard's work so powerfully illustrates, the religious group must now unite against an outside enemy.[25] Contributions and resources may come to the group from marginal members who, in the absence of conflict and violence, would not identify with the group. In a situation of holy war, you are either with the group or against the group, and violence makes it nearly impossible for a coreligionist to remain neutral. Religious heroes dying in battle inspire and intensify the commitment of all.

Violence can be efficacious and does change reality to the benefit of the more powerful group. Territory can come under religious control if the group is strong enough to demand territorial and political concessions from religious adversaries and the threat of potential violence itself can wrest compromises from competing groups. Holy wars have winners and losers, and winners can succeed in having their religious visions realized and their scriptures vindicated. Violence, of course, is not always successful and may lead to defeat and submission. But given the religious beliefs of many groups, violence is a legitimate means of achieving religious vindication. There is, as Mark Juergensmayer tells us in his review of worldwide religious violence, a "logic to religious violence."[26] The scriptures, traditions, and communal life of religion all come together to make sense of and justify religious violence. These violent events are not haphazard, nor are they random acts of hysteria. Instead, they are attempts on the part of religious actors to achieve specific goals deemed appropriate in the particular religious world view. The study of religious violence shows that despite continued criticism and condemnation, violence remains integral to religious life.[27]

An Agenda for the Future:
Reducing Religious Violence

It is reasonable to be pessimistic and to despair of ever finding solutions to what appears to be the unbreakable connection between religion and violence. John Hall has suggested, however, that understanding the complex nature of religious violence can help sensitize the religious protagonists to seek alternative means to resolve religious tension and conflict.[28] Religious scholars, activists, and social scientists studying religious wars and civilizational clashes have, in recent years, developed a series of highly creative strategies and techniques for mediating religious conflict and violence. Some of these strategies have worked well in different settings and appear to have considerable promise of larger applicability, while other approaches, more theoretical and innovative, have yet to be proved workable. The whole field of religious conflict resolution is new, and while some successes have been notable and have attracted much media attention, there is a not-unjustified wariness about the whole approach. From the accumulated work of social scientists, religious thinkers, and community activists, we will review and discuss several possibilities for reducing religious conflict and violence.

An Informed Laity

R. Scott Appleby, the distinguished Catholic historian, has argued that a committed and theologically informed laity that knows scripture and is at home with sacred texts and traditional practices can be mobilized as an important resource for stopping extremist groups and a militant leadership from promoting violence and religious confrontation.[29] An informed laity can question the legitimacy of religious violence and can object to religious confrontation on religious grounds. A pious and committed laity cannot easily be ignored or viewed as outsiders who object to violence on secular humanistic grounds without appreciating the sacred dimensions of religious faith. The power of a worldly, economically advantaged, and religiously sophisticated laity is in its ability to hold a dialogue with and challenge the militants from within the theological tradition itself, and additionally, if necessary, threaten to withhold its continued financial support.

Appleby's work on the "ambivalence of the sacred" is particularly relevant in this connection. As Appleby illustrates, religious traditions are never monolithic; there are always areas of ambivalence in responding to conflict and calls for violence.[30] Theological guidelines and proclamations which appear to be clear-cut calls to religious conflict are, in reality, open to different interpretations and may well be rejected by other schools in the same tradition. However, the discussions and even arguments over what is right can only take place within the acceptable parameters of the faith community. Tradition always changes, but the form, degree, and style of change must be determined by those who know the inner life and are committed to the system. Put differently, secularists may share common peacemaking goals with religious groups, but only the committed religious community will have the power to influence the behavior of militant fellow religionists. The vocabulary and dynamics of avoiding violence may be as important as conflict resolution. An example of the power of religious motivation and theological understanding to avoid war can be seen in the response of large sectors of the Muslim world to Saddam Hussein's call for religious war against the West in the 1990–1991 Persian Gulf crisis. There was much in Saddam's rhetoric and in the proclamations of jihad by sympathetic Muslim religious leaders to inspire and encourage an acceptance of religious war in the larger Muslim community. However, the bulk of the Muslim community, including some of the most devout and traditional elements, rejected Saddam's call as being unworthy and religiously inappropriate from someone who had a record of persecution against religious Muslim communities in Iraq. Of course, there were political considerations as well on the part of the Saudis and others who were looking for continued support from the United States, but it was the Muslim communities' refusal on religious grounds to define Saddam's military venture as a legitimate Muslim war which undermined the attempt to engage the Muslim world in a jihad against America at that time. Statements and arguments against joining the war with Saddam by American and European peace activists did not carry weight with Muslims, but the stance of learned theological positions by fellow religionists did matter.[31] At the close of the Gulf War in 1993, as well, Muslim clerics joined with American and coalition forces in calls to prevent looting, violence, and bloodshed.

Central to understanding religious attitudes toward violence and peacemaking is the existence of multiple subgroups in any religious community. Some of these subgroups, because of their unique history, location, and leadership, may be disposed toward violence and conflict, while other groups, as committed and as central to the tradition, may be more open to compromise and conciliation. Attempts to mediate conflicts need not only focus on the groups prone to violence but must be, as well, attuned to those elements that can argue for reconciliation from within the particular religion's traditions of moderation and compromise. A example of an internal Jewish religious conflict with the potential for real violence was the organization by feminist groups of communal prayer meetings involving the reading of the Torah, an activity traditionally limited to male communal prayer, at the Western Wall in Jerusalem. Local ultraorthodox Jerusalemites, both men and women, saw this as sacrilege, and verbally and physically attacked the women participants. But moderate but still Orthodox scholars and rabbis, using the same ultraorthodox texts, were able, with the help of the secular courts, to demonstrate that by some readings of Orthodox Jewish law, women's prayer groups could be accommodated. This did not eliminate all violence against the women, but it did limit the extent of confrontation and served to legitimate the inaction of those ultraorthodox locals who refused to engage in violence against the women's groups.[32]

The Role of the State

Some religious conflicts can be stopped by the intervention of the state through the exercise of political and military power. This means that all the power of the state apparatus, including limited violence, can be used to limit religious conflict and stop religious terrorism. The state which refuses or is unable to intervene in ongoing terrorism and violence encourages chronic religious conflict and silences religious moderates. The judicious use of state violence, Mark Juergensmeyer argues, is an important factor in curing violence.[33] The conflicts and violence in India between Muslims and Hindus and the attacks and assassinations by Sikh militants, while serious, have been limited by strong governmental action. Similar action had been taken by the Japanese authorities against Aum Shinrikyo as police destroyed the group's infrastructure and ability to undertake attacks on Japanese society. The powerful legal and police response to antiabortion violence also accounts for the low incidence of murders and has prevented these groups from becoming a more acceptable movement among sympathetic Christian groups. Still, these are serious civil rights issues for a democratic society. At what point does a government intervene to protect its citizens and at what point is government action a limitation on freedoms of assembly, speech, and religion?

The Role of Charismatic Leadership

Ron Hassner, a political scientist at Stanford University, has called for the inclusion of charismatic leaders in political solutions to religious violence, particularly as these conflicts relate to sacred space.[34] Hassner has shown that political solutions that do not include authoritative religious leaders may appear logical and just to secular politicians but will not work because notions of sacred space and religious privilege are not amenable to diplomatic solutions alone. Charismatic religious leaders help redefine the parameters of sacred space so that the diplomatic solutions will be acceptable to their religious followers. Many diplomatic negotiations, like the ill-fated Israeli-Palestinian 2000 Camp David summit with President Bill Clinton, have failed because the agreements did not include a sufficient awareness of sacred space and did not include charismatic leaders who could cooperate with the diplomats and make the compromise religiously acceptable. Charismatic leaders, through their religious standing, can encourage violence, but they have also been instrumental in helping mediate religious conflict in several critical disputes, including Israeli claims to the Northern Sinai and fundamentalist Muslim attacks on the Grand Mosque in Mecca, and they have also helped to avoid bloodshed over the Temple Mount in Jerusalem. In these cases, religious leaders have demonstrated that including them in compromise arrangements can help ameliorate the conflict over sacred space.

Recognizing Symbols of Religion

Similar to the work of Ron Hassner, other scholars have called for a recognition and empowerment of religion so that religious communities, particularly politically unpopular ones, do not have to struggle for recognition and respect from governmental institutions. Western conceptions of pluralism and freedom of religion, these scholars claim, do not mean that religious symbols must be eliminated from the public square.[35] The sensitivities of religious belief and tradition can be incorporated in civil society so that religious values and goals are accepted as legitimate forms of education and public discourse. Empowering religion as a central element of political and economic discourse will, in this view, help introduce religious themes to societal decision making and defuse religious resentment over marginalization and noninclusion. Mark Juergensmeyer reports that a great deal of anger is generated among militants and born-again fundamentalists in all religious communities by their view that their emphasis on spirituality and their transcendental understanding of the human condition is not accorded sufficient respect and dignity.[36] A militant, unthinking secularity, in this view, encourages a militant response on the part of traditionalists who see themselves cut off from the central power positions of state and society.

Secular and Religious Cooperation

Secular organizations involved in conflict resolution and international cooperation, particularly the nongovernmental organizations (NGOs) affiliated with the United Nations, can play an important role in mediating religious conflict. The very fact that they do not have a religious stake in the conflict and the neutral personnel and environment they provide helps initiate dialogue and contact between the warring factions. Combined with economic aid and technical acumen in conflict resolution, these groups have had a measure of success in identifying a core of dialogue partners from opposing sides who can work as a front-line defense and communicate with each other in crisis situations, limiting the degree of confrontation and violence. In the Palestinian-Israeli conflict, the Seeds of Peace International Camp for Conflict Resolution and Neve Shalom/Wha al-Salam Village in Galilee are examples of programs that bring together moderates from both sides for an experience of empathy and understanding. Some limited success has also been reported by NGOs working with Muslims, Serbs, and Croatians in the former Yugoslavia. Frankly, these are modest attempts with a mixed record in many parts of the world, but they have identified a core constituency that is willing to support peacemaking across religious boundaries.[37]

Conflict, Dialogue, and Religious Camaraderie

There is a meaningful dialogue that unites even religions in conflict. This is a dialogue of overarching concerns and common goals which transcends the particular conflict and makes comrades of the religious antagonists. These are theological concerns and sociological dilemmas which religions share as communities of faith. This does not mean that religions necessarily share common values or similar beliefs, but it does mean that some religions share problems specific to their traditions, and it is only in dialogue with their religious siblings that these issues can be meaningfully discussed. The conflict between Islam and Judaism, for example, severe as it is, is nonetheless also an example of religious communities facing similar issues as they confront the modern world.[38] The issues of adapting to a revealed scriptural tradition, the adjustment of the sharia and halacha to the world of modernity, and the religious education of young Jews and Muslims brought up in the secularized world, are common to the two religions. Islam and Judaism are examples of religions that the distinguished Jewish philosopher Norman Lamm has termed "faith in action."[39] Both traditions not only specify principles of faith and dogma but also require conformity to religiously based rules and guidelines for everyday life and behavior. These rules, governing food consumption and preparation, dress and modesty regulations, and the necessity for family, community, and government to be under religious authority, have resulted in tensions with secular modernity. Meetings and encounters between Muslim imams and Jewish rabbis that occur regularly in the Middle East, Europe, and the United States have certainly not resolved the political impasse, but the communality and theological understandings forged at these meetings raise hopes for peacemaking.

Strategies, dialogues, and activities for mediating religious conflict and promoting peace and harmony between religions, as R. Scott Appleby correctly puts it, are entirely necessary and laudatory "acts of civic responsibility in today's world."[40] In the current situation of global religious violence, with thousands being routinely killed and maimed in the name of religion, people all over the world are intent upon finding ways of eliminating ongoing religious wars and struggles. There is much that has been learned about religious violence and many programs operating in trouble spots all over the world that have shown some promise of reducing the terrifying toll of human life and suffering in violence and war waged in the name of God and religion. Many religious leaders and theologians hold out the view—perhaps the hope—that with increasing globalization and religious interaction will come a religious maturity that will do away with violence as an element in religious life. This is an optimistic and worthy goal. The nature of religious life and faith, however, makes this unlikely. So long as religion is about ultimate truth and commitment to the sacred, to a vision of a utopia described in holy scripture, men and women will be defenders of the faith and willing soldiers in the battles for God.

Notes

1. Jonathan Fox, "The Ethnic-Religious Nexus: The Impact of Religion on Ethnic Conflict," *Civil Wars* 3, no. 3 (2000): 1–21.

2. See Ted Robert Gurr, "Terrorism in Democracies: When it Occurs, Why it Fails," in *The New Global Terrorism*, ed. Charles Kegley Jr. (Upper Saddle River, N.J.: Prentice Hall, 2003), 213–215. For a discussion of the thesis that poverty and powerlessness cause religious violence, see Daniel Pipes, "God and Mammon: Does Poverty Cause Militant Islam?" *National Interest*, Winter 2001–2002, 14–21.

3. Fox, "Ethnic-Religious Nexus," 11–17.

4. Pipes, "God and Mammon," discusses the mood in academia, where many scholars have argued that religious violence and terrorism are not really religious but an expression of anger and frustration over international inequality and economic deprivation. One author Pipes cites claims that religious fury against America will rise without American help for education, the elimination of poverty, and economic progress, and the Middle East will see the rise of new Osama bin Ladens until economic issues are resolved. See also Samuel P. Huntington, *The Clash of Civilizations and the Remaking of World Order* (New York: Simon and Schuster, 1996), chap. 5, for the place of economics and competition in religious and civilizational violence

5. Karen Armstrong, *The Battle For God* (New York: Alfred A. Knopf, 2000), 278–316. Also see Pipes, "God and Mammon."

6. Gershon Gorenberg, *The End of Days: Fundamentalism and the Struggle for the Temple Mount* (New York: Free Press, 2000).

7. David Bukay, *Total Terrorism in the Name of Allah: The Emergence of the New Islamic Fundamentalists* (Sharei Tikvah, Israel: ACPR Publications, 2002), 107–110.

8. Ehud Sprinzak, *Brother Against Brother: Violence and Extremism in Israeli Politics From Altalena to the Rabin Assassination* (New York: Free Press, 1999), 244–285; Geneive Abdo, *No God But Allah: Egypt and the Triumph of Islam* (New York: Oxford University Press, 2000), 13–14.

9. Salman Rushdie, *The Satanic Verses* (New York: Viking, 1988). See Lisa Appignanesi and Sara Maitland, *The Rushdie Files* (Syracuse, N.Y.: Syracuse University Press, 1996), for documents and a history of the controversy.

10. Mark Juergensmeyer, *Terror in The Mind of God: The Global Rise of Religious Violence* (Berkeley and Los Angeles, University of California Press, 2000), 19–23.

11. Bruce Hoffman, " 'Holy Terror': The Implications of Terrorism

Motivated by a Religious Imperative," *Studies in Conflict and Terrorism* 18 (October–December 1995): 272.

12. Jonathan R. White, *Terrorism: An Introduction* (Belmont, Calif.: Wadsworth, 2002), 51–57. For the historical roots, see the analysis by Jack Hawley, "Pakistan's Longer Border" (paper presented at the conference, "Understanding Religious Violence," St. Bartholomew's Church, New York, N.Y., February 2002).

13. Jonathan Fox, "The Salience of Religious Issues in Ethnic Conflicts: A Large-N Study," *Nationalism and Ethnic Politics* 3, no. 3 (1997): 1–14.

14. Fox, "Salience of Religious Issues," 14.

15. Fox, "The Ethnic-Religious Nexus," 51–59.

16. Abdo, *No God But Allah*, 3–19. See also Juergensmeyer, *Terror in the Mind of God*, 30–36.

17. Huntington, *Clash of Civilizations*, 163–167, 254–258.

18. Ron Hassner, "Charismatic Authority and the Management of Religious Conflict" (paper presented at the Society for the Scientific Study of Religion, Salt Lake City, November 2002).

19. Hans Gerth and C. Wright Mills, eds., *From Max Weber* (New York: Oxford University Press, 1958), 245–252.

20. Yossef Bodansky, *Bin Laden: The Man Who Declared War on America* (New York: Random House, 2001), 91–114.

21. John R. Hall with Philip D. Schuyler and Sylvaine Trinh, *Apocalypse Observed: Religious Movements and Violence in North America, Europe, and Japan* (New York: Routledge, 2000), 111–148.

22. Sprinzak, *Brother Against Brother*, 180–216.

23. For a contemporary postmodernist view, see Zygmunt Bauman, *Life in Fragments: Essays In Postmodern Morality* (London: Blackwell, 1998). See Jonathan Schell, "The Unconquerable World," part 2 of "No More Unto The Breach," *Harper's*, April 1993, 41–56. Also see Barbara A. Strassberg, "Religion, Moral Competence, and Violence" (paper presented at the Society for the Scientific Study of Religion, Salt Lake City, November 2002).

24. Lewis Coser, *The Functions of Social Conflict* (New York: Free Press, 1956); Juergensmeyer, *Terror in the Mind of God*, 187–215.

25. Rene Girard, *Violence and the Sacred* (Baltimore: Johns Hopkins University Press, 1977).

26. Juergensmeyer, *Terror in the Mind of God*, 117.

27. See Rene Girard, *The Scapegoat* (Baltimore: Johns Hopkins University Press, 1986).

28. John R. Hall, "Religion and Violence: Social Processes in Com-

parative Perspective," in *Handbook For the Sociology of Religion*, ed. Michele Dillon (Cambridge: Cambridge University Press, forthcoming).

29. R. Scott Appleby, *The Ambivalence of the Sacred: Religion, Violence, and Reconciliation* (Lanham, Md.: Rowman & Littlefield, 2000), 284–288.

30. Appleby, *Ambivalence of the Sacred*.

31. Appleby, *Ambivalence of the Sacred*, 282–286.

32. See Phyllis Chesler and Rivka Haut, eds., *Women of the Wall: Claiming Sacred Ground at Judaism's Holy Site* (Woodstock, Vt.: Jewish Lights, 2000).

33. Juergensmeyer, *Terror in the Mind of God*, 218.

34. Hassner, "Charismatic Authority."

35. Richard John Neuhaus, *The Naked Public Square: Religion and Democracy in America* (Grand Rapids, Mich.: Eerdmans, 1984).

36. Juergensmeyer, *Terror in the Mind of God*, 218.

37. Appleby, *Ambivalence of the Sacred*, 292–305

38. See Charles Selengut, ed., *Jewish-Muslim Encounters: History, Philosophy, and Culture* (St. Paul, Minn.: Paragon, 2002).

39. Quoted in Selengut, *Jewish-Muslim Encounters*, viii.

40. Appleby, *Ambivalence of the Sacred*, 306.

Glossary

Abu Sayyef. A Muslim militant group in the Philippines responsible for the kidnapping and murder of tourists and Christian missionaries.

Al-Qaeda. A Muslim extremist and terrorist group under the leadership of Osama Bin Laden responsible for the September 11, 2001, attacks on the World Trade Center and other American targets around the world.

Apocalypse. The violent and catastrophic events which will usher in the end of the world according to biblical religious traditions.

Aum Shinrikyo. A Japanese extremist cult responsible for the killing of civilians in a poisonous gas attack in the Tokyo subway system.

Brainwashing. The attempt to psychologically coerce an individual to convert or join a religion or to encourage violent and terroristic acts of behalf of an extremist group.

Branch Davidians. An extremist and unconventional sect of the Seventh-day Adventist Church headed by David Koresh, whose members died in a confrontation with United States law enforcement officials in Waco, Texas, in 1993.

Charisma. A quality of leadership and personality that endows a religious or political leader with unquestioned authority. The pronouncements of the charismatic leader are considered to be true and divinely inspired by his or her followers. Charisma can be used for good or evil purposes.

Christian Identity. An American Christian extremist group proclaiming a theology of racism and white supremacy.

Cognitive Dissonance. The psychological stress experienced when an individual holds two opinions or beliefs—cognitions—that are contradictory and mutually exclusive, for example, being a pacifist who is opposed to war and supporting a nation's war.

243

Cult. An unconventional religious group, usually headed by a charismatic leader, or a group which proclaims a new revelation or religious truth. Cults are generally opposed by more established religious groups.

Dar al Islam. An "abode of Islam," referring to a country under Muslim sovereignty where the rules of Islam are legally established.

Dhimmi. A member of a non-Muslim "protected" community living in a Muslim society under Muslim rule.

Eschatology. The study of the "eschaton," the end of the world, as described in religious and philosophical writings.

Fatwa. A religious decision or edict promulgated by a Muslim cleric or religious authority.

Gush Emunim. Literally the "Bloc of the Faithful," Zionist nationalist settlers who have established Jewish communities in the Israeli-controlled West Bank, which they consider the ancient Jewish area of Judea and Samaria.

Hajj. A Muslim religious pilgrimage to the holy city of Mecca and considered one of the "five pillars" of Islam.

Hamas. Formed in 1987 as the militant Islamic Resistance Movement, the group opposes the state of Israel and engages in political and military action, including the organization of suicide bombings.

Haram al Sharif. The Muslim holy site in Jerusalem where, by tradition, the prophet Muhammad ascended to heaven.

Heaven's Gate. An unconventional religious group whose members committed collective suicide as they awaited the arrival of a spaceship from another planet to take them to another place in the universe where, according to their beliefs, they would live in a higher consciousness.

Hijab. The traditional veil or head covering worn by Muslim women.

Irish Republican Army (IRA). A revolutionary and militant Irish terrorist group fighting for a united Ireland.

Jahiliyya. The "age of ignorance" in Islamic theology, referring to the immoral culture in Arabia before the teachings of the prophet Muhammad. Also used to describe any society living with the absence of an ethical and moral code.

Jihad. A Muslim religious obligation involving a "struggle" for faith and overcoming evil. Jihad can be a psychological or political struggle but it can also involve war and violence on behalf of religion and faith.

Kach. A militant political party, now declared illegal by the Israeli government, and movement in Israel founded by Rabbi Meir Kahane that is committed to the transfer of Arabs to Muslim lands.

Kiddush Hashem. Literally the "sanctification of God's name," a concept in Jewish theology of bringing honor to God by performing acts of charity and surrendering to God's will to the point of religious martyrdom.

Martyr. An individual of faith who is willing to die in defense of his or her religious beliefs or religious community. The word was originally used to describe a Christian who was willing to announce publicly his or her faith even in the face of death.

Milchemet Mitzvah. An obligatory war ordained by God in which killing and destruction are sanctioned by divine command.

Militia Groups. American extremist paramilitary groups that tend to espouse a right-wing political agenda centering on white supremacy, opposition to gun control and abortion rights, and support for local community rights as opposed to centralized governmental authority.

Mimetic Desire. A term used by Rene Girard to describe the human experience of envy and desire to have the admirable and desirable characteristics of another person or collectivity. Girard believed that mimetic desire was a central feature in understanding human violence.

Peoples Temple. An unconventional religious community established by Rev. Jim Jones in California which founded a commune in Guyana where over 900 people died in what is believed to have been a mass religious suicide.

Postmillennialism. A way of interpreting Christian scriptures to predict that Jesus Christ will return to proclaim his kingdom on earth only after widespread conversions to the Christian faith and the organization of a Christian society faithful to Jesus and his teachings.

Premillennialism. A way of interpreting Christian scriptures to predict that Jesus Christ will return to earth to set up a Godly kingdom for a thousand-year period before the time of the final judgment.

Rapture. The belief among some premillenialist Christians that they will be miraculously taken to heaven and spared the suffering of the sinful that will occur before the return of Christ.

Scapegoating. Blaming the troubles of an individual or society on an innocent victim and in this way avoiding responsibility .The term is taken from the Hebrew Bible, which describes a sacrificial ritual in which a goat is sacrificed as an atonement for the sins and transgressions of the community.

Shahid. A pious Muslim who dies in a religious holy war or by otherwise offering his life on behalf of God and the Islamic community.

Sharia. Islamic religious law based upon the Koran and the authoritative religious traditions as interpreted by Muslim scholars and religious teachers.

Temple Mount. The traditional site of the ancient Jewish Jerusalem temple.

Temple Mount Faithful. A fundamentalist Jewish movement in Israel supported by American Christian fundamentalists that seeks to rebuild the ancient Jerusalem temple.

Terrorism. Unconventional, illegitimate, and frequently violent means, such as bombing, assassination, hijacking, or kidnapping, used by religious or political movements to achieve their goals.

Theodicy. Religious explanations for evil and human suffering.

Torah. The first five books of the Hebrew Bible. The word also refers to the collective teachings of Judaism.

Ummah. The worldwide Muslim community following Islamic teachings.

Zionism. The religious and political movement which supports the establishment of the state of Israel as the national home for Jews.

Bibliography

Abanes, Richard. *Rebellion, Racism, and Religion: America's Militias.* Downers Grove, Ill.: Intervarsity Press, 1966.

Abdo, Geneive. *No God but Allah: Egypt and the Triumph of Islam.* New York: Oxford University Press, 2000.

Abu-Amr, Ziad. *Islamic Fundamentalism in the West Bank and Gaza: Muslim Brotherhood and Islamic Jihad.* Bloomington: Indiana University Press, 1994.

Ahlstrom, Sydney E. *A Religious History of the American People.* New Haven: Yale University Press, 1972.

Aho, James. *This Thing of Darkness: A Sociology of the Enemy.* Seattle: University of Washington Press, 1994.

Alexander, Yonah. *Osama bin Laden's al-Qaida: Profile of a Terrorist Network.* Ardsley, N.Y.: Transnational, 2001.

Ali, Abdullah Yusuf, trans. *The Meaning of the Holy Qur'an.* Brentwood, Md.: Amana, 1989.

Ammerman, Nancy Tatom. *Bible Believers: Fundamentalists in the Modern World.* New Brunswick, N.J.: Rutgers University Press, 1987.

Appignanesi, Lisa, and Sara Maitland. *The Rushdie Files.* Syracuse, N.Y.: Syracuse University Press, 1996.

Appleby, R. Scott. *The Ambivalence of the Sacred: Religion, Violence, and Reconciliation.* Lanham, Md.: Rowman & Littlefield, 2000.

Armstrong, Karen. *The Battle For God.* New York: Alfred A. Knopf, 2000.

Audi, Robert, and Nicholas Wolterstorff. *Religion in the Public Square: The Place of Religious Convictions in Political Debate.* New York: Lanham, Md., 1997.

Bainbridge, William. *The Sociology of Religious Movements.* New York: Routledge, 1997.

Baird-Windle, Patricia. *Targets of Hatred: Anti-Abortion Terrorism*. New York: St. Martin's Press, 2000.

Barker, Eileen. *New Religious Movements: A Practical Introduction*. London: HMSO, 1992.

Barkun, Michael, *Religion and the Racist Right: The Origins of the Christian Identity Movement*. Chapel Hill: University of North Carolina Press, 1994.

————, ed. *Millennialism and Violence*. London: Frank Cass, 1996.

Bauman, Zygmunt. *Life in Fragments: Essays in Postmodern Morality*. London: Blackwell, 1998.

Begin, Menachem. *The Revolt*. New York: Dell Publishing, 1977.

Ben-Horin, Michael. *Boruch Hagever*. Jerusalem: n.p., 1995.

Bennet, David H. *The Party of Fear: The American Far Right from Nativism to the Militia Movement*. New York: Vintage Books, 1995.

Berger, Peter L. *Facing Up to Modernity: Excursions in Society, Politics, and Religion*. New York: Basic Books, 1977.

————. *The Heretical Imperative*. New York: Doubleday, 1979.

————. *The Sacred Canopy: Elements of a Sociological Theory of Religion*. New York: Doubleday, 1967.

————. "Some Sociological Comments on Theological Education." *Perspective*, Summer, 1968.

Berger, Peter L., and Thomas Luckman, *The Social Construction of Reality*. New York: Doubleday, 1967.

Berkovits, Eliezer. *Faith after the Holocaust*. New York: Ktav, 1973.

Blanchard, Dallas A., and Terri J. Prewitt. *The Gideon Project*. Gainesville: University Press of Florida, 1993.

Bodansky, Yossef. *Bin Laden: The Man Who Declared War on America*. New York: Random House, 2001.

Boston Globe Investigative Staff, *The Crisis in the Catholic Church*. Boston: Little, Brown, 2002.

Boulding, Elise. "Two Cultures of Religion." *Zygon* 21, no. 4 (1986): 501–516.

Bowersock, G.W. *Martyrdom and Rome*. Cambridge: Cambridge University Press, 1995.

Bray, Michael. *A Time to Kill: A Study Concerning the Use of Force and Abortion*. Portland, Ore.: Advocates for Life, 1994.

Bromley, David G. "Constructing Apocalypticism: Social and Cultural Elements of Radical Organizations." In *Millennium, Messiahs, and Mayhem*, edited by Thomas Robbins and Susan J. Palmer. New York: Routledge, 1997.

Bromley, David G., and James Richardson, eds. *The Brainwashing/De-*

programming Controversy: Sociological, Psychological, Legal, and Historical Perspectives. New York: Edwin Mellon Press, 1983.

Bukay, David. *Total Terrorism in the Name of Allah: The Emergence of the New Islamic Fundamentalists.* Sharei Tikvah, Israel: ACPR Publications, 2002.

Burkert, Walter, Rene Girard, and Jonathan Z. Smith. *Violent Origins: Ritual Killing and Cultural Formation.* Edited by Robert G. Hamerton-Kelly. Stanford, Calif.: Stanford University Press, 1987.

Bushart, Howard, John R. Craig, and Myra Barnes. *Soldiers of God: White Supremacists and their Holy War for America.* New York: Kensington, 1998.

Capps, Donald. "Religion and Child Abuse," *Journal for the Scientific Study of Religion* 31 (1992): 1–14.

Chesler, Phyllis, and Rivka Haut, eds. *Women of the Wall: Claiming Sacred Ground at Judaism's Holy Site.* Woodstock, Vt.: Jewish Lights, 2000.

Cohn, Norman. *Cosmos, Chaos, and the World to Come.* New Haven: Yale University Press, 1993.

Condland, Christopher. *The Spirit of Violence: An Interdisciplinary Bibliography of Religion and Violence.* New York: Harry Frank Guggenheim Foundation, 1992.

Coppola, Vincent. *Dragons of God: A Journey through Far-Right America.* Atlanta: Longstreet Press, 1996.

Coser, Lewis. *The Functions of Social Conflict.* New York: Free Press, 1956.

Crespo, Virgilio Pinto. "Thought Control in Spain." In *Inquisition and Society in Early Modern Europe,* edited by Stephen Haliczer, 17–188. Totowa, N.J.: Barnes & Noble, 1987.

Davies, John Gordon. *Christians, Politics, and Violent Revolution.* Maryknoll, N.Y.: Orbis, 1976.

Dees, Morris, with James Corcoran. *Gathering Storm: America's Militia Threat.* New York: HarperCollins, 1996.

Durkheim, Emile. *The Elementary Forms of the Religious Life.* New York: Free Press, 1965.

Ellison, Ralph. *Invisible Man.* New York: Vintage, 1995.

Ellul, Jacques, *Violence: Reflections from a Christian Perspective.* London: SCM, 1970.

Elwood, Robert. *Many Peoples, Many Faiths: An Introduction to the Religious Life of Mankind.* Englewood, N.J.: Prentice Hall, 1976.

Esposito, John L. *The Islamic Threat: Myth or Reality?* New York: Oxford University Press, 1983.

————. *Voices of Resurgent Islam*. New York: Oxford University Press, 1983.

Fanon, Frantz. *The Wretched of the Earth*. Harmondsworth: Penguin, 1967.

Festinger, Leon, Henry W. Riecken, and Stanley Schachter. *When Prophecy Fails*. Minneapolis: University of Minnesota Press, 1956.

Firestone, Rueven. "Conceptions of Holy War in Biblical and Qur'anic Tradition." *Journal of Religious Ethics* 24, no. 1 (Spring 1996): 99–123.

Flynn, Kevin, and Gary Gerhardt. *The Silent Brotherhood: Inside America's Racist Underground*. New York: Free Press, 1989.

Fox, Jonathan, "The Ethnic-Religious Nexus: The Impact of Religion on Ethnic Conflict." *Civil Wars* 3, no. 3 (2000): 1–22.

————. "The Salience of Religious Issues in Ethnic Conflicts: A Large-N Study." *Nationalism and Ethnic Politics* 3, no. 3 (1997): 1–14.

Freud, Sigmund. *Civilization and its Discontents*. Translated by Joan Riviere. London: Hogarth, 1963.

————. *The Future of an Illusion*. New York: Norton, 1990.

Friedman, Robert I. *The False Prophet: Rabbi Meir Kahane*. New York: Lawrence Hill, 1990.

Friedman, Robert I., and Sheik Abdel Rahman. *The World Trade Center Bombing and the CIA*. Westfield, N.J.: Open Media, 1993.

Fromm, Erich. *Psychoanalysis and Religion*. New Haven: Yale University Press, 1950.

Gerth, Hans, and C. Wright Mills, eds. *From Max Weber*, 245–248. New York: Oxford University Press, 1958.

Gibb, H. A. R., and J. H. Kramers. *Shorter Encyclopedia of Islam*, 515–518. Ithaca, N.Y.: Cornell University Press, 1965.

Girard, Rene. *The Scapegoat*. Translated by Yvonne Freccero. Baltimore: Johns Hopkins University Press, 1986.

————. *Things Hidden Since the Foundation of the World*. Stanford, Calif.: Stanford University Press, 1987.

————. *Violence and the Sacred*. Translated by Patrick Gregory. Baltimore: Johns Hopkins University Press, 1977.

Glucklich, Ariel. *Sacred Pain: Hurting the Body for the Sake of the Soul*. New York: Oxford University Press, 2001.

Goldberg, Jeffrey. "The Martyr Strategy." *New Yorker*, July 9, 2001, 34–39.

Gorenberg, Gershom. *The End of Days: Fundamentalism and the Struggle for the Temple Mount*. New York: Free Press, 2000.

Gurr, Ted Robert. "Terrorism in Democracies: When it Occurs, Why it Fails." In *The New Global Terrorism*, edited by Charles Kegley Jr. Upper Saddle River, N.J.: Prentice Hall, 2003.

Hall, John R. *Gone from the Promised Land: Jonestown in American Cultural History.* New Brunswick, N.J.: Transaction, 1987.
————. "Religion and Violence: Social Processes in Comparative Perspective." In *Handbook For the Sociology of Religion,* ed. Michele Dillon. Cambridge: Cambridge University Press, forthcoming.
Hall, John R., with Philip Schuyler and Sylvaine Trinh. *Apocalypse Observed: Religious Movements and Violence in North America, Europe, and Japan.* New York: Routledge, 2000.
Halpern, Thomas. *Beyond the Bombing: The Militia Menace Grows.* New York: Anti-Defamation League, 1995.
Hassan, Nasra. "An Arsenal of Believers." *New Yorker.* November 19, 2001, 36–41.
Hassner, Ron E. "Charismatic Authority and the Management of Religious Conflict." Paper presented at the Society for the Scientific Study of Religion, Salt Lake City, November 2002.
Haught, James A. *Holy Hatred.* Amherst, N.Y.: Prometheus, 1995.
Heggen, Carolyn Holderread. "Religious Beliefs and Abuse." In *Women, Abuse, and the Bible,* edited by Catherine Clark Kroeger and James Beck. Grand Rapids, Mich.: Baker Books, 1996.
Heikal, Mohammed. *Autumn of Fury: The Assassination of Sadat.* London: Andre Deutsch, 1983.
Hoffman, Bruce. "'Holy Terror': The Implications of Terrorism Motivated by a Religious Imperative." *Studies in Conflict and Terrorism* 18 (1995): 271–284.
Hoffman, David S. *The Oklahoma City Bombing and the Politics of Terror.* Venice, Calif.: Feral House, 1998.
Huntington, Samuel P., *The Clash of Civilizations and the Remaking of World Order.* New York: Simon and Schuster, 1996.
Jacquard, Roland. *In the Name of Osama bin Laden: Global Terrorism and the bin Laden Brotherhood.* Durham. N.C.: Duke University Press, 2002.
Jansen, Johannes J.G., *The Neglected Duty: The Creed of Sadat's Assassins and Islamic Resurgence in the Middle East.* New York: Macmillan, 1986.
Juergensmeyer, Mark. *The New Cold War? Religious Nationalism Confronts the Secular State.* Berkeley and Los Angeles: University of California Press, 1993.
————. *Terror in the Mind of God: The Global Rise of Religious Violence.* Berkeley and Los Angeles: University of California Press, 2000.
————, ed. *Violence and the Sacred in the Modern World.* London: Frank Cass, 1991.
Kahane, Meir. *Listen World, Listen Jew.* Jerusalem: Institute of the Jewish Idea, 1978.

————. *They Must Go.* Jerusalem: Institute of the Jewish Idea, 1981.

————. *Never Again: A Program For Survival.* New York: Pyramid Books, 1972.

Kanter, Rosabeth Moss. *Commitment and Community: Communes and Utopias in Sociological Perspective.* Cambridge: Harvard University Press, 1972.

Kaplan, Jeffrey. *Radical Religion in America: Millenarian Movements from the Far Right to the Children of Noah..* Syracuse, N.Y.: Syracuse University, 1997.

Kedar, B. Z. *Crusade and Mission: European Approaches toward the Muslims.* Princeton, N.J.: Princeton University Press, 1988.

Kelsay, John. *Islam and War: A Study of Comparative Ethics.* Louisville, Ky.: Westminster, 1979.

Kelsay, John, and James Turner Johnson, eds. *Cross, Crescent and Sword: The Justification and Limitation of War in Western and Islamic Tradition.* New York: Greenwood Press, 1991.

————. *Just War and Jihad: Historical and Theoretical Perspectives on War and Peace in Western and Islamic Traditions.* New York: Greenwood Press, 1991.

Klausner, Samuel Z. "Martyrdom." In *The Encyclopedia of Politics and Religion,* edited by Robert Wuthnow, 2 vols., 494–497. Washington, D.C.: Congressional Quarterly, 1998.

Kramer, Jane. "The Patriot." *New Yorker,* May 6, 2002, 104–118.

Kuhs, William. *In Pursuit of Dietrich Bonhoeffer.* Garden City, N.Y.: Doubleday, 1969.

Kutzman, Charles, ed. *Liberal Islam.* New York: Oxford University Press, 1998.

Lawrence, Bruce B. *Shattering the Myth: Islam Beyond Violence.* Princeton, N.J.: Princeton University Press, 1998.

————. *Defenders of God: The Fundamentalist Revolt Against the Modern Age.* Columbia: University of South Carolina Press, 1995.

Lehay, Tim, and Jerry Jenkins. *Left Behind.* Carol Stream. Ill.: Tyndale House, 2000.

Levin, Jack, and Jack McDevitt. *Hate Crimes.* New York: Plenum Press, 1993.

Lewis, Bernard. *The Jews of Islam.* Princeton, N.J.: Princeton University Press, 1984.

————. *What Went Wrong? Western Impact and Middle Eastern Response.* New York: Oxford University Press, 2002.

Lewis, James R., ed, *From the Ashes: Making Sense of Waco.* Lanham, Md.: Rowman & Littlefield, 1994.

Lindsay, Hal, with C.C. Carlson. *The Late Great Planet Earth.* New York: Bantam Doubleday Dell, 1999.

Mack, John. Foreword to *Cyprus—War and Adaptation: A Psychoanalytic Study of Groups in Conflict,* by Volkan Vanik. Charlottesville: University of Virginia Press, 1979.

Maitland, Sara. *The Rushdie Files.* Syracuse, N.Y.: Syracuse University Press, 1996.

Marty, Martin E., and R. Scott Appleby, *Fundamentalism Observed.* Chicago: University of Chicago Press, 1991.

Neitz, Mary Jo, and Marion S. Goldman, eds., *Sex, Lies, and Sanctity: Religion and Deviance in North America.* Greenwich, Ct.: JAI Press, 1995.

Neuhaus, Richard John. *The Naked Public Square: Religion and Democracy in America.* Grand Rapids, Mich.: Eerdmans, 1984.

Noble, Kerry. *Tabernacle of Hate: Why They Bombed Oklahoma City.* Prescott, Canada: Voyageur, 1998.

North, Gary. *Backward Christian Soldiers? An Action Manual for Christian Reconstruction.* Tyler, Tex.: Institute for Christian Economics, 1984.

North, Gary, and Gary DeMar. *Christian Reconstruction: What It Is, What It Isn't.* Tyler, Tex.: Institute for Christian Economics, 1991.

O'Brien, Conor Cruise. *Ancestral Voices: Religion and Nationalism in Ireland.* Dublin: Poolbeg Press, 1994.

Orlinsky, Harry M. "The Situational Ethics of Violence in the Biblical Period." In *Violence and Defense in the Jewish Experience,* edited by Solo W. Baron and George S. Wise. Philadelphia: Jewish Publication Society, 1997.

Ozelsel, Michaela. *Forty Days: The Diary of a Traditional Solitary Sufi Retreat.* Brattleboro, Vt.: Threshold, 1996.

Partner, Peter. *God of Battles: Holy Wars of Christianity and Islam.* London: HarperCollins, 1997.

Peters, Edward. *Inquisition.* New York: Free Press, 1988.

Peters, Joan, *From Time Immemorial: The Origins of The Arab-Jewish Conflict over Palestine.* New York: Harper & Row, 1988.

Peters, Rudolph. *Islam and Colonialism: The Doctrine of Jihad in Modern History.* The Hague: Mouton, 1979.

Peterson, Anna. *Martyrdom and the Politics of Religion: Progressive Catholicism in El Salvador's Civil War.* Albany: State University of New York, 1997.

Pipes, Daniel. "God and Mammon: Does Poverty Cause Militant Islam?" *National Interest,* Winter 2001–2002, 14–21.

Potok, Chaim. *Wanderings.* New York: Ballantine, 1978.

Rapaport, Era. *Letters From Tel Mond Prison: An Israeli Settler Defends His Act of Terror*. New York: Free Press, 1996.

Rapoport, David C., ed. *Inside Terrorist Organizations*. New York: Columbia University Press, 1988.

Rappaport, Roy. *Ritual and Religion in the Making of Humanity*. Cambridge: Cambridge University Press, 1999.

Reich, Water. *Origins of Terrorism: Psychologies, Ideologies, Theologies, States of Mind*. Cambridge: Woodrow Wilson International Center for Scholars and Cambridge University Press, 1990.

Richardson, James, "Manufacturing Consent About Koresh: A Structural Analysis of the Role of Media in the Waco Tragedy." In *Armageddon in Waco: Critical Perspectives on the Branch Davidian Conflict*, ed. Stuart A. Wright. Chicago: University of Chicago Press, 1995.

Rippin, Andrew. *The Contemporary Period*. Vol. 2 of *Muslims: Their Religious Beliefs and Practices*. London: Routledge, 1993.

Risen, Jim, and Judy L. Thomas. *Wrath of Angels: The American Abortion War*. New York: Basic Books, 1998.

Roker, Patrick Michael. *This Troubled Land: Voices from Northern Ireland and the Front Lines of Peace*. New York: Ballantine, 2002.

Roy, Joseph T., ed. *False Patriots: The Threat of Antigovernment Extremists*. Montgomery, Ala.: Southern Poverty Law Center Klanwatch Project, 1996.

Rushdie, Salman. *The Satanic Verses*. New York: Viking, 1988.

Schell, Jonathan. "The Unconquerable World." Part 2 of "No More Unto the Breach." *Harper's*, April 1993, 41–56.

Scherman, Nosson, and Meir Zlotowitz, eds. *The Complete Artscroll Machzor: Yom Kippur*. Brooklyn. N.Y.: Mesorah, 1993.

Selengut, Charles. "Eschatology and the Construction of Alternative Realities: Towards a Social Conflict Perspective on Millennialism." In *The Return of the Millennium*, edited by J. Bettis and S. K. Johannesen. Barrytown, N.Y.: New Eras, 1984.

———, ed., *Jewish-Muslim Encounters: History, Philosophy, and Culture*. St. Paul, Minn.: Paragon, 2001.

Sells, Michael A. *The Bridge Betrayed: Religion and Genocide in Bosnia*. Berkeley and Los Angeles: University of California Press, 1996.

Sennett, Charles. *Broken Covenant: The Story of Father Bruce Ritter*. New York: Simon & Shuster, 1992.

Sivan, Emmanuel. *Radical Islam: Medieval Theology and Modern Politics*. New Haven: Yale University Press, 1985.

Spencer, Robert. *Islam Unveiled: Disturbing Questions About the World's Fastest Growing Faith*. San Francisco: Encounter, 2002.

Sprinzak, Ehud. *The Ascendance of Israel's Radical Right.* New York: Oxford University Press, 1991.

———. *Brother Against Brother: Violence and Extremism in Israeli Politics From Altalena to the Rabin Assassination.* New York: Free Press, 1999.

Stark, Rodney. *For the Glory of God: How Monotheism Led to Reformations, Science, Witch Hunts, and the End of Slavery.* Princeton, N.J.: Princeton University Press, 2003.

Stark, Rodney, and William Sims Brainbridge. *The Future of Religion: Secularization, Revival, and Cult Reformation.* Berkeley and Los Angeles: University of California Press, 1985.

———. "Secularization, Revival, and Cult Formation." *Annual Review of the Social Sciences* 4 (1980): 85–119.

Stern, Kenneth S. *A Force Upon the Plain: The American Militia Movement and The Politics of Hate.* New York: Simon & Schuster, 1996.

Strozier, Charles B. *Apocalypse: On the Psychology of Fundamentalism in America.* Boston: Beacon Press, 1995.

Sutherland, Charles W. *Disciples of Destruction: The Religious Origins of War and Terrorism.* Buffalo, N.Y.: Prometheus Press, 1987.

Urbach, Ephraim. "Jewish Doctrines and Practices in Halachic and Aggaddic Literature." In *Violence and Death in the Jewish Experience: Papers Prepared for a Seminar on Violence and Defense in Jewish History and Contemporary Life,* edited by Salo W. Baron and George S. Wise. Philadelphia: Jewish Publication Society, 1977.

Victoria, Brian. *Zen at War.* New York: Weatherhill, 1988.

Walsh, Andrew. "Bishops Against the Wall." *Religion in the News,* Spring 2002, 30.

Walzer, Michael. *Just and Unjust Wars.* New York: Basic Books, 1977.

Wasserman, Elchanan, *Yalkut Maimorim and Michtavim.* Brooklyn, N.Y.: n.p., 1986.

Weber, Max. *The Protestant Ethic and the Rise of Capitalism.* New York: Scribner's, 1958.

Weightman, Judith. *Making Sense of the Jonestown Suicides: A Sociological History of People's Temple.* New York: Edwin Mellon, 1983.

Weil, Simone. *Gravity and Grace.* New York: Octagon, 1983.

Weisburd, David. *Jewish Settler Violence: Deviance as Social Reaction.* University Park: Pennsylvania State University Press, 1989.

Wentz, Richard E. *Why Do People Do Bad Things in the Name of Religion?* Macon, Ga.: Mercer, 1987.

Wessinger, Catherine. *How the Millennium Comes Violently: From Jonestown to Heaven's Gate.* New York: Seven Bridges, 2000.

White, Jonathan R. *Terrorism: An Introduction.* Belmont, Calif.: Wadsworth, 2002.

Williams, James G. *The Bible, Violence, and the Sacred: Liberation from the Myth of Sanctioned Violence.* San Francisco: Harper, 1991.

Wolfe, Michael. *The Hadj: An American's Journey to Mecca.* New York: Atlantic Monthly Press, 1999.

Wright, Stuart A., ed. *Armageddon in Waco: Critical Perspectives on the Branch Davidian Conflict.* Chicago: University of Chicago Press, 1995.

Zilboorg, Gregory. *Freud and Religion.* Westminster, Md.: Newman Press, 1958.

Zulaika, Joseph, and William A. Douglass. *Terror and Taboo.* London: Routledge, 1996.

Index

About The Author

CHARLES SELENGUT is an expert on the sociology, psychology, and politics of religious fundamentalism and new religious movements and has published articles and monographs on the significance of Islamic and Jewish fundamentalists in international relations. He has been a member of the MacArthur Foundation–sponsored University of Chicago Project on Fundamentalism and has been a visiting scholar and has lectured at meetings and conferences across Europe, Asia, and the United States. He has been active in interreligious studies and is the editor of *Jewish-Muslim Encounters: History, Philosophy, and Culture*, a volume of essays based on an international conference of Muslim and Jewish scholars held in 1999 in Cordova, Spain, that he organized with Professor Mumtaz Ahmad of Hampton University.

He is professor of sociology at County College of Morris in Randolph, N. J., and visiting professor of religion at Drew University in Madison, N.J. He was a National Endowment for the Humanities fellow at Harvard University and a 1997 finalist for the Carnegie Professor of the Year Award. He is also the author of *Seeing Society: Perspectives on Social Life*. His current project is an ethnographic study of the beliefs, lifestyles, and reality construction in Islamic and Jewish messianic fundamentalist movements.